Once More Astonished

ONCE MORE ASTONISHED

The Parables of Jesus

JAN LAMBRECHT, S.J.

CROSSROAD · NEW YORK

1981
The Crossroad Publishing Company
575 Lexington Avenue, New York, NY 10022

Originally published as *Terwijl Hij tot ons sprak.*
Parabels van Jezus
© Uitgeverij Lannoo, Tielt and Amsterdam 1976

First English edition published in 1978 under the title
Parables of Jesus: Insight and Challenge
by Theological Publications in India
(Bangalore)

Library of Congress Cataloging in Publication Data

Lambrecht, Jan.
    Once more astonished.

    Translation of: Terwijl Hij tot ons sprak.
    Includes bibliographies and index.
    1. Jesus Christ—Parables. I. Title. II. Title:
Parables of Jesus.
BT375.2.L3513   225'.8   81-5411
ISBN 0-8245-0093-8 (pbk.)   AACR2

Contents

Foreword   ix
Preface   xi
Abbreviations   xv

Chapter One   1
Parables in the Synoptic Gospels   1
   I. The Many Meanings of the Word "Parable"   2
  II. Insight and Appeal   12
 III. Overview of the Synoptic Parables   17
      Bibliography   20

Chapter Two   24
Parables in Luke 15: What Was Lost   24
   I. A Closer Look at Chapter 15   25
  II. The Lost Sheep   35
 III. The Prodigal Son   45
  IV. Actualization   51
      Bibliography   53

Chapter Three   57
The Good Samaritan (Luke 10:25–37)   57
   I. No Problems?   57
  II. Redacted Tradition   60
 III. The Message of Jesus   68
  IV. A Plea for Luke   75
   V. Fruitful Exegesis   80
      Bibliography   83

Chapter Four 85
Parables in Mark 4 85
   I. Defining the Problem 86
  II. Mark's Redactional Role 89
 III. The Explanation of the Sower (Verses 14–20) 97
  IV. The Similitudes and the Parable 99
   V. The Secret of the Kingdom of God 104
      Bibliography 107

Chapter Five 110
Parables Elsewhere in Mark's Gospel 110
   I. Discussion about Beelzebul (Mark 3:22–30) 112
  II. Clean and Unclean (Mark 7:1–23) 121
 III. The Wicked Tenants (Mark 12:1–12) 127
  IV. The Budding Fig Tree and the Doorkeeper (Mark 13:28–29
      and 34–36) 132
   V. A Marcan Parable Theory? 139
      Bibliography 143

Chapter Six 146
The Wise and Foolish Virgins (Matthew 25:1–13) 146
   I. Matthew's Eschatological Discourse (Chapters 24–25) 147
  II. Uncertainties and Disturbing Elements in Matthew
      25:1–13 153
 III. Tradition and Redaction 157
  IV. Jesus' Original Parable 161
   V. Matthew's Allegorizing 163
      Bibliography 166

Chapter Seven 167
The Talents and the Pounds
(Matthew 25:14–30 and Luke 19:11–27) 167
   I. Comparison of the Talents and the Pounds 169
  II. The Parable in Early Christian Preaching 180
 III. The Parable in Jesus' Preaching 183
  IV. The Parable in Luke's Gospel 187
   V. The Parable in Matthew's Gospel 191
      Bibliography 194

Chapter Eight 196
The Last Judgment (Matthew 25:31–46) 196
  I. The Context 197
  II. The Text of the Last Judgment 211
  III. The Pre–Matthean Tradition or Text 217
  IV. Matthew's Interpretation 220
  V. "Smallness" and Poverty 227
  VI. The Last Judgment in the Parousia Discourse 228
    Bibliography 234

Index of Biblical References 237
Index of Authors 243

Foreword

A basic approach to the Gospels, shared by the vast majority of centrist scholars, is that these works contain *authentic* memories of Jesus' words and deeds, *elaborated* in the course of thirty to sixty years of Christian preaching and reflection. ("Authentic" is emphasized against a radical skepticism; "elaborated," against a literalistic fundamentalism.) If one analyzes the Gospels, then, they cast light on the ministry of Jesus, on subsequent Christian concerns, and (most directly) on the view of Christ held by the evangelist as he instructed a Christian community several generations after Jesus.

Nowhere is this approach more graphically verified than in the parables, which scholars tend to regard as the most extensive legacy of the authentic words of Jesus. What did a given parable mean on his lips? How was it modified and interpreted by the apostolic preachers to convey a message to a subsequent generation? Finally, what did the parable mean in the evangelist's overall plan for presenting Jesus to his readers?

In the instance of the parables these are not merely academic questions, for they illustrate the genius of parabolic communication. Jesus did not come teaching an organized body of doctrine. Rather he proclaimed the kingdom in figurative language that lends itself to adaptation. The very fluidity of such a symbolic medium urges those who comprehend it to keep the message current and relevant through creative reuse of the parable. Thus, attention to the stages of development in the parable tradition from Jesus to the evangelists is not an exercise in curiosity, but a recognition of the fruitful flexibility inherent in Jesus' chosen style of communication. Jesus did not simply inform minds; he challenged them. By their unexpected twists the parables opened to question set religious ways of looking at things and invited consideration of divine values different from those to which the hearers were accustomed. Simple repetition of the parables by the apostolic preachers and by the evangelists would have reduced them to learned answers to past problems. Adapting the parables to new church situations not envisaged by Jesus enabled the preachers and the evangelists to open to question Christian ways of thought, which were now just as fixed as those that confronted Jesus. And so the challenge was kept alive.⌋

If a careful study of the Gospels unfolds this first-century history of parable use and reuse, the true seeker of Gospel meaning must ask a further question. To stop the study of Jesus' parables with the stage of adaptation reached when the evangelist wrote would also reduce the parables to learned answers to past problems, except that now the past would be the time of the evangelists in the last third of the first century instead of the time of Jesus in the first third of that century. Do we not need urgently to discover how the parables of Jesus can challenge a twentieth-century audience with its fixed religious views?

Attempts to "actualize" the parables for today have led scholars to bring into parable research suggestions from literary theory, philosophy, and psychology. Alas, despite the best intentions, the end result has too often been a highly complicated theoretical approach, phrased in structural jargon, which further obscures the impact of the parables. It is delightful, therefore, to find a concise book on the parables that is scholarly, perceptive, and clear. Professor Lambrecht knows the extensive literature on parables and has a masterful control of the methodology. He shows this in the abstract by explaining lucidly the principles of parable interpretation. More important he devotes most of the book to practice, taking some of the most important parables of Jesus and working through them. Readers who follow this exercise step by step will come away with a new appreciation of the radical way in which the parables functioned for Jesus and for the early church. They will also gain an idea of how those parables may function as a challenge in their own lives today.

RAYMOND E. BROWN, S.S.

Preface

This book has its immediate origin in a series of lectures which I was asked to give during an intensive one-week course, in July 1975 and 1976, organized by the American College Theological Institute of Louvain. Substantial parts of chapters one, three, four, and eight have already appeared in print, either in Dutch or English, but these have been reworked for this new publication.

On several occasions, people have urged me to publish my courses in the Faculty of Theology of the Catholic University of Louvain (K.U.L.). This request has come from colleagues, students, and friends as well as my Belgian publisher, Lannoo. All of them have stressed the need for literature on New Testament exegesis, especially on the Gospels. Priests and religious, religion teachers, and catechists are longing for such publications. It is especially for them, but also for every interested Christian, that these pages have been written.

This book is a study of the parables in the Synoptics; those contained in the Gospel of John, which are of a very different sort, are beyond the scope of this work. After the introductory chapter dealing with the parable as a literary form and the history of research on the parables, two chapters are devoted to the parables of Luke, the two following to the Marcan parables, and the three last to some parables of Matthew. Thus, not all the Synoptic parables are dealt with. The more thorough and paradigmatic treatment of a number of different types of parables, however, justifies the hope that the reader will become familiar with modern methods of parable exegesis and, at the same time, gain a better insight into what is typical in Jesus' speaking in parables.

In each chapter of this book my aim has been to present the results of specialized biblical research. Now and then some personal views have been proposed. Footnotes have been deliberately omitted, since they would have altered the nature and purpose of the work. A fairly large bibliography, however, has been added at the end of each chapter. These bibliographical lists provide a selection of scientific publications which were used in the various chapters and, moreover, document the ongoing discussion on different parable topics. It should be noted here that commentaries have not been included in these bibliographies and, further, that works which deal in a single volume with all (or most of) the parables are mentioned only once, i.e., at the end of the first chapter.

For the English translation of this book, the original Dutch version has been revised and, in certain places, slightly expanded. Furthermore, our earlier English publications to which we already referred have been thoroughly rewritten for this work, and some titles have been added to the bibliographies. The Bible translation used is, with few exceptions which are indicated as they come up, the Revised Standard Version.

Once More Astonished, the English title of this work, is taken from Paul Ricoeur's "Listening to the Parables: Once More Astonished," a homily which was published in the journal *Christianity and Crisis* 34 (1975) 304–8. This title, stressing as it does the decision-provoking quality of the parable, is meant as a pointer to the character of the parable.

At the completion of this English translation, I wish to thank René Van de Walle, S.J., Professor of Old Testament at Pune (India), who suggested the possibility of having the translation of this book published in India and who, in the midst of his many responsibilities, found time to prepare the first draft of the translation, and the Rev. Fr. Raymond Rossignol, M.E.P., Bangalore (India), who accepted the book in the series Theological Publications in India and supervised the printing of a first edition there. I also wish to express my sincere gratitude to the Rev. Christopher Begg, S.T.D. (Louvain), and Florence Morgan, S.T.L. (Louvain), who have read and carefully reworked the English text and with whom I have discussed numerous questions of translation.

This work is dedicated to my present and former students.

Abbreviations

AnBib	Analecta biblica
AssSeign II	*Assemblées du Seigneur* (second series)
AusBR	*Australian Biblical Review*
BETL	Bibliotheca ephemeridum theologicarum lovaniensium
BEvT	Beiträge zur evangelischen Theologie
Bib	*Biblica*
BibLeb	*Bibel und Leben*
BJRL	*Bulletin of the John Rylands (University) Library of Manchester*
BR	*Biblical Research*
BTB	*Biblical Theology Bulletin*
BWANT	Beiträge zur Wissenschaft vom Alten und Neuen Testament
BZ	*Biblische Zeitschrift*
CBQ	*Catholic Biblical Quarterly*
EBib	*Etudes bibliques*
ETL	*Ephemerides theologicae lovanienses*
ETR	*Etudes théologiques et religieuses*
EvQ	*Evangelical Quarterly*
EvT	*Evangelische Theologie*
ExpT	*Expository Times*
FRLANT	Forschungen zur Religion und Literatur des Alten und Neuen Testaments

Interp	*Interpretation*
JBL	*Journal of Biblical Literature*
JR	*Journal of Religion*
JTS	*Journal of Theological Studies*
KD	*Kerygma und Dogma*
KuBANT	Kommentare und Beiträge zum Alten und Neuen Testament
LB	*Linguistica biblica*
NovT	*Novum Testamentum*
NovTSup	Supplements to *NovT*
NRT	*Nouvelle revue théologique*
NThTij	*Nederlands theologisch Tijdschrift*
NTS	*New Testament Studies*
Pittsburgh TMS	Pittsburgh Theological Monograph Series
RB	*Revue biblique*
RHPR	*Revue d'histoire et de philosophie religieuses*
RScR	*Recherches de science religieuse*
RThPh	*Revue de théologie et de philosophie*
RTL	*Revue théologique de Louvain*
SBT	Studies in Biblical Theology
ScEccl	*Sciences ecclésiastiques*
ST	*Studia theologica*
StANT	Studien zum Alten und Neuen Testament
TQ	*Theologische Quartalschrift*
TT	*Tijdschrift voor Theologie*
TZ	*Theologische Zeitschrift*
WMzANT	Wissenschaftliche Monographien zum Alten und Neuen Testament
ZNW	*Zeitschrift für die neutestamentlichen Wissenschaft*
ZRGG	*Zeitschrift für die Religions- und Geistesgeschichte*
ZThK	*Zeitschrift für Theologie und Kirche*

One

Parables in the Synoptic Gospels

Understanding the Parables

In Acts 8:30 Philip asks the Ethiopian, "Do you understand what you are reading?" This question will recur as a driving force through all the chapters of this book. Our aim is to reach a fuller understanding of what we read in the parables. For, in fact, the reproach which Jesus made to those asking him to explain the parable of the Sower can also be applied to us: "Do you not understand this parable? How then will you understand all the [other] parables?" (Mk 4:13).

Though our situation bears a certain similarity to that of the Ethiopian, it is nevertheless far more complex than that of Jesus' hearers. If we fail to understand the parables, this is partly due to the ancient and foreign language in which they are told. The literal meaning of what we read has to be clarified first. Only then can the text confront us with the challenge which Jesus intended; only then are we, like his hearers, faced with the risk of not understanding on a deeper level. One of the tasks of the exegete is to remove this first type of obstacle to our understanding, as far as that is possible, so that Jesus' own words or the written message of the evangelist can directly reach us, the Christians of today.

In this introductory chapter our attention is, first of all, directed to the many possible meanings which the term "parable" can have in the Bible. This investigation will give us the opportunity to briefly expose some data concerning the evolution which has taken place within parable research (I). We shall then discuss the method to be followed in our successive chapters, dealing at the same time with the double purpose which has guided us in writing this book, i.e., to give an insight into the parables and to elucidate their direct, personal appeal (II). A list of the parables which occur in the Synoptic gospels concludes this chapter (III).

I. The Many Meanings of the Word "Parable"

In the New Testament the term "parable" is often used in a vague and general sense and includes, therefore, a whole range of possible meanings. In their specialized studies, scholars distinguish several main categories: similitudes, parables in the strict sense, exemplary stories, and allegories. We shall first consider the differences between a similitude and a parable in the strict sense.

Similitude
"From the fig tree learn its lesson [parabolē]: as soon as its branch becomes tender and puts forth its leaves, you know that the summer is near. So also, when you see these things take place, know that he [it?] is near, at the very gates" (Mk 13:28–29). "And he called them [the scribes] to him and said to them in parables, 'How can Satan cast out Satan? If a kingdom is divided against itself, that kingdom cannot stand. And if a house is divided against itself, that house will not be able to stand. And if Satan has risen up against himself and is divided, he cannot stand, but is coming to an end' " (Mk 3:23–26).

In both of these examples we are dealing with similitudes, i.e., comparisons which may or may not be elaborated upon. Although in Mk 13:29 the subject of the sentence is lacking (hence our hesitation as to the translation), in both instances a "figurative half" and an "application," i.e., the part concerning the matter compared, have obviously to be distinguished. The application is respectively introduced by, "So also, when you see these things . . . , know that . . . ," and, "And if Satan has risen up against himself. . . ." One may further remark that the figurative part deals with a typical, regularly recurring event, or with an event that can be observed. Consequently, the verbs used are generally in the present tense. In two other similitudes, the Seed Growing by Itself (Mk 4:26–29) and the Mustard Seed (Mk 4:30–32), the application is lacking; but the introductory formula fulfills its function: "The kingdom of God is as if a man should scatter . . ." (4:26) and, "With what can we compare the kingdom of God or what parable [similitude] shall we use for it? It is like . . ." (4:30–31). The comparison could not be stated more plainly.

Parable in the Strict Sense

A parable in the strict sense is written in a different style: it tells a story. A narrative of this type does not need an introductory formula; it goes straight to the point: "There was a man who had two sons; and the younger of them said to his father . . ." (Lk 15:11–12); "There was a rich man who had a steward, and charges were brought to him that this man was wasting his goods . . ." (Lk 16:1); "Listen! A sower went out to sow. And as he sowed, some seed fell along the path, and the birds came . . ." (Mk 4:3–4). In a parable, the verbs are in the historic past tense ("aorist" in Greek). No comparison is made with what recurs regularly or with what can be repeatedly observed. The narrative does not involve a typical case, but relates something which happened just once. Neither is the parable an exemplary story about something which can be proposed as a model to be imitated. A parable is also not an allegory, i.e., a fictitious story, artificially conceived, containing many details whose meanings are hidden to most and understood only by those initiated.

Exactly what is a parable then? A parable may involve something unusual which will attract the attention of the hearer—think of the extraordinary field containing the hidden treasure, the peculiar family (of the Prodigal Son), and the strange steward! The teller of parables might even use metaphors, as long as they remain within the grasp of his audience. Such metaphors would have to be familiar to his hearers and derived from their shared cultural heritage. Though the story may seem somewhat of a *suprise,* it must remain realistic, meaningful, and sufficiently plausible so as not to force the hearer to have recourse to an allegorical interpretation.

Moreover, when someone starts to narrate a parable, he unavoidably gives the impression of abruptly changing the subject to something which, at first sight, has nothing to do with the present situation. His parable seems to deviate from what is going on, and his partner in dialogue is forced to ask himself what relevance this kind of story might have. The parable creates a certain distance, an estrangement; it is apparently unconnected with the given situation. David must indeed have been startled when the prophet Nathan entered his house and, without any sort of introduction or invitation, began to speak, "There were two men in a certain city, the one rich and the other poor. The rich man had very many flocks and herds; but the poor man had nothing but one little ewe lamb, which he had bought . . ." (2 Sam 12:1–3).

It is precisely because a parable is a sort of "kill-joy" or an irritant in a sense that it possesses a thought-provoking power. It appeals to the reflective capacities of the hearers. It obliges them to ask themselves why such a story is being told at this point. It is normal that the hearer will want to examine more closely, will wish to understand, what appears to be odd. Then whenever the *insight* after an initial resistance suddenly breaks through, whenever the clouds of the image are penetrated by the light of meaning, whenever a "disclosure" occurs, then the hearer recognizes with full certainty that the concrete situation has been illuminated and explicated by the parable. German exegetes rightly state, *"Die Parabel deutet, sie kann nicht gedeutet werden"* ("The parable explains, but cannot itself be explained"), as one could explain, e.g., a similitude or an allegory). Once the enigmatic parable has been understood, it takes hold of its hearers; it has convinced them. They perceive the connection between image and reality. They acknowledge the parable's message. The evidence becomes luminous and the complex, obscure situation itself has become much more transparent and clear. David has to acknowledge that Nathan is right: "I have sinned against the Lord" (2 Sam 12:13).

However, at the very same moment that a carefully constructed and skillfully narrated parable produces this effect (i.e., *insight*, conviction, acknowledgment on the part of the hearer), there is also the recognition that this is not a matter of an intellectual game or theory which leaves the hearer unaffected. No! *Mea res agitur*— this concerns me! The suddenly evoked insight, in itself, urges the hearer on to the response which is asked of him. A good parable is thus a challenge and inexorably demands a *decision*. Once I have heard and understood a parable, I am no longer the same person as before. I am affected at the core of my being, at the center of my decision-making. I must react, whether in a positive or negative way. I cannot remain a coldly judging, neutral hearer. It is true, of course, that the narrator cannot know beforehand how his hearers will react. To tell a parable is to take a risk. But this much is certain: the parable creates an opportunity which cannot be avoided; it must either be accepted or rejected. The parable is a word-event. If successful, it changes the situation. As such, it is "performative" language; the parable-word does not return empty.

It should be clear by now that the difference between a similitude and a parable in the strict sense is great indeed. A similitude is instructive, explanatory. It is addressed to the mind and makes a rather cold, matter-of-fact impression. It appeals to evidence, to ascertainable facts which possess a probative force in the argument of the one using them. A parable in the strict sense, on the other hand, is not so explicit. To be successful, it must be a fascinating story which appeals to the hearer, captivates him, and moves him deeply. However the meaning of the parable has to be discovered and worked out by the hearer himself. The parable initiates a process in which the entire person, with his understanding and power of decision, is involved. It has been said, and with a great deal of truth, that a similitude *in*-forms, but a parable *re*-forms.

Allegorizing and Moralizing

Three names come up again and again in connection with contemporary research into the meaning of the parables. At the end of the last century the German exegete, A. Jülicher, categorically affirmed that allegorizing should be considered secondary, a product of the early church. In his view the parables of the Synoptic gospels originally had nothing to do with such ingenious allegories. Rather, they were simple comparisons or stories involving images, usually taken from everyday life in Palestine. In his massive two-volume work, *Die Gleichnisreden Jesu* (I, 1888; II, 1899), Jülicher tried to prune the parable stories of all their allegorical overgrowth. He was also of the opinion that Jesus' main purpose in using the parables was to give an illustration of general truths concerning morality and religion. Jülicher's own approach was strongly moralistic and influenced by the nineteenth century Protestant image of man.

In 1935 the well-known English scholar, C. H. Dodd, published his short book *The Parables of the Kingdom*. With respect to allegorizing, he agrees with Jülicher; he does not, however, endorse the view that the parables of the kingdom are concerned with general moral or religious truths. These parables can only be understood in the context of Jesus' eschatological proclamation. They convey the definite message of the kingdom of God, which is inaugurated and realized in Jesus himself.

The third name is that of J. Jeremias whose book, *Die Gleichnisse Jesu*, appeared in 1947. He too subscribes to Jülicher's view on allegorizing and also accepts Dodd's attempt to explain the parables on the basis of the situation and message of Jesus. However, he disagrees with Dodd's understanding of eschatology. The final stage is not fully realized with Jesus' coming; in Jeremias's view the phrase "eschatology in the process of realization" (*sich realisierend*) is a more accurate description. Moreover, Jeremias's whole approach aims at uncovering the original meaning of the parables as intended by Jesus.

> Jesus spoke to men of flesh and blood; he addressed himself to the situation of the moment. Each of his parables has a definite historical setting, and to discover that setting is the task before us. What did Jesus intend to say at this or that particular moment? What effect must his words have had on his hearers? These are the questions that we must ask, so that we may, as far as possible, recover the original meaning of the parables, and hear again his authentic voice. (*The Parables of Jesus*, p. 22)

It is due to these three remarkable studies that, for over a quarter of a century, many Bible readers have come to recognize that the allegories (and perhaps also the exemplary stories) do not derive directly from Jesus himself. Today there is fairly general agreement that Jesus told few exemplary stories (or none according to some recent exegetes) and certainly no allegories. Very soon, however, there arose among the early Christians a tendency to adapt the parables to their own situation in a moralizing way and to allegorize, i.e., to interpret the parables as abounding in allegorical features. Such tendencies then influenced the evangelists so that one can say, although with a certain exaggeration, that Matthew allegorizes and Luke moralizes. Matthew does so because he was writing his gospel for Jewish–Christians, while Luke had more non–Jewish Christians in mind in composing his gospel.

Exemplary Story

There are several ways to moralize. Taking a given parable as their starting point, the evangelists often make all kinds of moralizing applications. But this in itself is not sufficient to categorize the narratives in question as exemplary stories. Consider, for example, the parable of the Doorkeeper:

> "Take heed, watch; for you do not know when the time will come. It is like a man going on a journey, when he leaves home and puts his servants in charge, each with his work, and commands the doorkeeper to be on the watch. Watch therefore—for you do not know when the master of the house will come, in the evening, or at midnight, or at cockcrow, or in the morning—lest he come suddenly and find you asleep. And what I say to you I say to all: Watch." (Mk 13:33–37)

This parable is not an exemplary story, for its moralizing is only clear when the images are understood. An explanatory application, a transposition from image to reality, is necessary.

In Lk 10:29, after the scribe has spoken with Jesus about what is necessary in order to inherit eternal life, he asks, "And who is my neighbor?" Jesus answers by telling the story of the Good Samaritan, ending with the question, "Which of these three, do you think, proved neighbor to the man who fell among the robbers?" (10:36). In the context of Luke's gospel, the parable of the Good Samaritan is a true exemplary story, for it obviously serves as an illustration of what is meant by "acting as a neighbor." Similarly, the parable of the Rich Fool (Lk 12:16–20) is an exemplary story. The fool enlarges his barn to store his harvest. He decides to take it easy, to eat, drink, and make merry, thinking himself to be secure, not knowing that he is to die the very same night. This narrative illustrates what Jesus says in the introductory exhortation in Lk 12:15: "Take heed, and beware of all covetousness; for a man's life does not consist in the abundance of his possessions." In the same gospel, we read the parable, or rather the exemplary story of the Pharisee and the Publican (Lk 18:10–14a). The publican went home justified, not the Pharisee, "for every one who exalts himself will be humbled, but the one who humbles himself will be exalted" (18:14b). The exemplary story of the Pharisee and the Publican is an illustration of this maxim.

From the instances just considered, we can conclude that the subject matter of an exemplary story is taken from the reality with which one is concerned. There is no comparison or image, but only a "specimen," a sample taken from real life. Consequently, no transfer is needed from image to reality. The illustration selected and narrated already belongs to the intended sphere, namely, the moral and religious world.

Allegory

Unlike the exemplary story, the allegory does involve an image. Like the parable in the strict sense, it is an imaginary narrative, or, as some authors prefer to put it, a developed metaphor. Both the terms metaphor and allegory are of Greek origin, as is also, incidentally, the term parable (=comparison). "Meta-phor" indicates that the meaning of the word used has been "trans-ferred." "Allegory" literally signifies that something different is said than what is really intended. One can, therefore, readily understand why metaphors and allegories easily give rise to a somewhat puzzling and enigmatic language. Ultimately there is, of course, something common to what is said and what is meant, but the relation between the two is often highly artificial. As a rule it is the author of the allegory himself who creates this conventional link. Consequently, the intended meaning is not immediately obvious; one needs a clue. Except for those initiated, the mysterious language of the allegory is unintelligible without an explanation. An allegory is veiled in secrecy; the insider will nod knowingly because, while listening, he can interpret the details of the narrative, but the outsider is puzzled and waits in frustration for an explanation. Moreover, whereas in a parable the details only serve as parts of a whole, in an allegory the various details each have their own well-determined, transferred sense: "He who sows the good seed is the Son of man; the field is the world, and the good seed means the sons of the kingdom; the weeds are the sons of the evil one, and the enemy who sowed them is the devil; the harvest is the close of the age, and the reapers are angels" (Mt 13:37b–39). All this must be told explicitly; for every word of the metaphorical half has its corresponding term in the part concerning the matter in question. Without such an explanation it is impossible to understand the allegory of the Weeds among the Wheat (Mt 13:24–30). The allegory of the Sower must be explicated in a similar way: see Mk 4:14–20.

Where a clear explanation is lacking, uncertainty prevails. Mt 22:7 is a case in point: "The king was angry, and he sent his troops and destroyed those murderers and burnt their city." Can it be taken for granted that this refers to the fate of Jerusalem in the year A.D. 70—a fate which was considered as a divine punishment? Is the parable of the Guests Invited to the Feast, taken as a whole (Mt 22:1–14), an allegory depicting God's saving initiative and man's response to it? The parables themselves and the gospel of Matthew in its entirety can of course help us in answering these questions. But the elucidation and interpretation of any allegory always remains a delicate matter.

Did Jesus, in fact, never employ a single allegory? Whether he did or not, this much is certain: the process of allegorizing started very early and is already apparent in the Synoptic gospels. In post-apostolic times it became extremely widespread. To illustrate this allegorizing process, we cite a passage from an article by C. H. Lindijer, in which he discusses the interpretation of the parable of the Good Samaritan:

> Widely propagated, especially in earlier times, is that type of explanation in accordance with which the majority of the other parables are interpreted. Generally, the explanation is worked out in such a way that it can be called an allegorical interpretation. With few exceptions, the commentators regard the Samaritan as a personification of Christ, while the vicissitudes of the traveler illustrate the fall and redemption of Adam. The interpretation proceeds as follows:
>
> The *traveler* is Adam, i.e., mankind.
>
> *Jerusalem* is paradise, the heavenly Jerusalem, the celestial city of peace.
>
> Adam descends from this heavenly Jerusalem to *Jericho,* the world. Jericho is then connected with the Hebrew word for moon. The moon, waxing and waning, represents mortal man, or—with reference to Sir 27:11—the fool, the sinner.
>
> The *robbers* are the demons who deprive Adam of virtue and immortality. He is left half-dead, i.e., alive in so far as man can know God, but dead in so far as he is in the power of sin; he is, therefore, not totally corrupt. At times another explanation is given: the soul is dead although the body is still alive.
>
> The *priest* is the Law. The *Levite* represents the Law or the prophets. Alternatively, both together signify the cult of the Old Testament.
>
> The *Samaritan* is Christ. *Oil* and *wine* are respectively the

word of consolation and admonition. The *mount*, the beast, is the body of Christ on which He bears our sins on the cross. To *be lifted onto it* is to believe in the Incarnation.

The *inn* is the Church. The *inn-keeper* represents the apostles Peter and Paul, or their successors. The *next day* is the day of the Resurrection or the time after the Resurrection. The two *silver coins* are interpreted in various ways: the two Testaments, the double commandment of love for God and neighbor; the promise of reward both in this life and the next (Mt 19:29); the preaching of the Law and the gospel, the four gospels, knowledge of both Father and Son.

The *return* of the Samaritan is the second coming of Christ.

The *extra expenses* refer either to Paul's advice about remaining celibate or to his doing manual labor.

This type of interpretation is very ancient and can already be found, in short form, in the writings of Irenaeus in the second century: ". . . the Lord commits to the Holy Ghost that man of His, who had fallen among thieves; whom He did Himself pity, and bound up his wounds, giving two royal pennies . . ." (*Adversus haereses* III 17,3). About the same period, Clement of Alexandria wrote, ". . . who could this be except the Saviour Himself? . . . who more than He has pitied us, all but put to death by world-rulers of the darkness . . . ? . . . This is He that poureth out on our wounded hearts wine, the blood of the vine of David; that brought and bestowed lavishly on us mercy [Note: The Greek word for "mercy" was pronounced much like that for "oil"] from the Father's heart" (*Quis Dives* 29). ("Oude en nieuwe visies op de gelijkenis van de barmhartige Samaritaan," *NThTij* 15 [1960–61], 11–23, pp. 12–13.)

Hermeneutics, Structuralism, and the Parables

Our survey of research concerning the parables is not yet complete with the mention and contextualization of the works of Jülicher, Dodd, and Jeremias. Today, to a greater extent than previously, scholars are examining the various types of language: spoken word and written text, living and dead, profane and religious, literary and technical, informative, emotive, and performative language. Furthermore, the intensive study of hermeneutics, the problematic of understanding, has radically revised our view of the parables. The classification of the parables into four different literary genres goes back to Jülicher. But, in our detailed analysis of the parable in the strict sense we have already taken into account these various new approaches. According to Jülicher, the parable in the strict sense is a developed comparison in which the figurative half has been expanded into a narrative. The parable helps to illustrate what is said or thought in order to make it more graphic and to clarify it. Today, however, there is a growing awareness that the parable involves a "metaphorical process." The metaphor can no longer be regarded in a negative way, as is clearly the case with Jülicher. The authentic, not yet petrified metaphor is not a static entity. It is more than a figure of speech with a merely decorative value. It does more than exemplify the matter at hand without giving any new information about it. On the contrary, by using a metaphor one sets a dynamic process in motion. Out of the tension between the apparently impossible literal sense and the transferred meaning still to be discovered, a semantic renewal emerges: the hearer gets a fresh, hitherto unsuspected insight into the matter under discussion. Today the parable is considered as a form of speech which employs such a metaphorical process within a narrative. In fact, when a parable is told it is precisely with the intention of evoking such a new insight.

In this context a word should be added about "structuralism," i.e., the analysis of the deep structures of language. One cannot a priori dismiss the structural analysis of the parables of the gospels as unjustified. Nevertheless, such studies as have been attempted till now have not proved very promising. This type of extremely "formal" investigation is characterized by a complicated and cryptic terminology. One often gets the impression that its lengthy descriptions tend to actually divert attention from the content of the text. Moreover, the method of structural analysis has been applied to the parables in rather divergent ways, and the results are disappointing. It might be asked whether these negative features are not to be attributed to the fact that the structural analysis of the parables is still in its initial stage. Many exegetes have adopted a cautious wait-and-see attitude, and understandably so. P. Ricoeur, the philosopher of language, is somewhat less reserved. Nevertheless, in his noteworthy article "Biblical Hermeneutics," he too warns against the antihistorical tendency of French structuralism which, for example, regards the narrative as a strictly autonomous, self-contained, aesthetic unit, without relation to realities other than the text itself and without any message from the author to the reader: i.e., structure for the sake of structure.

II. Insight and Appeal

From Jesus to the Evangelist

In our brief exposition of the four types of parables, we were already confronted with the problem of "original" and "secondary" elements. We have also mentioned the attempt made by modern exegetes to isolate and reconstruct the most ancient versions of the parables, i.e., the ones narrated by Jesus himself. It is very important from the outset to be aware of the stages through which the parable tradition has gone before reaching the written form now available to us. Four such stages must be clearly distinguished: The later interpretations made by the early church, mainly of a moralizing and allegorizing character, will not be considered even though contemporary Christians in their understanding of the parables are still guided and conditioned by those interpretations.

(a) In his preaching, *Jesus* narrated a certain number of parables. In every case he did so in concrete circumstances: at a certain time, in a certain place, to a definite group of people, and on a particular occasion. In short, the parables as originally spoken by Jesus were clearly situated. This implies that the images which he used were well-known to his contemporaries, related to the customs and usage of the people to whom his hearers belonged. In fact, the whole economic and social background of the parables was self-evident to them. But there is an additional factor of still greater importance: the specific character of the message which Jesus wanted to convey by his parables was illustrated and corroborated by the context of his own life. The people around Jesus who listened to his parables were witnesses of his way of life and could refer to his previous words and deeds. Although perhaps only vaguely, they suspected what the aim of Jesus' life was, and, they themselves constituted a part of the occasion and the situation when the parable was narrated. All this undoubtedly helped them to understand the particular parable and to experience the full impact of his word. But it was still up to them to react to Jesus' challenge and make the difficult, existential decision called for by the parable.

(b) After Jesus' death and resurrection the parables began, as it were, a new life, a second phase. They were told anew by people other than Jesus, although these people were inspired by his

Spirit. During the first postpaschal period of *apostolic preaching*, the parables were still a part of the oral tradition and did not yet belong to a written text. Each preacher had to repeat the parables in his own way in order to bring them to life, and thus to give them a new impact on his hearers. In doing so he presented them as parables of Jesus and spoke in his name. But by this time, Jesus had become the "Lord," and the postpaschal situation was basically different from that which had existed before the resurrection. The parables were now narrated to Christians, or used with a missionary purpose in view. Very soon they had to be told in another language, addressed to people belonging to another culture. In many respects the distance between the original narrative and the new actualizations grew steadily greater. This gap rendered the understanding of the parables more difficult and could give rise to a sort of mental block. This led the preacher to introduce changes, adaptations, and additional explanations into the parables.

It was not only the foreign cultural background or the change of language, however, which affected the original narratives. Christians of this early postpaschal period had their own new insights and specific needs. The preacher of parables, conscious of his pastoral responsibility, spontaneously began to discover his own personal view of the salvific events or the views of his religious community in the parables, and if need be he would even read them into the text. Thus allegorizing began. He would also use the parables to comfort his fellow believers, to admonish or reproach them. Allegorization and moralization can be traced back to these early days.

(c) A further decisive step was taken when the parables, which until then had circulated orally, were written down for the first time; they were, so to speak, poured into objective, fixed, and always accessible forms. On the one hand, one should not regard this transition to *fixation in writing* in too radical a fashion since the first written formulations of the parables did not necessarily give rise to the later officially known and accepted versions. Moreover, for the ancient culture to which the first Christians belonged, oral tradition was something more fixed and thus more accessible than we might easily suppose. On the other hand, one must recognize the new element at this stage and its possible implications: from that point on the Christian community possessed the parables in a written form. Every preacher who knew of its existence could use this formulation and compare the other oral versions with it; he could always refer back to this fixed form. The written text could now be used as a point of reference. The stream of tradition, which formerly could flow forward rather freely, came to a halt. A standard text was now available. The written version was, it is true, not yet "sacred," not yet "canonical"; it could still be—and was—altered, rewritten, and adapted. Nevertheless, this first fixation in written form was an extraordinarily important moment in the tradition process.

(d) A fourth and final stage was the *incorporation of the parables into the gospels*. The narratives were taken up and integrated into a larger literary work. The number of parables taken over varies with each evangelist. One must naturally keep in mind the theoretical possibility that, before the gospels, collections of orally-fixed or even written parables might have existed. There is also the probability, if not the certainty, that prior to the evangelists documents existed which contained parables (e.g. the so-called sayings-source). Nevertheless, the important new development in this fourth stage is the fact that the gospel gives a written context to the parables. They now function within a wider whole. The evangelist makes use of them in light of the purpose of his whole work. The parables are thus henceforth provided with a gospel framework. It can now practically be taken for granted that the biographical data which forms part of this framework—time, place, circumstances—need not always be considered as strictly historical. The concrete literary context which the evangelist created during this fourth stage, around A.D. 70–90, does not as a rule correspond to the historical situation in Jesus' public life, some time in the thirties. The various situations of the parables, determined to a great extent by the written contexts in which they stand, differ at times from one evangelist to another and must in the first place be understood on the basis of the distinct literary and theological viewpoints of the different evangelists.

The Way Back: Insight into the Process

Having come this far in our introductory chapter, we are now better equipped to describe more fully the reasons which inspired us to write this book. When modern Christians come to know all the intricacies of the tradition and redaction process through which the parables of the Synoptic gospels have passed, their first reaction may be one of perplexity. Most will, nevertheless, accept the demanding method which has to be followed if the parables are to be understood. First of all, the parables available to us are found only in the gospels, i.e., in a written form and within the literary context of those documents. The way back to Jesus must therefore begin from the gospel narratives; no other starting point is possible. And the way back must also take into account all the stages of the tradition process; no shortcut exists. If we wish to acquire a better understanding of the parables, it is clear that we have to follow this path. Today's Christians also wish to know whether there is a continuity between what Jesus intended in preaching a given parable and what the early church or the evangelist has made it say. The first major objective of this book is therefore to help the reader acquire a better insight into this tradition process, so that he or she will be able to come to a responsible position on the question of whether or not there is a real link between Jesus and the evangelist.

Where Now? The Parables Today and Tomorrow

Our second objective is related to the first. The Christian believer is not only interested in acquiring some deeper knowledge. His or her faith is not merely a matter of rational understanding. If Jesus is the still-living Lord, if what he did continues to happen now, then his voice must remain audible, it must resound ever again. How then shall we actualize the parables today, for ourselves and for others? Are the best means to achieve this actualization moralizing and allegorizing, as so often in the past? If it is true that Jesus spoke mostly, though not exclusively, in parables in the strict sense and used few or no allegories, should not then the actualization also consist in a real reproduction of the word-event with its three essential elements of *surprise, insight, and decision* (cf. the description on pp. 3–5)? *N.B.*

Undoubtedly, there are many difficulties besetting our understanding of the parables. These arise from the parables' different cultural background, from the loss of their original contexts within Jesus' public life and from the fact that the evangelists have already to a certain extent moralized and allegorized the original parables.

All these obstacles must be removed as far as possible. But, even then the greatest problem would still remain to be faced: How can one create the same awareness of a direct, personal message, of the challenge which Jesus intended with the original parable? How can the preacher or catechist actualize these narratives in accordance with the use Jesus originally made of them? In a homily P. Ricoeur characterized a successful actualization: "Listening to the Parables: Once More Astonished." The parable should once again puzzle us, provoke once more a startled surprise. The three elements of the parable as word-event, which we have just recalled, are often referred to by contemporary authors. In fact, some of the parables themselves illustrate what takes place when a true parable is told:

> The kingdom of heaven is like a treasure hidden in a field, which a man found and covered up; then in his joy he goes and sells all that he has and buys that field.
> Again, the kingdom of heaven is like a merchant in search of fine pearls, who, on finding one pearl of great value, went and sold all that he had and bought it. (Mt 13:44–46)

(a) Somebody finds the treasure or the pearl. This is the moment of amazement, the surprise. While Ricoeur simply states "he finds," J. D. Crossan calls it a revelation, the "advent" or dawn of something new. (b) But then, suddenly, the finder comprehends what has happened; he realizes the value of the treasure or the pearl. He starts acting. He sells everything. "He loses," says Ricoeur; Crossan speaks of this second moment as a "revolution." (c) Finally, the person concerned takes the decisive step. He accepts the risk, puts his entire existence on the line, spurred on by his newly acquired insight. He buys the treasure or the pearl. According to Ricoeur, "he chooses"; for Crossan this is the "resolution."

These three moments of the word-event are, moreover, linked with the three time dimensions: (a) *The future* becomes visible, a secret is revealed. One is puzzled and perplexed, surmises a new world with the possibility of authentic existence. The kingdom of God is announced. (b) The hearer must break with *the past*; an "inversion," a reversal of this past is demanded of him; a "revolution" is required. He is placed in an Exodus situation; he must leave the familiar country behind, sell his possessions, and give up his old certainties. (c) As for *the present*, a far-reaching decision must be taken here and now; a "resolution," a "decision," is asked of him, implying a "total commitment" (I. T. Ramsey). The hearer opts for authenticity, places himself under God's dominion and kingship, and thus becomes a "new creation."

With respect to this systematization (Ricoeur: "finds, loses, chooses"; Crossan: "revelation, revolution, resolution"), it can be questioned whether these and other authors (e.g., R. W. Funk and D. O. Via) conceive of the three moments in exactly the same way, or, further, whether a clearcut distinction between the three stages can be maintained. But nevertheless, the importance of such an analysis cannot be denied. In modern research on the parables one can no longer ignore the study of the language-event. The word-event, which a parable in the strict sense is, effects something. A parable is "performative"; it aims at and brings about an existential change.

The second objective of this book thus concerns the actualization of the parables. It is not only necessary to gain intellectual insight into the New Testament events as they happened in the past in order to be able to justify one's faith with full knowledge of the facts. There is a still greater need to bring the parables to bear on one's life, to discern what decision they are intended to evoke here and now. How are the parables to be actualized today and tomorrow?

III. Overview of the Synoptic Parables

In order to realize the double purpose which we have just outlined, we shall study representative parables and collections of parables. Our intention is not an exhaustive treatment of the entire material. Nevertheless, it does seem useful to begin by presenting an overview of all the parables contained in the Synoptic gospels. Two preliminary remarks should be made before doing this however. First, this list does not include those short utterances, sayings, and metaphors which for Jesus and the evangelists may have constituted full-fledged parables. For instance, we omit from our list Mk 3:23b–27, even though in 3:23a Mark himself introduces these verses with the words "He [Jesus] said to them in parables":

> "How can Satan cast out Satan? If a kingdom is divided against itself, that kingdom cannot stand. And if a house is divided against itself, that house will not be able to stand. And if Satan

> has risen up against himself and is divided, he cannot stand,
> but is coming to an end. But no one can enter a strong man's
> house and plunder his goods, unless he first binds the strong
> man; then indeed he may plunder his house."

While conceding that it is not always easy to draw the line between the too short and the long enough, we have incorporated
into our list only those parables which have a certain length and
involve a kind of narrative, i.e., those which are, in fact, usually
called parables or similitudes by contemporary commentators.

The second remark concerns the sequence followed: the parables are listed according to the two-source theory, which we accept
here as a working hypothesis. Mark is the oldest gospel. Matthew
and Luke used, beside Marcan material, a second source, the so-
called *Quelle* (Q, *Logienquelle* = sayings-source). In addition to
these two sources, Matthew and Luke also each have their proper
material, which the Germans call *Sondergut*, i.e., special material.
It is possible that Matthew and/or Luke did not take all the nine
common parables listed under Q from this sayings-source, but
rather from their *Sondergut* (this might, e.g., be the case for the
two versions of the Talents, Mt 25:14–30, and the Pounds, Lk
19:12–27). Neither do we exclude the possibility that one or another of the parables listed as *Sondergut* are actually Q-texts
which, for some reason of his own, one of the two evangelists did
not take up into his gospel (this might be the case, e.g., for the
Lost Coin, Lk 15:8–10).

There are in all 42 parables included in the list: 6 from Mk, 22
from Mt, and 31 from Lk. Of these 42, there are 29 which are
found in only one of the three gospels: 2 in Mk, 9 in Mt, and 18
in Lk.

(a) *Marcan Material* (6 parables)

	Mk	Mt	Lk
The Sower	4:3–9	13:3–9	8:5–8
The Mustard Seed	4:30–32	13:31–32	13:18–19
The Wicked Tenants	12:1–11	21:33–44	20:9–18
The Budding Fig Tree	13:28–29	24:32–33	21:29–31
The Seed Growing by Itself	4:26–29		
The Doorkeeper	13:34–36		

(b) *Q-Material* (9 parables)

	Mt	Lk
Going before the Judge	5:25–26	12:58–59
The Children in the Market Place	11:16–19	7:31–35
The Return of the Evil Spirit	12:43–45	11:24–26
The Leaven	13:33	13:20–21
The Lost Sheep	18:12–14	15:4–7
The Guests Invited to the Feast	22:2–14	14:16–24
The Burglar at Night	24:43–44	12:39–40
The Faithful or Wicked Servant	24:45–51	12:42–46
The Talents/The Pounds	25:14–30	19:11–27

(c) *Sondergut* (27 parables; Mt: 9; Lk: 18)

	Mt
The Weeds among the Wheat	13:24–30
The Hidden Treasure	13:44
The Pearl	13:45–46
The Fisherman's Net	13:47–50
The Unforgiving Servant	18:23–35
The Workers in the Vineyard	20:1–16
The Two Sons	21:28–32
The Wise and Foolish Virgins	25:1–13
The Last Judgment	25:31–46

	Lk
The Two Debtors	7:41–43
The Good Samaritan	10:30–37
The Persistent Friend	11:5–8
The Rich Fool	12:16–21
The Watchful Servants	12:35–38
The Barren Fig Tree	13:6–9
The Closed Door	13:24–30
The Places of Honor	14:8–11
Inviting Guests	14:12–14
Building a Tower	14:28–30
Planning a War	14:31–32
The Lost Coin	15:8–10

The Prodigal Son   15:11–32
The Unjust Steward   16:1–8
The Rich Man and Lazarus   16:19–21
The Useless Servant   17:7–10
The Unjust Judge   18:1–8
The Pharisee and the
  Publican   18:9–14

BIBLIOGRAPHY

The works listed are divided into two categories. First, a number of books and articles are mentioned which more or less continue the Jülicher–Dodd–Jeremias line of research. Then follow some studies which aim at a new approach, e.g., from the perspective of word-event, symbol and metaphor, and structuralism:

1.

Jülicher, A., Die Gleichnisreden Jesu, I: Die Gleichnisreden Jesu im Allgemeinen, Tübingen, 1888; II: Auslegung der Gleichnisreden der Drei Ersten Evangelien, Tübingen, 1899.
Dodd, C. H., The Parables of the Kingdom, London, 1935.
Jeremias, J., Die Gleichnisse Jesu, Zurich, 1947; The Parables of Jesus, 2nd ed. of ET of 6th revised and expanded German ed. (1962) by S. H. Hooke; 3rd rev. ed., London, 1972.

Armstrong, E. A., The Gospel Parables, London, 1967.
Berger, K., "Materialien zu Form und Überlieferungsgeschichte neutestamentlicher Gleichnisse," NovT 15 (1973) 1–37.
Bultmann, R., The History of the Synoptic Tradition, 2nd ed. of ET of 2nd German ed. (1931) by J. Marsh, Oxford, 1968.
Buzy, D., Les paraboles, traduites et commentées, 16th ed., Paris, 1948.
Cadoux, A. T., The Parables of Jesus: Their Art and Use, New York, 1931.
Carlston, C. E., The Parables of the Triple Tradition, Philadelphia, 1975
Cerfaux, L., The Treasure of the Parables, ET by M. Bent, De Pere, Wis., 1968.
Dupont, J., Pourquoi des paraboles? La méthode parabolique de Jésus, Lire la Bible 46, Paris, 1977.
Eichholz, G., Einführung in die Gleichnisse, Neukirchen, 1963.
———, Gleichnisse der Evangelien, Neukirchen, 1971.
George, A., "Parabole," Dictionnaire de la Bible. Supplément 6 (1960) cols. 1149–77.
———, "Les paraboles," Lumière et Vie 23 (1974) 35–48.
Goulder, M. D., "Characteristics of the Parables in the Several Gospels," JTS 19 (1968) 51–69.

————, *Midrash and Lection in Matthew*, London, 1974 (see pp. 47–69: "The Midrashic Parable").

Harrington, W. J., *He Spoke in Parables*, Dublin, 1964.

Hermaniuk, M., *La Parabole Evangélique*. *Enquête exégétique et critique*, Dissertationes ad gradum magistri in Facultate Theologica (Universitas Catholica Lovaniensis), Ser. II 38, Bruges-Paris-Louvain, 1947.

Jones, G. V., *The Art and Truth of the Parables: A Study in their Literary Form and Modern Interpretation*, London, 1964.

Kahlefeld, H., *Parables and Instructions in the Gospels*, ET by A. Swidler, Montreal, 1966.

Lambrecht, J., "Parabels in Mc. 4," *TT* 15 (1975) 26–43.

Meinertz, M., *Die Gleichnisse Jesu*, 4th ed. Münster, 1948.

Michaelis, W., *Die Gleichnisse Jesu*, Die urchristliche Botschaft 32, 3rd ed., Hamburg, 1956.

Smith, B.T.D., *The Parables of the Synoptic Gospels*, Cambridge, 1937.

TeSelle, S., *Speaking in Parables*, Philadelphia, 1975.

2.

Alexandre, J., "Note sur l'esprit des paraboles, en réponse à P. Ricoeur," *ETR* 51 (1976) 367–72.

Almeida, Y., *L'opérativité sémantique des récits-paraboles. Sémiotique narrative et textuelle. Herméneutique du discours religieux*, Bibliothèque des Cahiers de l'Institut de Linguistique de Louvain 13, Leuven–Paris, 1978.

Aurelio, T., *Disclosures in den Gleichnissen Jesu. Eine Anwendung der disclosure-Theorie von I. T. Ramsey, der modernen Metaphorik und der Theorie der Sprechakte auf die Gleichnisse Jesu*, Regensburger Studien zur Theologie 8, Frankfurt, 1977.

Biser, E., *Die Gleichnisse Jesu. Versuch einer Deutung*, Munich, 1965.

Boucher, M., *The Mysterious Parable: A Literary Study*, CBQ Monograph Series 6, Washington, 1977

Crossan, J. D., "Parable as Religious and Poetic Experience," *JR* 53 (1973) 330–58.

————, *In Parables: The Challenge of the Historical Jesus*, New York, 1973.

————, *The Dark Interval: Towards a Theology of Story*, Niles, Il., 1975.

————, "Paradox Gives Rise to Metaphor: Paul Ricoeur's Hermeneutics and the Parables of Jesus," *BR* 24–25 (1979–1980) 20–37. (For Ricoeur's response, see pp. 70–80 of the same issue.)

Fuchs, E., *Hermeneutik*, 2nd ed., Bad Cannstatt, 1958 (see especially pp. 211–30: para. 16, "Die Metapher, das Bildwort, die Allegorie"; para. 17, "Gleichnis und Parabel").

————, "Bemerkungen zur Gleichnisauslegung," in Fuchs, *Zur Frage nach dem historischen Jesus*, Tübingen, 1960, pp. 136–42.

————, "Die Frage nach dem historischen Jesus," in Fuchs, *Zur Frage nach dem historischen Jesus*, Tübingen, 1960, pp. 143–67.

Funk, R. W., "Language as it Occurs in the New Testament: Parable," in Funk, *Language, Hermeneutic and Word of God*, New York, 1966, pp. 123–222.

———, "The Narrative Parables: The Birth of a Language Tradition," in *God's Christ and His People: Studies in Honour of N. A. Dahl*, ed. J. Jervell and W. A. Meeks, Oslo–Bergen–Tromsö, 1977, pp. 43–50.

Güttgemanns, E., "Die linguistische didaktische Methodik der Gleichnisse Jesu," in Güttgemanns, *Studia linguistica neotestamentica*, BEvT 60, Munich, 1971, pp. 99–183.

———, "Narrative Analyse synoptischer Texte," *LB* (1973) no. 25/26, pp. 50–73.

Harnisch, W., "Die Sprachkraft der Analogie. Zur These vom 'argumentativen Charakter' der Gleichnisse Jesu," *ST* 28 (1974) 1–20.

Huffman, N. A., "Atypical Features in the Parables of Jesus," *JBL* 97 (1978) 207–220.

Jörns, K. P., "Die Gleichnisverkündigung Jesu. Reden von Gott als Wort Gottes," in *Der Ruf Jesu und die Antwort der Gemeinde. Exegetische Untersuchungen J. Jeremias zum 70. Geburtstag gewidmet*, ed. E. Lohse, Göttingen, 1970, pp. 157–78.

Jüngel, E., *Paulus und Jesus*, Hermeneutische Untersuchungen zur Theologie 2, Tübingen, 1962 (see especially pp. 71–214).

Klauck, H. J., *Allegorie und Allegorese in synoptischen Gleichnistexten*, Neutestamentliche Abhandlungen, n.s. 13, Münster, 1978.

Klemm, H. G., "Die Gleichnisauslegung Ad. Jülichers im Bannkreis der Fabeltheorie Lessings," *ZNW* 60 (1969) 153–74.

Linnemann, E., *Parables of Jesus: Introduction and Exposition*, ET of 3rd German ed. (1964) by J. Sturdy, London, 1966.

Linton, O., "Coordinated Sayings and Parables in the Synoptic Gospels: Analysis versus Theories," *NTS* 26 (1979–1980) 139–63.

Magass, W., "Bemerkungen zur Gleichnisauslegung," *Kairos* 20 (1978) 40–52.

Maillot, A., *Les paraboles de Jésus aujourd'hui*, Geneva, 1973.

Mees, M., "Die moderne Deutung der Parabeln und ihre Probleme," *Vetera Christianorum* 11 (1974) 416–33.

Patte, D., ed., *Semiology and Parables: Exploration of the Possibilities offered by Structuralism for Exegesis. Papers of the Vanderbilt University Conference, May 15–17, 1975*, Pittsburgh TMS 9, Pittsburgh, 1976.

Pépin, J., *Mythe et allégorie. Les origines grecques et les contestations judéo-chrétiennes*, 2nd ed., Paris, 1976.

Perrin, N., "The Parables," in Perrin, *The New Testament: An Introduction*, New York, 1974, pp. 291–95.

———, *Jesus and the Language of the Kingdom: Symbol and Metaphor in New Testament Interpretation*, Philadelphia, 1976.

Ricoeur, P., "La métaphore et le problème central de l'herméneutique," *Revue philosophique de Louvain* 70 (1972) 93–112.

———, "Biblical Hermeneutics," *Semeia* (1975) no. 4, pp. 27–145.

————, "Listening to the Parables: Once More Astonished," *Christianity and Crisis* 34 (1975) 304–8.

————, *La métaphore vive*, Paris, 1975.

Robinson, J. M., "Jesus' Parables as God Happening," in *Jesus and the Historian. Written in Honor of E. C. Colwell*, ed. F. T. Trotter, Philadelphia, 1968, pp. 134–50.

Schillebeeckx, E., *Jesus: An Experiment in Christology*, ET by H. Hoskins, London, 1979.

Via, D. O., *The Parables: Their Literary and Existential Dimension*, Philadelphia, 1967.

Weder, H., *Die Gleichnisse Jesu als Metaphern*, FRLANT 120, Göttingen, 1978.

Wilder, A., "The Parable," in Wilder, *Early Christian Rhetoric: The Language of the Gospel*, 2nd ed., Cambridge, Mass., 1971, pp. 71–88.

Good surveys of recent parable research:

Harrington, W. J., "The Parables in Recent Study (1960–1971)," *BTB* 2 (1972) 219–41.

Klauck, H.–J., "Neue Beiträge zur Gleichnisforschung," *BibLeb* 13 (1972) 214–30.

Little, J. C., "Parable Research in the Twentieth Century," *ExpT* 87 (1975–1976) 356–60; 88 (1976–1977) 40–43, 71–75.

Perrin, N., "The Modern Interpretation of the Parables of Jesus and the Problem of Hermeneutics," *Interpr* 25 (1971) 131–48.

J. D. Crossan has compiled a rather extensive bibliography: "A Basic Bibliography for Parables Research," *Semeia* (1974) no. 1, pp. 236–74. A more recent bibliography is that provided by W. S. Kissinger: *The Parables of Jesus: A History of Interpretation and Bibliography*, ATLA Bibliography Series 4, Metuchen–London, 1979.

Two

Parables in Luke 15
What Was Lost

Few parables lend themselves more readily to reinterpretation than that of the Prodigal Son. André Gide published his version of it in 1906 under the title "Le retour de l'enfant prodigue." In Gide's presentation the father is as hardhearted as the older son. In addition, there is also a third son, younger than the other two, who in a conversation with the returned prodigal gives voice to his own adventurous longings. Similar alterations of the gospel data can also be found in more recent publications in which the attempt is made to relate the parable to the contemporary generation gap. Young people clash with their parents and demand their freedom; the older generation—it is said—usually reacts in the wrong way. It would be better for them to imitate the father in the parable and to allow the young person to find his own way and thus develop his own personality, if need be even at the cost of some harm and disgrace to himself. In our opinion, such free manipulations of the text do not deserve to be called exegesis. Moreover, it is questionable whether this kind of actualization is advisable or even responsible. But how then ought it to be done? In our exposition of Lk 15 we shall try to propose an answer to this question.

There are also other reasons which lead us to the study of the Lucan parables. The third evangelist has preserved the greatest number of parables. Although his tendency to moralize is well-known, one has nonetheless the impression that some of his parables have remained closer to the form in which Jesus spoke them than have those of Matthew and Mark. In any case, Luke does not seem to accept the famous hardening of heart theory which Mark formulates in 4:11–12 even though Luke himself includes it in shortened form in 8:10. Luke's gospel deserves our attention then because it contains a great number of parables and narrates them with a certain simplicity, a feature which may perhaps be considered as a sign of his fidelity to the original spoken version.

Chapter 15 of Luke's gospel contains three parables dealing with "what was lost." These parables are very well-known, in fact so well-known that they have lost their evocative power and are no longer able to make an impact on many Christians. It might be good to regard this situation as a challenge to us to find a way of bringing the message of these parables to expression once again.

In content, practically the whole of Lk 15 belongs to the Lucan *Sondergut;* only the parable of the Lost Sheep (15:3–7 = Mt 18:12–14) contains a Q-text. The presence of this Q-fragment is an additional reason for studying chapter 15. Via a detailed comparison of the two versions of the Lost Sheep it may be possible to reconstruct, at least partially, the Q-text which is older than the versions found in the gospels, and thus to ascertain whether our initial impression concerning Luke's simplicity and fidelity in the rendition of the parables is well-founded.

This study of Lk 15 proceeds in four steps: first, the composition and structure of the chapter as a whole are examined (I); then the parable of the Lost Sheep is analysed—comparing Luke's version with that of Matthew, we try to work back to their common source in order thereafter to define the aim and message of this reconstructed older version (– Q?), on the basis of which we may see how Luke and Matthew, each in his own way, understood and reinterpreted this older parable (II); next, attention is directed to the story of the Prodigal Son (III); by way of conclusion, we take another overall view of chapter 15 and investigate the possibility of a modern actualization (IV).

I. A Closer Look at Chapter 15

It is well-known that Luke's gospel, in contrast to the other two Synoptics, contains an extensive travel narrative which starts at 9:51: "When the days drew near for him to be received up, he [Jesus] set his face to go to Jerusalem." Jesus arrives in Jerusalem in 19:45: "He entered the temple and began to drive out those who sold . . ." In between these two events the evangelist repeatedly reminds us that Jesus is on the way: see 13:22, e.g., "He went on his way through towns and villages, teaching and journeying toward Jerusalem"; cf. also 9:51, 53, 56, 57; 10:1, 38; 13:33; 14:1; 17:11; 18:31, 35; 19:1, 11, 28, 29, 37. It is obvious, however, that Luke has used this framework of Jesus' going up to Jerusalem to situate a whole mass of gospel material, notwithstanding the fact that this material for the most part has little or nothing to do with that journey.

Chapter 15 stands within the Lucan travel narrative. It constitutes a well-rounded whole made up of three parables dealing with "what was lost." After chapter 14, the introduction (15:1–2) describes a new situation: "Now the tax collectors and sinners were all drawing near to him. And the Pharisees and the scribes murmured, saying, 'This man receives sinners and eats with them.' " Jesus addresses himself in these three parables to the murmuring scribes and Pharisees. From 16:1 onwards he speaks to his disciples.

The structure of Lk 15 is very simple: (a) Two verses describe the new situation and the reason why Jesus speaks (vv. 1–2). (b) Then two succinct similitudes follow, the Lost Sheep (vv. 4–7) and the Lost Coin (vv. 8–10). (c) These are followed by the long parable of the Prodigal Son (vv. 11–32). Connecting links are minimal. Verse 3 is an introductory formula: "So he told them this parable"; the two short similitudes are coupled by a single particle "or" (v. 8); the transition to the narrative of the Prodigal Son is also extremely simple: "And he said further . . ." (v. 11).

The Twin–Similitudes (vv. 4–10)

The Lost Sheep and the Lost Coin in Lk 15 are a typical example of a "twin-similitude." Similar double similitudes are found elsewhere in the Synoptics, e.g., the Mustard Seed and the Leaven (Lk 13:18–21 = Mt 13:31–33); the Hidden Treasure and the Pearl (Mt 13:44–46); and Building a Tower and Planning a War (Lk 14:28–32). The story of the Lost Sheep concerns a man, that of the Lost Coin a woman. With their applications these two narratives belong to the genre "similitude." In both the figurative part begins with a rather lengthy question. They are separated from one another merely by the single small particle "or." They have a similar content and verbally almost the same application. They are constructed according to the same pattern, although the second being a kind of repetition of the first is somewhat shorter. It is worthwhile to place the two texts parallel to one another. The figurative part with its two long sentences itself comprises two parts: the search and what happens after the finding. Together with the applications there are, then, three sentences which can be considered as the three subsections:

(1) *Search*

4 What man of you,	8 Or what woman,
having a hundred sheep,	having ten silver coins,
if he has lost one of them,	if she loses one coin,
does not leave the ninety-nine	does not light a lamp
in the wilderness	and sweep the house
and go after the one which is lost,	and seek diligently
until he finds it?	until she finds it?

(2) *Actions after the finding*

5 And when he has found it	9 And when she has found it,
he lays it on his shoulders, rejoicing.	
6 And when he comes home,	
he calls together his friends,	she calls together her friends
and his neighbors	and neighbors,
saying to them,	saying,
"Rejoice with me,	"Rejoice with me,
for I have found my sheep	for I have found the coin
which was lost."	which I had lost."

(3) *Application*

7 Just so, I tell you,	10 Just so, I tell you,
there will be more joy	there is joy
in heaven	before the angels of God
over one sinner who repents	over one sinner who repents.
than over ninety-nine	
righteous persons	
who need no repentance.	

The two similitudes exhibit so many identical features both in form and content that the term "twin-similitude," used above in connection with them, appears fully justified. Apparently these two similitudes belonged together from the first, and it is therefore probable that both were told on the same occasion. And if this is the case, we may perhaps conclude that Luke found them together in his Q-source, i.e., the Lost Coin would not derive from his *Sondergut*. The question thus arises whether Matthew knew not only the Lost Sheep (Mt 18:12–14), but also the Lost Coin. We shall then have to examine the text of Mt 18 more closely to see if it contains a clue which would explain why Matthew would have omitted the story of the Lost Coin.

The application is given in vv. 7 and 10: "Just so . . . there will be more joy in heaven . . . ," and "Just so . . . there is joy before the angels of God. . . ." Very often the expressions "heaven" and "angels of God" are interpreted as Semitic paraphrases referring to God himself. And as a matter of fact, the Jews of Jesus' time did avoid pronouncing the name of God. Nevertheless, one must also take into account that in the figurative parts (vv. 6 and 9) friends and neighbors are summoned to a common joy. Consequently, the expressions used in the applications may also refer to a joy that is shared by God and the inhabitants of heaven. Moreover, vv. 7 and 10 leave no doubt as to the message of the similitudes: God and his angels rejoice at the conversion of one single sinner. On the other hand, the applications do not correspond fully to the figurative parts of the similitudes in their entirety. For while the figurative parts stress not only the call to rejoice but also the active search by the shepherd and the housewife, in the application the latter element is not even mentioned. The focus is exclusively on the joy. While the image underlines the initiative and the activity of God, we get the impression that the application is more concerned with the response of the man "who is found," i.e., his conversion. This shift of emphasis creates a certain tension and raises the question whether this tension was already present in the original similitudes or is to be explained in some other way. A comparison with Matthew's version of the Lost Sheep may throw some light on this problem. First, however, the structure and literary form of the Prodigal Son must be examined.

The Prodigal Son (vv. 11–32)

The Prodigal Son is not a similitude but a parable in the strict
sense. It is an imaginary narrative which captivates the hearer by
its delicacy of feeling, its psychological descriptions, and graphic
depiction. Of course it requires a transposition from metaphor to
reality, from the fictive to the factual, but that application is not
explicitly made by the narrator. He seems to urge his hearers to
do their own further reflection so that they will understand the
deeper meaning. With his parable he also confronts the hearers
with an invitation, a challenge.

11 And he said, "There was a man who had two sons;
12 and the younger of them said to his father, 'Father, give me
the share of property that falls to me.' And he divided his living
between them.
13 Not many days later, the younger son gathered all he had and
took his journey into a far country, and there he squandered his
property in loose living.
14 And when he had spent everything, a great famine arose in
that country, and he began to be in want.
15 So he went and joined himself to one of the citizens of that
country, who sent him into his fields to feed swine.
16 And he would gladly have fed on the pods that the swine ate;
and no one gave him anything.
17 But when he came to himself he said, 'How many of my father's hired servants have bread enough and to spare, but I perish
here with hunger!
18 I will arise and go to my father, and I will say to him, "Father,
I have sinned against heaven and before you;
19 I am no longer worthy to be called your son; treat me as one of
your hired servants."'
20 And he arose and came to his father. But while he was yet at
a distance, his father saw him and had compassion, and ran and
embraced him and kissed him.
21 And the son said to him, 'Father, I have sinned against heaven
and before you; I am no longer worthy to be called your son.'
22 But the father said to his servants, 'Bring quickly the best robe,
and put it on him; and put a ring on his hand, and shoes on his
feet;

23 and bring the fatted calf and kill it, and let us eat and make merry;

24 for this my son was dead, and is alive again; he was lost, and is found.' And they began to make merry.

25 Now his elder son was in the field; and as he came and drew near to the house, he heard music and dancing.

26 And he called one of the servants and asked what this meant.

27 And he said to him, 'Your brother has come, and your father has killed the fatted calf, because he has received him safe and sound.'

28 But he was angry and refused to go in. His father came out and entreated him,

29 but he answered his father, 'Lo, these many years I have served you, and I never disobeyed your command; yet you never gave me a kid, that I might make merry with my friends.

30 But when this son of yours came, who has devoured your living with harlots, you killed for him the fatted calf!'

31 And he said to him, 'Son, you are always with me, and all that is mine is yours.

32 It was fitting to make merry and be glad, for this your brother was dead, and is alive; he was lost, and is found.' "

The story of the Prodigal Son is more than twice as long as those of the Lost Sheep and the Lost Coin taken together. In this extensive narrative two sections can easily be distinguished: one dealing with the younger son (vv. 12–24; cf. v. 12, "And the younger of them said to his father, 'Father, give me . . .' "), the other centering on the elder brother (vv. 25–32; cf. v. 25, "Now the elder son was in the field; and as he came . . ."). Each section ends with a statement, couched in practically the same words, which functions as a sort of refrain. Compare vv. 24 and 32:

> For this my son was dead, and is alive again;
> he was lost, and is found.
> And they began to make merry (v. 24).

> It was fitting to make merry and be glad,
> for this your brother was dead, and is alive;
> he was lost, and is found (v. 32).

The explanation of v. 24 is directed by the father to the servants, that of v. 32 to the elder son. In v. 24, the reason for the feast is placed first; in v. 32 it comes last. But v. 32 is not a mere parallel to v. 24. In the latter the father refers to the returning boy as "this son of mine" while in the former he calls him "this your brother." This expression is obviously used in reaction to what the elder son says in v. 30: "But when *this son of yours* came, who has devoured his living with harlots, you killed for him the fatted calf!" The language of the elder son is unusually harsh. The younger son may still be a "son" for the father, but he is no longer a "brother" to the elder son. The father refuses to accept this view. By his response, "this your brother," he repudiates the derogatory "this son of yours" (v. 30) of the older son. For him the returning boy is still brother to the elder son. In fact, in between vv. 30 and 32, the father addresses the elder son with another word which is full of endearment: *teknon*, i.e., "my dear boy." The man still has two sons (cf. v. 11)! This intentional contrast between the two sons is one of the most striking features of the parable of the Prodigal Son. Using such contrasts is a well-known rhetorical device to which Jesus often had recourse in preaching the parables: cf. e.g., the Two Sons (Mt 21:28–31), the Pharisee and the Publican (Lk 18:9–14), and the Ten Virgins, five wise and five foolish (Mt. 25:1–13).

Leaving aside the second section which deals with the elder son (vv. 25–32), one cannot but notice the close resemblance between the first part of the narrative and the preceding twin-similitudes, especially with respect to the teaching implied. It seems obvious that here also the narrator intends to stress the joy of the father (God) caused by the return of his son. He finds "what was lost." This first section corresponds to the applications of vv. 7 and 10: God rejoices. Just as in the applications, the motif of conversion appears here also. This conversion is more fully developed in the Prodigal Son, however, where the psychological process is described at length. In the applications of vv. 7 and 10, no further mention is made of the earnest search, the preoccupation and exertion of the shepherd and the housewife. Similarly, this aspect is absent in the first part of the Prodigal Son, for it would be reading too much into the text to interpret the statement of v. 20, "while he was yet at a distance, his father saw him and had compassion, and ran. . . ," as referring to an active search on the father's part. It is the son himself who comes to his senses and decides to return. It might be admitted that the narrator intentionally interrupts the son's prepared confession (compare v. 21 with vv. 18–19); it is also possible that the father was already inclined to forgive

before the son came to repentance. It must be conceded that the
actual forgiveness and restoration of the prodigal to his full rights
as a son imply astonishingly more than the mere pardoning of his
offenses. Nevertheless, the main difference between the first part
of the Prodigal Son and the similitudes of the Lost Sheep and the
Lost Coin clearly lies in the fact that in it the "going out and seeking" of the latter has no place. The joy of the finder is only briefly
mentioned in the applications of vv. 7 and 10; but the attitude of
the merciful father is fully described in vv. 12–24. Verses 17–24
develop in more detail what in vv. 7 and 10 is briefly indicated as
the application of the two similitudes.

Verse 24 has all the appearance of a conclusion. It summarizes
and explains what precedes and adds as a final statement: "they
began to make merry." But, in fact, the parable does not end
there; it starts anew and moves towards a second climax. Other
parables also have a double climax and a twofold moral. There is,
e.g., the Workers in the Vineyard (Mt 20:1–16) which illustrates
both a reversal of normal procedures and God's goodness. In Matthew's version of the Guests Invited to the Feast (Mt 22:2–14), the
first part comes to a climax when all those who are found in the
streets and at the crossroads have filled the wedding hall (vv. 2–
10), while the second section deals with worthy attendance at the
banquet, i.e., with the wedding garment (vv. 11–14). The story of
the Rich Man and Lazarus (Lk 16:19–31) also contains two lessons:
first, that "things can change" (the situation of the two men is re-
versed) and secondly, that here on earth people have to be satisfied with the revelation given through Moses and the prophets. In
each of these cases one would have to examine whether the double
climax is original—it could have been added by a later redactor.
However, this does not seem to be the case for the Prodigal Son.
The second section, concerning the elder brother, constituted an
integral part of the parable right from the beginning. Actually, this
second focal point can be considered as an application of one of the
general laws in parable narration, the law of end-stress (*Achtergewicht* in German), i.e., the greater emphasis is placed on what
comes last. The tension in the parable builds up to a final climax.
All the various elements of the narrative function within this movement; they are not allowed to divert attention as independent developments in isolation from the whole. With respect to the Prodigal Son, this would imply that the first half functions primarily as

a preparation for the second part of the story. Although it is much more than just one of the elements of the narrative, it would then no longer possess a fully independent character. And, in fact, in the context of the whole chapter greater importance is attached to the latter part of the story. More attention is given to the elder son than to his younger brother. The latter undoubtedly represents the typical sinner. The elder with his pretentiousness, his heartless adherence to duty, his appeal to his own merits and virtue, clearly typifies the Pharisees and the scribes concerning whom the opening description of the situation states, "Now the tax collectors and sinners were all drawing near to hear him. And the Pharisees and the scribes murmured, saying, 'This man receives sinners and eats with them.' " (15:1–2). In Luke's view it is precisely because they grumble that Jesus rebukes them through his similitudes and the parable. They too are invited to share the joy and take part in the feast. The description of the indignant elder brother is given for their benefit and fits them perfectly. What is most prominent in the narrative is not only the conversion of the sinner and his forgiveness, but—much more—the rejoicing occasioned by his return, even though this rejoicing does not seem equally appropriate to all. Taking the phenomenon of end-stress into account here, one can understand why commentators have often suggested changing the title of the parable from "The Prodigal (younger) Son" to "The Grumbling (elder) Brother."

There has been another—but apparently less justified, at least in the Lucan context—proposal for a change of title. Some scholars assert that the father is more prominent than either son. They base their idea on the preceding similitudes wherein the lost sheep and the lost coin give way to the man and woman who lose, seek, and find again. In a similar way, it is said, the sons recede into the background and the father comes to the fore. So, for example, J. Jeremias in consideration of these and similar observations, suggests as a title for Lk 15:11–32, "The Parable of the Father's Love." Inasmuch as this discussion about the correct title is of relevance for the determination of the original meaning of the parable we will consider it again in our third section.

Chapter 15 as a Whole

Having successively examined the twin-similitudes and the parable of the Prodigal Son, we will now briefly analyze chapter 15 as a whole. The description of the situation at the beginning of the chapter clarifies the purpose of the Prodigal Son, especially its second part, vv. 25–32. This last section of the chapter clearly refers back to the introduction and both "extreme sections" are intended as an inclusion to the whole. It has been noted that the chapter has a double bipartite division. The longer narrative of the Prodigal Son forms the counterpart to the twin-similitude. The Lost Sheep is parallel to the Lost Coin, while the Prodigal Son also consists of two parts, dealing respectively with the younger and the elder son. From a structural point of view, however, the build-up to the climax is even more important than this framework and double division. While numerically speaking there is a gradual decrease (a hundred, ten, and two), from the point of view of content there is an undeniable crescendo: in the parable of the Prodigal Son "that which was lost" is no longer an animal or a coin but a human being; what is at stake is no longer a possession but the unity or breakup of a family.

The composition, structure, and build-up of a chapter such as Lk 15 is normally considered to be the work of the gospel writer or evangelist, and not of the original narrator of the parables, Jesus. Is there still other data in this chapter which confirms this contribution of the evangelist? A detailed analysis of style and vocabulary can be of help here. That analysis is restricted to three considerations which seem to confirm that Luke was actively at work in the composition of this chapter: (a) Most critics agree that Luke himself wrote the introduction (15:1–2). Moreover, the linking formula of v. 11a, "and he said" (*eipen de*), is also typical for Luke. (b) There is a remarkable similarity in structure between chapter 15 and Lk 13:1–9. Both have a bipartite division and a climax. After the introduction, "There were some present at that very time who told him [Jesus] of the Galileans whose blood Pilate had mingled with their sacrifices" (13:1), we note two parallel references to a disastrous incident, linked by the particle "or"; both incidents are described in the form of a question and are followed by an application:

13:2b Do you think that   4 Or
these Galileans   those eighteen
(cf. lb: whose blood Pilate   upon whom the tower in Siloam

had mingled with their sacrifices)	fell and killed them,
	do you think that they
were worse sinners than all the other Galileans,	were worse offenders than all the others who dwelt in Jerusalem?
because they suffered thus?	
3 I tell you, No; but unless you repent you will likewise perish.	5 I tell you, No; but unless you repent you will all likewise perish.

Then, as a climax, follows the somewhat longer narrative of the Barren Fig Tree, a parable in the strict sense. The entire passage clearly centers around the theme of the urgent need for conversion. Although some scholars have asserted that Luke took the structure of both Lk 13:1–9 and Lk 15 from his source, it seems far more likely that both compositions, which moreover are thematically related by the Lucan motif of conversion, owe their structure to the evangelist himself. (c) In the course of our study we have already pointed to a third corroborating indication: Luke has a distinct preference for the theme of conversion. It is therefore quite plausible that he himself is at least partly responsible for the tension between the applications of vv. 7 and 10 and the figurative parts of the twin-similitudes. The applications give a strong emphasis to the motif of conversion, and more specifically to the common joy resulting from this conversion.

On the basis of this consideration of chapter 15 as a whole, the question arises whether or not it was Luke himself who combined the double-similitude and the parable and whether, by that combination and by his creation of the introductory verses, he has not imposed on the double-similtitude the same point taught by the Prodigal Son. To see if this is the case the Matthean version of the Lost Sheep must first be examined.

II. The Lost Sheep

Matthew's Version (18:12–14)

Mt 18 is usually regarded as the fourth discourse of Matthew's gospel, the ecclesial discourse. The following chapter begins, "Now when Jesus had finished these sayings, he went away from

Galilee and entered the region of Judea beyond the Jordan" (19:1). This discourse is actually a series of different sayings and similitudes. Elements of dialogue are also present. Thus, right at the beginning we meet the question, "Who is the greatest in the kingdom of heaven?", and in v. 21 Peter asks, "Lord, how often shall my brother sin against me, and I forgive him? As many as seven times?" In the discourse itself the following short units can be distinguished: Jesus' exhortation to become like little children (vv. 2–5); a warning against giving scandal (vv. 6–10); teaching concerning God's will that the erring brothers be sought out and won back (vv. 12–14); instruction about admonition (vv. 15–18); common prayer (vv. 19–20); and mutual forgiveness (vv. 21–35). In all these subsections Jesus addresses the disciples. It is, however, not certain whether all disciples are meant here or only those among them who have some special responsibility. From v. 6 on (certainly until v. 20), mention is made of the "little ones who believe in Jesus," who can be scandalized, go astray, and are in danger of being lost. In these verses a distinction does seem to be made between those believers whose faith is weak and the church leaders.

The similitude of the Lost Sheep stands within this discourse:

(1) *Search*
12 What do you think? If a man has a hundred sheep, and one of them has gone astray, does he not leave the ninety-nine on the hills and go in search of the one that went astray?

(2) *Joy after the finding*
13 And if he finds it, truly, I say to you, he rejoices over it more than over the ninety-nine that never went astray.

(3) *Application*
14 So it is not the will of my Father who is in heaven that one of these little ones should perish.

The resemblance to Luke's version is striking; Matthew's text can be subdivided into the same three sections. Moreover, as in Luke, the first of these sections is in question form. Matthew first has a short question, designed to stimulate interest: "What do you think?" Then follows the longer question about the search.

Comparison of Lk 15:4–7 and Mt 18:12–14

Emphasis here will be placed on the differences between the two versions, which can be enumerated as follows: (1) Luke places the similitude in a parable chapter; in Mt it stands in the middle of a discourse. (2) Luke includes, in addition to the Lost Sheep, its "twin," the similitude of the Lost Coin; Matthew incorporates only the Lost Sheep. (3) In Lk the story is told to the Pharisees and scribes; Matthew addresses it to the disciples (i.e., to those in the Christian community who have a certain responsibility). (4) According to Luke the Lost Sheep is narrated as an answer to the Pharisees and scribes who grumble because of Jesus' association with sinners and tax collectors; Matthew places it after 18:10 as a positive explication of the command not to despise the "little ones" spoken of in that verse. (5) In Lk the shepherd *loses* one sheep; in Mt one of the sheep is said to *go astray*. (6) In his application Luke identifies the sheep with the sinner; according to Matthew it is "one of these little ones," i.e., a marginal Christian. (7) In Lk the application concerns the joy of God and in heaven at the conversion of the sinner; in Mt the similitude is meant to teach that God does not want one of the little ones to get lost and thus serves to remind the church leaders of their pastoral responsibility. (8) In Matthew's version the appeal to friends and neighbors which we find in Lk 15:6 ("Rejoice with me!") is lacking.

Other less important differences could also be noted: (9) Matthew starts the story by posing two questions; Luke has only one. (10) In Mt both sentences of the figurative part begin with a conditional clause introduced by "if", Luke uses participles: ". . . having a hundred sheep, and having lost one of them . . . having ten silver coins . . ." (in 15:8 however we read, "Or what woman, having ten silver coins, *if* she loses one. . . ."—The RSV translation overlooks these slight differences). (11) The ninety-nine other sheep are left "on the hills," according to Matthew; "in the wilderness," according to Luke. (12) The shepherd "goes after" (Lk) or "goes in search of" (Mt) the lost sheep. (13) Only Luke mentions that the shepherd takes the sheep on his shoulders.

The Q-Version

The enumeration of the above differences is only a first step. The unavoidable question as to which of the two versions is more faithful to their common source, the Q-text, must now be ad-

dressed. This Q-version is older than either of those found in the
two Synoptics. For each of the differences listed above we must
investigate which version is more likely to preserve that of Q. The
analysis will be restricted to the main points.

It can readily be admitted that the Matthean discourse context
is secondary. The initial question "What do you think?" is Matthew's own (cf. e.g., 17:25; 22:17, 42). By his use of the second
person plural in this phrase, Matthew anticipates the pronoun of
the single question in Q, "What man *among you* . . ." which he
thereafter drops in his second question. It is very likely that Matthew's source contained the two similitudes, but that Matthew left
out the story of the Lost Coin, because in his view it was less in
line with the application which he wished to make: a housewife
looking for a lost coin may not have seemed to be a very suitable
image for a concerned church leader. As long as we confine our
attention to the figurative part no great distinction can be made
between the expressions "going astray" (Mt) and "losing" (Lk). But
when we consider the Matthean application it appears that Matthew does make a distinction between the two terms: the little
ones who "went astray" (cf. 18:12, 13) are not irretrievably "lost"
because they can still be found again (cf. 18:14; the RSV's "perish"
is a translation of the same verb, *apollumai*, rendered as "be lost"
in Lk 15:4, 6). It is then highly probable that Matthew substituted
the term "going astray" in vv. 12, 13, for the sake of his application
in v. 14 where the presence of the verb "lose" may be an indication that this was the term used throughout his source. Finally,
Matthew's application is closely linked to its discourse context and
can therefore most probably be considered as secondary and Matthean. Matthew took up the similitude of the Lost Sheep and inserted it into his discourse to thereby illustrate the pastoral duty
of those invested with ecclesial responsibility.

If there are, then, secondary elements in Matthew's version—
e.g., the omission of the Lost Coin, the discourse context, the use
of the term "going astray," and the application—this does not yet
necessarily mean that Luke has preserved the original text. A close
examination of the vocabulary and the style of Lk 15:4–7 reveals
that Luke has also in some measure recast his source text. As
noted earlier, the structure of chap. 15 may be the work of the
evangelist himself. Perhaps the expression "on the hills" in Mt

18:12 is more original than "in the desert" in Lk 15:4. But the crux of the problem of Luke's redactional activity has to do with the application in v. 7. Consider the following points: (a) Conversion is one of Luke's favorite themes. (b) There is a certain tension in the similitude between the application in which the initiative of "that which is found," i.e., the sinner's repentance, gets the greater emphasis, and the figurative part which concerns the anxious activity of the seeker. (c) Studies of the parables have established that the applications are often secondary, added at times by the redactors themselves. (d) An even more significant consideration is that a comparison of Lk 15:7 (application) with Mt 18:13 (still in the figurative part) gives the impression that Luke composed this verse on the basis of the figurative part of the similitude as found in the Matthean verse:

Lk 15:7	Mt 18:13
Just so, I tell you,	. . . truly, I say to you,
there will be more joy in heaven	he rejoices
over one sinner who repents	over it more
than over ninety-nine righteous persons	than over the ninety-nine
who need no repentance.	
	that never went astray.

If the foregoing supposition is accepted, the question then arises whether Luke himself has not constructed vv. 5–6 (more specifically the actions after the finding of the sheep) substituting them for the more original statement concerning the rejoicing, which however he did use in his application, although he interpreted it in an "allegorical" fashion (i.e., the sinner who converts and the ninety-nine righteous people who have no need of repentance). But what would be the motive for such a redactional reworking? Did Luke make this change under the influence of the. Prodigal Son parable (to stress the theme of conversion) and of the context (to appeal for greater rejoicing, directed to the grumbling Pharisees and scribes)? In such a conception of the matter the redactional activity of Luke is exaggerated. This opinion is supported by the following reasons: Both Matthew and Luke give an application, introduced by the particle "so." The very fact that both versions have an application—however divergent these may be from one another—seems to indicate that the Q-version most probably had one as well. Furthermore, the twin-similitudes of the Lost Sheep and the Lost Coin in Lk have a very similar structure: compare vv. 5–6 and 9; vv. 7 and 10. One might suppose that Luke would have expanded the text each time in the same way with an application. But it seems more probable that the basic structure, including the application, was already found in Q, and that it was Matthew who, for the sake of his application with its particular and precise aim, shortened the text and omitted the Q-appeal which Luke retains in vv. 5–6. Nevertheless, it must be readily conceded that Luke has made important redactional changes in v. 7, especially by his addition of the phrase "righteous persons who need no repentance" (cf. 16:15 and 10:29). Consequently, it is practically impossible to reconstruct the wording of the application such as it appeared in Q. Nonetheless, we must with all due reserve now attempt a reconstruction of the source text:

(1) *Search*
What man of you, having a hundred sheep and having lost one of them, does not leave the ninety-nine behind on the hills and go after the one which is lost, until he finds it?

(2) *Actions after the finding*
And when he has found it, he lays it on his shoulders, goes home and calls together his friends and his neighbors and says to them, "Rejoice with me, for I have found my sheep which was lost!"

(3) *Application*
I tell you, just so there will be joy in heaven over one sinner . . . more than over ninety-nine . . .

If our reconstruction is accurate, then the Lost Sheep as well as the Lost Coin at the Q-level belonged to the genre which we have called "similitude." The figurative part began with an introductory question. The application, introduced by the words "just so," was the part concerning "reality." In the figurative part the joy in heaven was compared to that of a shepherd who loses one of his hundred sheep and finds it again, a joy which is shared by his neighbors. The image was thus taken from the concrete life of that time and place. It is a happening that took place more than once. The narrator refers to events which his hearers could observe and verify for themselves. With his question "What man of you . . . ?" the storyteller wants to draw his hearers into the picture; they are supposed to agree with what is so obvious. An appeal is made to their common sense: they too would leave their flocks behind and go searching; they too would greatly rejoice and invite their friends and neighbors to share their joy when they had found the lost sheep.

The application attached to the figurative part revealed the intention of the comparison, its point. Attention was focused exclusively on the second element of the metaphorical part, the joy. In Luke's version, on the other hand, we have noted a certain tension arising from the fact that in the figurative part the emphasis is on the anxious activity of the seeker—the sheep itself does nothing!—while the application includes not only the rejoicing but also the initiative, i.e., the repentance, of the sinner who is found; moreover, the ninety-nine others are qualified as "righteous persons who need no repentance." Even if the expressions "a sinner who repents" and "ninety-nine righteous"—or equivalent terms—were present already in the Q-version, and even if already in Q the application had become one-sided in that it took up only the second aspect of the figurative part (the joy), the tension at this level should nevertheless not be exaggerated. In fact, it seems that the application follows quite normally from the second part of the metaphorical half and does not in any way exclude the active care of the shepherd, God. Moreover, once the transition is made from the animal which is found to a sinful human being, the necessity arises of mentioning the minimum requirement expected of the sinner, i.e., his being open to conversion.

The Lost Sheep and the Lost Coin were thus at the Q-level already similitudes and as such had the character of explicit instructions. Their purpose was to stimulate reflection and to stress a given truth by illustration and comparison, i.e., the truth that God loves the sinner who converts. The Christians who knew and used this Q-version and tried to live up to its message recognized that this love of God had been revealed in a definitive and eschatological way in Jesus Christ.

The Version in the Gospel of Thomas

Before studying the question of how Jesus himself formulated the similitude of the Lost Sheep, the text will first be considered as it is found in the apocryphal gospel of Thomas. This gospel was found among other writings at Nag Hammadi in Egypt in 1945 and was published in 1958. It contains a collection of sayings of Jesus, of which about half also appear in the canonical gospels. The collection has a distinctly Gnostic flavor. The Greek text, of which the existing Coptic version is a translation, derives from the second or third century.

Saying 107 reads as follows:

> Jesus said: "The kingdom is like a shepherd who had a hundred sheep. One of them went astray; it was the largest. He left the ninety-nine (and) sought for the one until he found it. After he had exerted himself, he said to the sheep, I love you more than the ninety-nine." (B. M. Metzger's translation, in K. Aland, *Synopsis quattuor evangeliorum* [Stuttgart, 1964], p. 529)

This version is a rather late recasting of the story. In place of an application it has an introduction: "The kingdom is like a shepherd who had a hundred sheep." The main difference, whereby it diverges sharply from the Lucan and Matthean similitudes, is the addition "it was the largest." This addition tells why the shepherd exerts himself in the search and why, after finding the sheep, he declares in direct address to it, "I love you more than. . . ." Here the stress undoubtedly lies on the great value of the sheep which was lost, whereas in the versions of the Synoptics and in the one that we have reconstructed attention is exclusively directed to the search and the joy in finding. The great value of what was lost is nowhere mentioned, not even in the application.

The Similitude as Told by Jesus

If we hesitated as to the precise reconstruction of the Q-version, a similar hesitation attends our response to the question of how the similitude was originally narrated by Jesus himself. Four reasons might lead us to think that Jesus told the story of the Lost Sheep (and also that of the Lost Coin) without giving it any explicit application. First of all, we know that in the normal process of tradition the parables were often made more explicit and applications were added. In addition there is also the possibility, already mentioned, that Mt 18:12–13 (without the application of v. 14) has—apart from a few details—preserved the Q-version more faithfully than Lk 15:4–7. (Recall however that we have rejected this supposition). Third, some authors refer, incorrectly in our view, to the (late) gospel of Thomas in which the application is lacking. None of these three reasons however appear to be decisive, and even taken together they remain unconvincing.

A fourth reason is based on the tension between the figurative part and the application. It was our opinion that at the Q-level this tension should not be overemphasized. One should, for instance, not suppose that the real point of the metaphorical part would be the joy of the seeker, while in the application what was found would stand in the foreground. The rejoicing is the focus of attention in both parts. The tension arises, rather, from the fact that the application concerns only the finding and not also the search. This last reason, however, taken in conjunction with the first, may perhaps be sufficient to make us suspend judgment concerning the possible absence of an application in the original narrative.

If Jesus did narrate the Lost Sheep and the Lost Coin without an application, then originally these two stories would not have been similitudes but parables in the strict sense thus involving the different key moments of the word-event which were described in our first chapter: disorientation, insight, decision. After being initially surprised—wondering what could be meant by these images of a shepherd seeking a lost sheep and a woman looking for a coin—the hearers would suddenly come to the realization that the parable actually depicts God's love for sinners, a love manifested here and now in Jesus' activity. They would at the same time recognize the challenge with which this insight confronts them: Do you agree with this attitude of God? And what does this imply for your own attitude? Later this parable in the strict sense would have been changed into a similitude by Christians of the postpaschal period. With this alteration the narratives became easier to understand, but also somewhat flatter; they had become well-constructed moral lessons.

The similitude genre, however, should not be denigrated in this way, as if it were unworthy of Jesus. Whatever the original form of the Lost Sheep may have been, whether a parable properly so called or a similitude, the focus of our inquiry concerns what Jesus meant by telling it. If the circumstances which led Jesus to narrate this story were known, it would be far easier to answer this question. Nowadays some scholars speak less about the concrete living context of Jesus' words, which existed "once and for all" and is no longer known; they concentrate, and rightly so, on the "life-setting of Jesus" (*Sitz im Leben Jesu*). This expression does not refer to a particular situation which happened only once, but to the typical context of Jesus' usual, recurrent behavior towards others—his disciples, the people, his enemies, the poor, sinners. This "life-setting" of Jesus can still be determined and is very important for the understanding of the parables.

In the story of the Lost Sheep, there is the animal, a symbol of the sinner, and—if our reconstruction of the Q-text is correct— also the neighbors and friends who are invited to share in the finder's joy. Does this data not point to a typical, often recurring situation in the life of Jesus, i.e., his search for sinners and the fact that this conscious concern of his was often taken amiss? In order to justify his conduct Jesus narrates the story of the Lost Sheep and the Lost Coin. Through the figures of the shepherd and the housewife, both searching for "what was lost," he depicts God's own concern. If God acts like the man who loses a sheep or the woman who mislaid a coin, if God rejoices and heaven with him when what was lost is found again, then Jesus' own behavior is fully justified and his hearers—whether friends or enemies—must share in his joy.

In his study "Les implications christologiques de la brebis perdue" J. Dupont points out that a mere "moral" explanation (as he calls it) of the story does not go far enough. According to this moral explanation, Jesus would justify himself indirectly here, reminding his audience of a universal religious truth: the God of love desires the salvation of sinners—a truth with which Jesus' actions are in agreement. This interpretation, according to Dupont, does not yet

fully reflect what is specifically proper to Jesus. Every compassionate person could justify himself in the same way. In order to understand fully what Jesus intended with these parables, we have to
connect them with God's definitive, eschatological action in Jesus
of Nazareth. In him it is not so much God's immutable essence
which becomes visible in an historical, concrete form. Rather, in
Jesus God's kingdom breaks into history. Jesus himself was aware
of this; it was the very soul of his being. His life was a fulfillment
of his God-given mission. All his words and actions were a continuous proof of that mission. He knew that God had linked the salvation of mankind to his own person. Without this eschatological
and Christological dimension every explanation remains on a
somewhat superficial level, dissociated from Jesus' own life.

In the course of our extended discussion the reader may have
wondered if this story of the Lost Sheep is truly authentic, i.e.,
whether it goes back to Jesus himself. The answer to this question
must be sought with the help of the foregoing discussion. Not only
do the images of the Lost Sheep and the Lost Coin stem from life
in Palestine and not only does the Greek version seem to presuppose an Aramaic underlying text—these two factors do not yet
however constitute a sufficient proof of authenticity—but these
parables also fit in very well with the whole context of Jesus' mission and preaching as these are known to us from the rest of the
gospel material. There is therefore no real reason to doubt the
genuineness of these narratives. Although it is precisely on the
basis of such parables that we form our conceptions of the historical Jesus—a fact which confronts us with the famous "circle" (from
our image of Jesus to the parables, from the parables to our image
of Jesus)—and although we can never of course have full certainty
as to the exact wording of the narrative as spoken by Jesus, this
answer seems nonetheless to be a satisfactory response to the reasonable claims of critically minded Christians.

III. The Prodigal Son

In the first section of this chapter a literary analysis of the Prodigal
Son was given (pp. 29–33). Luke probably rewrote this parable in
his own style and perhaps thematically reworked it to some extent.
The parable comes from the Lucan *Sondergut*. In contrast to the

Lost Coin, it is hardly thinkable that Matthew found this parable
in his Q-source and dropped it. On the other hand, it is not a
priori excluded that the parable could already have been linked to
the twin similitudes in Luke's source, his own version of Q. However, reasons have already been given (cf. pp. 33–35) for adopting
a negative position vis à vis this latter hypothesis. Even very recently it has been claimed that the story of the Prodigal Son originally consisted only of the first part (15:11–24) or that the whole
narrative is Luke's own creation, but few scholars take such asser-
tions seriously, and rightly so. On the other hand, the fact that
only Luke preserves this parable makes the reconstruction of its
pre–Lucan form extremely difficult.

After our previous detailed analysis of the Lost Sheep, we can
now deal with the parable of the Prodigal Son more briefly. Two
questions concerning it are yet to be answered: What was the function of the narrative within the preaching of Jesus? And how did
Luke make use of this parable in his gospel and, more specifically,
within the context of chap. 15?

The Parable as Told by Jesus

The Prodigal Son is a parable in the strict sense, i.e., a story
which comes straight to the point and narrates an imaginary event
in the past tense: "There was a man who had two sons; and the
younger of them said to his father. . . ." We can easily recognize
the three typical elements of the word-event within it. First there
is disorientation. Certain exegetes have left no stone unturned in
their attempts to interpret the narrative as true to life and to explain it within the context of contemporary conditions. They study
the customs of the time, the elder brother's right to the inheritance, the agricultural situation in Palestine, the practices associ
ated with the younger son's being re-acknowledged and restored
to his rights. Notwithstanding all these investigations, it remains
the story of a strange family, and the real aim is not immediately
evident. But the story is indeed captivating. The hearer is invited
to enter into the drama of the family and to approve the loving,
forgiving response of the father. Yet he cannot but stand back and
ask himself what the story really means. He has to discover its
sense, decode its symbolic meaning, and personally make the
transposition to the realm of reality. As soon as he attains this in-

sight and grasps the full significance of the parable he is confronted
with a choice. The story does not let him go free until he takes a
stand. This parable too is, as a word-event, performative: disorientation, insight, decision! But what in fact has to come about
through the parable? What did Jesus actually intend with the
Prodigal Son?

(a) One of the central themes of Jesus' message and activity was
the proclamation that guilt can be removed, that the sickness of
sin can be healed. He came for the salvation of sinners, went out
in search of them, associated, and ate with them. It was precisely
for these reasons that he was criticized and attacked. The so-called
righteous people were scandalized. They opposed him and censured his behavior. With the story of the Prodigal Son Jesus once
more underlines God's mercy. It is not at all a general, abstract
teaching about God. On the contrary, the parable illustrates what
Jesus himself did daily. It throws light on his way of life as God's
ultimate envoy and gives expression to his conviction. Therefore
the parable as a teaching about God's love for sinners must be
understood in a Christological and eschatological way. This first
consideration leads to an important conclusion. To deny the parable any kind of *informative* value appears unwarranted. The understanding of the parable as a word-event, as valuable as that is,
should not obscure this dimension of the narrative.

(b) Because of the criticism which he encountered, Jesus could
not restrict himself to speaking of the forgiveness of sins alone. He
had to justify his message and also himself as the bearer of that
message and the one who puts it into effect. To explain this apologetic dimension of the Prodigal Son, one cannot refer to the introductory vv. 15:1–2. For although it remains theoretically possible that such an introduction accompanied the parable in Luke's
source, it is more probable, as we have already shown, that these
verses are Luke's own redactional creation. Besides the introduction, however, there is also the second part of the story concerning
the elder brother. Even apart from the data of the introduction,
the attitude of the elder son in this second section can only refer
to Jesus' opponents who disapprove of his activities. The Prodigal
Son is therefore also an *apologetic* parable by means of which Jesus
justifies his conduct. By showing that the father (God) restores the
sinner as his son, Jesus legitimates his own activity. Through his

words and actions Jesus is doing nothing more or less than realizing God's present plan of salvation. Ultimately that is his only apology!

(c) Many commentators have pointed out that the narrative ends abruptly with the words of the father without mentioning the final reaction of the elder brother. Did the father convince his elder son? Did that son stubbornly persevere in his refusal, or did he finally go in and take part in the feast? The parable remains open. May we not infer from this that Jesus aimed not only at instruction but also conversion, not only self-defence but also convincing and winning over his opponents? If so, the parable involves a third, *missionary*, dimension. Through the figure of the older son, Jesus' adversaries are once again invited to change their view of God and of Jesus. The father in the parable goes out twice: once with open arms to receive his younger son; the second time with excuses and pleas to win over his elder son: "My boy . . . it was fitting to make merry and to be glad for this your brother was dead and is alive . . ." (15.01-02).

Do the elder sons, the proud and heartless people, the self-consciously righteous ones, not run the danger of going even further astray than the younger son? J. Jeremias writes:

> The parable was addressed to men who were like the elder brother, men who were offended at the gospel. An appeal must be addressed to their conscience. To them Jesus says: "Behold the greatness of God's love for his lost children, and contrast it with your own joyless, loveless, thankless and self-righteous lives. Cease then from your loveless ways, and be merciful. The spiritually dead are rising to new life, the lost are returning home, rejoice with them." Hence we see that . . . the emphasis falls on the second half. The parable of the Prodigal Son is therefore not primarily a proclamation of the Good News to the poor, but a vindication of the Good News in reply to its critics. Jesus' justification lies in the boundless love of God. But Jesus does not remain on the defensive; the parable breaks off abruptly, and the issue is still open. No doubt this is a reflection of the situation which confronted Jesus. His hearers were in the position of the elder son who had to decide whether he would accept his father's invitation and share his joy. So Jesus does not yet pronounce sentence; he still has hope of moving them to abandon their resistance to the gospel, he still hopes that they will recognize how their self-righteousness

and lovelessness separate them from God, and that they may come to experience the great joy which the Good News brings (v. 32a). The vindication of the Good News takes the form of a reproach and an appeal to the hearts of his critics. (*The Parables of Jesus*, pp. 131–32)

It requires no further argument to show that it is above all, although not exclusively, in this third dimension that the Prodigal Son functions as performative language. A parable is a word-event; a successful parable changes the situation for the better. Did Jesus' parable succeed in doing this? His death on the cross, the result of a crime for which the leaders of his people were mainly responsible, would seem to indicate that it did not.

As a conclusion to this discussion it may be useful to make two further observations. Previously we did not wish to categorically affirm that Jesus could not have made use of literary genres other than that of the parable in the strict sense. In the same way we wish to emphasize here that a parable can have more than one dimension. It is an appeal, and at the same time an apology and teaching. Conversely, the parable with its explicit teaching is also word-event and appeal. Our second observation concerns those to whom the narrative is addressed and those for whose benefit it is told. Are these two groups necessarily identical? We do not think so. Nevertheless, since in each of us there is something of the disciple and of the missionary, but also something of the unbeliever and adversary, in any effective actualization of the Prodigal Son the three dimensions of lesson, apology, and conversion will each spontaneously have to receive their due.

Luke's Version

To ascertain to what extent the narrative of the Prodigal Son has been altered and rewritten either by Luke or in the tradition prior to him is no easy task. It can however be regarded as practically certain that Luke made at least two redactional changes. He wrote the introduction (15:1–2) and placed the Prodigal Son after the twin-similitudes, in this way constituting chap. 15 as a balanced whole, centered around the theme of "what was lost." Through the first of these redactional interventions, Luke creates the concrete literary (i.e., non-historical) situation. Jesus directs these parables to the Pharisees and scribes who protest against his contacts with sinners and tax collectors. Those addressed are therefore the same people—the Pharisees and the scribes—who are the target of the final part of the chapter which concerns the older son. Apparently it was on the basis of this second part of the Prodigal Son that Luke conceived his introduction, since the twin-similitudes, in which the friends and neighbors are not presented in a bad light, would not have suggested such a situation. Consequently, the redactional introduction and the section concerning the elder brother form a kind of inclusion to all three intervening narratives and also determine the meaning of the whole to a certain extent, as we shall now try to show in greater detail.

Since the theme of repentance and conversion is typical of Luke, it is possible that he has emphasized this motif in the applications of vv. 7 and 10, and in v. 7 above all by setting up the explicit contrast between the one "that was lost" and "righteous persons who need no repentance." This last expression apparently represents a Lucan addition. If we read the first part of the Prodigal Son immediately after the twin-similitudes, we cannot fail to note the younger son's conversion process: he repents, he takes the initiative. The reader retrospectively will spontaneously fill the term "to convert" in vv. 7 and 10 with the content and meaning which he derives from reading vv. 11–24. By placing the parable immediately after the twin-similitudes Luke has conditioned our understanding of the latter.

But this is not all. Although Luke shows a marked preference for the theme of conversion, the main emphasis in this chapter is not on the process of conversion as such. Taking our clue from the applications of the similitudes wherein God and his angels rejoice exceedingly at the return of a sinner, we realize that the point concerns rather the shared joy. Due to their new context between 15:1–2 and 11–32, the meaning of the two short similitudes has been somewhat modified, i.e., the murmuring of the Pharisees and the scribes (vv. 1–2), and the stubborness of the elder brother (vv. 25–32) give a new and greater relevance to the appeal of the shepherd and the housewife who invite their friends and neighbors to share their joy. Their appeal is identical to that which the father directs to his elder son. Ultimately it is Jesus himself who tries to win over the Pharisees and the scribes, inviting them to share in the joy. He challenges them to come out of their hardened isolation, to give up their sterile religiosity, and to surrender themselves to God's salvific plan. Luke has given these similitudes a new meaning and interpretation by placing them in the context of his fifteenth chapter and addressing them to the same persons who heard the parable of the Prodigal Son. The active repentance of the sinner and especially the appeal to those who complain about Jesus' concern for sinners: these are the two Lucan accentuations which characterize chapter 15.

IV. Actualization

After having thus traversed the way from the evangelist to Jesus and from Jesus back to the evangelist, the Christian exegete has not yet accomplished his or her task as an interpreter of the Scriptures. Of course the foregoing complex, demanding investigation, has borne appreciable fruit in the form of better insight into the various stages through which the traditional material has passed. The critically-minded Christian of this modern age cannot but welcome such an analysis; it satisfies intellectual needs and a desire for rationality. But beyond that Christians also want to know the relevance of such parables today, their actual value. Do they contain a message for this generation as well? Can the language-event happen again so that we might stand "once more astonished" before these parables? This question concerns the possibility of actualization.

The Example of the Synoptics

We should not forget that Christians began actualizing right from the start. Circumstances forced them to do so. After Easter their situation was radically changed: the Lord was risen to life, the disciples had undergone a process of conversion and were confirmed in their faith, times and places had changed, they faced new problems. The two versions of the Lost Sheep, that of Matthew and that of Luke—Q and the Gospel of Thomas are not considered here—were each actualized in a specific way. Matthew uses the similitudes to remind church leaders of their responsibility, to stimulate them to a greater zeal and concern for the weaker members who go astray. Matthew the pastor would never have been content with a self-satisfied elite church or with closed groups of ghetto Christians. The church in which he lived probably showed signs of waning enthusiasm. Matthew reacts strongly against this tendency; he exhorts. His entire gospel is motivated by such parenetical considerations. This same concern is manifest in his actualization of the Lost Sheep. He rewrites the story, altering it on the basis of that concrete danger which in his view the hierarchy must help to ward off.

Luke also, in composing his fifteenth chapter, did not simply intend to give information about the historical situation which led Jesus to tell his parables. What contemporary ecclesial situations did he have in mind then? Possibly, writing c. A.D. 80, Luke wanted to remind his readers of the painful struggle which divided Christians in the first decades after Jesus' resurrection, caused by the acceptance of non–Jewish converts. If so, his readers were to identify the elder brother with the Christians of Jewish origin who stood on their principles. The younger brother would be the non–Jewish converts whose sinful past was a source of scandal to the Jewish–Christians. More probably however, Luke's actualization and exhortation are concerned with the situation of his own time. In his own community there may also have been some tension between fervor and tepidity, rigorism and a so-called compromise with sin. In this case, Luke in his fifteenth chapter would be in dialogue with the more fervent Christians, those of strict observance. He would be pleading with them to accept repentant sinners, fighting for a Christianity that could continue to believe in God's forgiveness as an unmerited grace.

And We?

There are then various possibilities of actualization, but there are also certain limits. The way in which the author of the gospel of Thomas alters the Lost Sheep is an example of an incorrect interpretation and application, whereas there can be no doubt that Matthew, with his exhortation to church leaders of his own time, and Luke, with his plea against an exaggerated rigorism, both stand in the line of what was intended by Jesus himself. But must we actualize, as the tradition and the evangelists did in the case of the Lost Sheep and the Lost Coin by using similitudes such as these and by adding explicit applications? Theoretically, there is no objection to doing this, but perhaps it is more advisable for us, aided by modern philosophical reflection and its new insight into what language is and can do, to devote greater attention to the parable in the strict sense. The transposition to the personal situation then becomes more of a task for the individual listener than for the preacher or teacher. The result is that the risk-aspect of challenge which so characterized Jesus' activity and speaking will confront us again within our own specific situations. Be that as it may, when we attempt to actualize either for our own benefit or for others, it is really a question of allowing Jesus himself to give expression to his unheard of, eschatological message which comes from God himself. Because that message has often been forgotten, today it is good that the Christian preacher, in the name of the church, proclaims God's forgiveness over against any exaggerated rigorism. God's grace is always there prior to our merits. His forgiveness is never restricted or conditioned by our human achievements. This does not mean that Christian living, morality, and repentance are of no consequence. But how can there be a converted life, unless it be on the basis of the experience of the healing, forgiving, undeserved, and joy-giving gifts of God?

Preaching these parables about "what was lost," Jesus announced wonderful news: there is still hope for those who are thought to be dead and irrevocably lost by their fellow men! With these parables and their reference to God, Jesus had to defend his own way of life. The same Jesus still addresses these parables to his adversaries as an appeal for assent, recognition, and joy. Actualizing, in fact, means nothing other than bringing Jesus and his "cause" to expression once again.

BIBLIOGRAPHY

To be noted is the collective work *Exegesis: Problems of Method and Exercises in Reading (Genesis 22 and Luke 15)*, Pittsburgh TMS 21, ed. F. Bovon and G. Rouiller, ET by D. G. Miller, Pittsburgh, 1978. In this work the following authors deal with Lk 15: F. Bovon, G. Antoine, L. Beirnaert, J. Leenhardt, and Y. Tissot.

Arai, S., "Das Gleichnis vom Verlorenen Schaf—Eine Traditionsgeschichtliche Untersuchung," in *Annual of the Japanese Biblical Institute* 2, ed. M. Sekine and A. Satake, Tokyo, 1976, pp. 111–37.

54   ONCE MORE ASTONISHED

Bonnard, P., "Approche historico-critique de Luc 15," *Foi et Vie* 72:3 (1973) (=Cahiers bibliques 12) 25–37.

Broer, I., "Das Gleichnis vom Verlorenen Sohn und die Theologie des Lukas," *NTS* 20 (1973–1974) 453–62.

Cantinat, J., "Les Paraboles de la Miséricorde," *NRT* 77 (1955) 246–64.

Carlston, C. E., "Reminiscence and Redaction in Luke 15:11–32," *JBL* 94 (1975) 368–90.

Crossan, J. D., "A Metamodel for Polyvalent Narration," *Semeia* (1977) no. 9, pp. 105–47.

Derrett, J.D.M., "Law in the New Testament: The Parable of the Prodigal Son," *NTS* 14 (1967–1968) 55–74; also in Derrett, *Law in the New Testament*, London, 1970, pp. 100–125.

――――, "The Parable of the Prodigal Son: Patristic Allegories and Jewish Midrashim," *Studia Patristica* 10 (1970) 219–24.

――――, "Fresh Light on the Lost Sheep and the Lost Coin," *NTS* 26 (1979–1980) 36–60.

Dupont, J., "La brebis perdue et la drachme perdue," *Lumière et Vie* (Suppl. bibl. de *Paroisse et Liturgie*) (1957) no. 34, pp. 15–23.

――――, "La parabole de la Brebis perdue," *Gregorianum* 49 (1968) 265–87.

――――, "Le Fils prodigue. Lc 15,1–3.11–32," *AssSeign II* (1969) no. 17, pp. 64–72.

――――, "Réjouissez-vous avec moi! Lc 15,1–32," *AssSeign II* (1974) no. 55, pp. 70–79.

――――, "Les implications christologiques de la parabole de la brebis perdue," in *Jésus aux origines de la christologie*, BETL 40, ed. J. Dupont, Louvain-Gembloux, 1975, pp. 331–50.

Fuchs, E., "Das Fest der Verlorenen. Existentiale Interpretation des Gleichnisses vom verlorenen Sohn," in Fuchs, *Glaube und Erfahrung*, Tübingen, 1965, pp. 402–15.

Giblet, J., "La parabole de l'accueil messianique (Lc 15,11–32)," *Bible et vie chrétienne* (1962) no. 47, pp. 17–28.

Giblin, C. H., "Structural and Theological Considerations on Luke 15," *CBQ* 25 (1962) 15–31.

――――, "Why Jesus Spoke in Parables—An Answer from Luke 15," *Chicago Studies* 7 (1968) 213–20.

Grelot, P., "Le père et ses deux fils: Luc, XV, 11–32," *RB* 84 (1977) 321–48, 538–65.

Groupe d'Entrevernes, *Signes et Paraboles. Sémiotique et Texte Evangélique*, Paris, 1977, pp. 94–142.

Güttgemanns, E., "Struktural-generative Analyse des Bildworts 'Die verlorene Drachme' (Lk 15,8–10)," *LB* (1972) no. 6, pp. 2–17.

Hickling, C.J.A., "The Tract on Jesus and the Pharisees? A Conjecture on the Redaction of Luke 15 and 16," *Heythrop Journal* 16 (1975) 253–65.

Hofius, O., "Alttestamentliche Motive im Gleichnis vom verlorenen Sohn," *NTS* 24 (1977–1978) 240–48.

Parables in Luke 15   55

Jeremias, J., "Tradition und Redaktion in Lukas 15," ZNW 62 (1971) 172–89.

Kossen, H. B., "Quelques remarques sur l'ordre des paraboles dans Luc XV et sur la structure de Matthieu XVIII 8–14," NovT 1 (1965) 75–80.

Le Du, J., Le fils prodigue ou les chances de la transgression, Saint–Brieuc, 1974.

Légasse, S., "Jésus et les prostituées," RTL 7 (1976) 137–54 (see pp. 146–50).

Lindijer, C. H., "Kerk en Israël in de gelijkenis van de verloren zoon," NThTij 20 (1965–1966) 161–70.

Lohfink, G., "Das Gleichnis vom gütigen Vater," BibLeb 13 (1972) 138–46.

———, " 'Ich habe gesündigt gegen den Himmel und gegen dich! (Lk 15, 18.21)," TQ 155 (1975) 51–52.

Magass, W., "Geben, Nehmen, Teilen als Tischsequenz in Lk 15,11–32," LB (1976) no. 37, pp. 31–48.

O'Rourke, J. J., "Some Notes on Luke XV.11–32," NTS 18 (1971–1972) 431–33.

Patte, D., "Structural Analysis of the Parable of the Prodigal Son: Toward a Method," in Semiology and Parables: Exploration of the Possibilities Offered by Structuralism for Exegesis, Pittsburgh TMS 9, ed. D. Patte, Pittsburgh, 1976, pp. 71–149 (with a discussion pp. 151–78).

Pesch, R., "Zur Exegese Gottes durch Jesus von Nazaret. Eine Auslegung des Gleichnisses vom Vater und den beiden Söhnen (Lk 15,11–32)," in Jesus, Ort der Erfahrung Gottes, ed. B. Casper, Freiburg–Basel–Wien, 1976, pp. 140–89.

Pöhlmann, W., "Die Abschichtung des Verlorenen Sohnes (Lk 15,12f.) und die erzählte Welt der Parabel," ZNW 70 (1979) 194–213.

Ramaroson, L., "Le coeur du Troisième Evangile," Bib 60 (1979) 348–60.

Rasco, E., "Les paraboles de Luc, XV. Une invitation à la joie de Dieu dans le Christ," in De Jésus aux Evangiles, BETL 25, ed. I. de la Potterie, Gembloux–Paris, 1967, 165–83.

Rengstorf, K. H., "Die Re–Investitur des Verlorenen Sohnes in der Gleichniserzählung Jesu. Luk. 15,11–32," Arbeitsgemeinschaft für Forschung des Lands Nordrhein–Westfalen, Geisteswissenschaft 137, Cologne, 1967.

Richards, W. L., "Another Look at the Parable of the Two Sons," BR 23 (1978) 5–14.

Sanders, J. T., "Tradition and Redaction in Luke XV.11–32," NTS 15 (1968–1969) 433–38.

Schnider, F., Die verlorenen Söhne. Strukturanalytische und historisch-kritische Untersuchungen zu Lk 15, Orbis biblicus et orientalis 17, Freiburg–Göttingen, 1977.

———, "Das Gleichnis vom verlorenen Schaf und seine Redaktoren. Ein intertextueller Vergleich," Kairos 19 (1977) 146–54.

Schottroff, L., "Das Gleichnis vom verlorenen Sohn," ZThK 68 (1971) 27–52.

Scott, B. B., "The Prodigal Son: A Structuralist Interpretation," *Semeia* (1977) no. 9, pp. 45–73.

Tolbert, M. A., "The Prodigal Son: An Essay in Literary Criticism from a Psychoanalytic Perspective," *Semeia* (1977) no. 9, pp. 1–20.

Van den Hougen, T., "Omgaan met een niet-vanzelfsprekend Evangelie," *TT* 17 (1977) 225–49.

Via, D. O., "The Prodigal Son: A Jungian Reading," *Semeia* (1977) no. 9, pp. 21–43.

Waelkens, R., "L'analyse structurale des paraboles. Deux essais: Luc 15,1–32 et Matthieu 13,44–46," *RTL* 8 (1977) 160–78.

Three

The Good Samaritan
(Lk 10:25–37)

C. H. Lindijer starts his short but informative survey of old and new views on the parable of the Good Samaritan by remarking that the average Christian, when asked about the meaning of the parable of the Good Samaritan, would probably answer straight away, "You should love your neighbor!" For most people the parable is without problems and Lindijer thinks they may well be right. It is hard for them, he says, to imagine that theologians can find problems even here.

I. No Problems?

Who Is My Neighbor?

The Christian who attentively reads or listens to this parable must, nevertheless, be struck by a peculiar shift of meaning which occurs within the pericope of the Good Samaritan (Lk 10:25–37). The lawyer asks the question, "And who is my neighbor?" In other words, whom must I regard as my neighbor? But at the end of the story, Jesus answers with the counter question, "Which of these three, do you think, proved neighbor to the man who fell among the robbers?" According to the first question the beaten, wounded traveler ought to be called neighbor; according to the second it is the Good Samaritan who has become the neighbor. At the beginning the neighbor is the object of the action; at the end the neighbor has become another person and the subject of the action!

It thus appears that the concept "neighbor" has a double meaning in the Good Samaritan parable. (1) In the *lawyer's* question and also in the quotation of the commandment "You shall love your neighbor as yourself" (cf. v. 27), the "neighbor" is the other person (i.e., anyone in need of my help) whom I encounter and ought to love. I must, in a human and Christian way, make a neighbor of the other person who is "near" me in a local sense. (2) *Jesus'* attention goes precisely to this latter task. He does not, however, speak of it as making *the other* my neighbor; his emphasis is rather on *my* becoming a neighbor to the other. "Neighbor" here is the equivalent of brother and friend; "to become a neighbor" means to act in a loving and compassionate, helpful and sympathetic way. I must feel with the other; I must become a real friend and brother to him.

This shift of meaning (from "neighbor," the other as the object of my action, to "neighbor," that which I myself as subject must become) may or may not be intended, but in any case it makes the reader pause and reflect. It sets him thinking and causes a tension within the story which is not removed by a superficial, unproblematic explanation.

Three Further Observations

It might seem sufficient to state that this shift of meaning is precisely the point of the parable: i.e., Jesus wanted it to be realized that love of neighbor involves an active, self-giving commitment. The exegete, however, has to raise further questions.

(a) In another passage of Luke's gospel a similar shift occurs. In the pericope about the woman who was a sinner (7:36–50), it is not immediately clear whether the woman's love is the cause or the result of Jesus' forgiveness. Compare "Her sins, which are many, are forgiven, for she loved much" (v. 47a) with "He who is forgiven little, loves little" (v. 47b). As in 10:36 ("Which of these three, do you think, proved neighbor to the man . . ."), Jesus here by his question in 7:42 after the parable of the Two Debtors ("Now which of the two debtors will love the creditor more?") wants the Pharisee himself to formulate the self-incriminating answer. In view of this striking parallelism the following questions might be posed: Does such a shift in meaning have to do with the fact that dialogue and parable together constitute one single pericope? Is a shift of this sort typical of Luke's gospel? Is it, perhaps, a Lucan stylistic device?

(b) A second observation is that the parable itself does not start until 10:30 with the phrase "a (certain) man" (*anthrōpos tis*). In the *Sondergut* of Luke's gospel there are several parables which begin in the same manner: 12:16 (the Rich Fool), 15:11 (the Prodigal Son), 16:1 (the Unjust Steward), 16:19 (the Rich Man and Lazarus), 18:10 (two men: the Pharisee and the Publican). These parables are introduced with a description of the situation, but with the exception of the Rich Fool (12:16–21), they appear as self-contained wholes and do not function within the context of a longer dialogue as do the two parables in 7:36–50 and 10:25–37.

This observation confronts us with a new range of questions: Did parable and dialogue stand together from the beginning? Was it this specific dialogue in Jesus' early life which led to the narrating of the story? Or is it possible that the combination of dialogue and parable was made only in a later phase? Could the combination be the result of Luke's redactional activity?

(c) This last is not an idle question as is clear from a third observation. In Mk 12:28–34 (= Mt 22:34–40) we have the well-known pericope of the Great Commandment. Luke surely read this passage in his source, the gospel of Mark (as could easily be demonstrated by a stylistic analysis of Lk 20:28, 39–40). He does not, however, preserve it in the same context as Mark. There must have been some reason for not doing so. Note that the pericope of the Great Commandment is very much like the dialogue which in Lk 10:25–28 gives rise to the parable of the Good Samaritan. One may ask, therefore, whether Luke omitted the Great Commandment in his twentieth chapter because he had already used it in chap. 10. Of course this supposition would in itself not exclude the possibility that Luke derived this preparatory occasion for his parable from a source other than Mark's gospel. Nor is the possibility excluded that dialogue and parable already stood together in that other hypothetical source.

But, from this third remark (as well as from the two foregoing observations) other problems besides the uncertainties surrounding the term "neighbor" arise, problems of a literary, redactional nature. It is not impossible that a better insight into the redaction of Lk 10:25–37 will throw additional light on the passage's varying use of the term "neighbor."

The Aim of Our Explanation

The new cycle of the liturgical year every three years (1983, 1986, etc.) includes many readings taken from Luke's gospel. It seems worthwhile therefore, on the basis of this well-delimited passage, to investigate some important Lucan themes, namely "love of neighbor" and "doing mercy" (cf. v. 37).

There are two reasons why every Christian feels deeply challenged by the parable of the Good Samaritan. He intuitively realizes that the credibility of his Christian faith as a whole stands or falls for himself and for the world around him with his active love of neighbor. Moreover, the Good Samaritan story does not let the believer off, because he himself has often passed his neighbor by on the other side. The implicit but pointed accusation present in this parable makes it ever actual.

Besides elucidating certain Lucan themes and confronting us with the personal call of Jesus' message, this chapter has a further aim. Time and again one hears the question, Is Holy Scripture still accessible to ordinary people like us? Hasn't the ingenuity of the biblical scholar, the specialist, complicated matters beyond comprehension? Having noted that the Good Samaritan poses problems of concern even for the nonspecialist but attentive, honest reader, a treatment of this pericope may help to show both the necessity and the fruitfulness of the modern exegetical approach. In personal prayer and preaching it may be preferable at times to let oneself be directly inspired by the text itself. But for the Christian of today, who rightly requires rational insight and justification for his faith, we may legitimately ask whether the laborious path of critical investigation and analysis can be avoided. To this question also an answer is suggested in the following pages. It is not stated in the abstract, but concretely by means of a sample investigation.

II. Redacted Tradition

The Text

In Lk 10:25–37 there are two sections of dialogue (vv. 25–29 and 36–37) separated by a monologue, i.e., the parable spoken by Jesus (vv. 30–35). In line with this division the text can be presented this way:

(a) *Dialogue* (vv. 25–29)

25 And behold, a lawyer stood up to put him to the test, saying, "Teacher, what shall I do to inherit eternal life?"

26 He said to him, "What is written in the law? How do you read?"

27 And he answered, "You shall love the Lord your God with all your heart, and with all your soul, and with all your strength, and with all your mind; and your neighbor as yourself."

28 And he said to him, "You have answered right; do this, and you will live."

29 But he, desiring to justify himself, said to Jesus, "And who is my neighbor?"

(b) *Parable* (vv. 30–35)

30 Jesus replied, "A man was going down from Jerusalem to Jericho, and he fell among robbers, who striped him and beat him, and departed, leaving him half dead.

31 Now by chance a priest was going down that road; and when he saw him he passed by on the other side.

32 So likewise a Levite, when he came to the place and saw him, passed by on the other side.

33 But a Samaritan, as he journeyed, came to where he was; and when he saw him, he had compassion,

34 and went to him and bound up his wounds, pouring on oil and wine; then he set him on his own beast and brought him to an inn, and took care of him.

35 And the next day he took out two denarii and gave them to the innkeeper, saying, 'Take care of him; and whatever more you spend, I will repay you when I come back.'

(a') *Dialogue* (vv. 36–37)

36 Which of these three, do you think, proved neighbor to the man who fell among the robbers?"

37 He said. "The one who showed mercy on him." And Jesus said to him, "Go and do likewise."

Some exegetes have proposed a different division. They distinguish two parallel discussions, i.e., vv. 25–28 and vv. 29–37. Both sections would contain the following elements:

(1) a question put by the lawyer: v. 25 and v. 29
(2) a counterquestion by Jesus: v. 26 and vv. 30–36 (here: parable and counterquestion)
(3) the answer of the lawyer: v. 27 and v. 37a
(4) the command given by Jesus: v. 28 and v. 37b.

The irregularity caused by the length of the parable (vv. 30–36) and its difference of content make it seem rather unlikely, however, that Luke intended such a parallel structure here.

With this parable most of the so-called laws of the parable genre can be well illustrated. The narrative is concise; the various details are chosen in function of the main point of the comparison; there are never more than two persons together on the scene at the same time (the Germans call this *szenische Zweiheit*); the characterization progresses in a straightforward fashion; the depiction is very vivid; there is repetition and sharp contrast (here: two negative figures and then one positive); and the most important element comes last (end-stress, *Achtergewicht*).

The Influence of Mk 12:28–34 and Lk 18:18–30

It is clear that the evangelist Luke did not mechanically or blindly reproduce the traditions which he received. In respect to his pericope, he was perhaps more active as a redactor than a first reading would lead us to believe. Is it possible to more exactly determine the extent of Luke's redaction? Two literary considerations form our starting point in this effort:

(a) In his editing of 10:25–28, Luke made use of the pericope Mk 12:28–34.

Mk 12:28–34	Lk 10:25–28
28 And one of the scribes came up	25 And behold, a lawyer stood up
and heard them disputing with one another,	
and seeing that he answered them well,	
	to put him to the test
asked him,	saying,
"Which commandment is the first of all?"	"Teacher, what shall I dó to inherit eternal life?"
	26 He said to him,

"What is written in the law?"
How do you read?"

29 Jesus answered,
"The first is,
'Hear, O Israel:
30 The Lord our God, the Lord
is one;
and you shall love the Lord
your God
with all your heart,
and with all your soul
and with all your mind,
and with all your strength.'
31 The second is this,
'You shall love your neighbor
as yourself.'
There is no other
commandment
greater than these."
32 And the scribe said to him,
"You are right, Teacher;
you have truly said
that he is one,
and there is no other but he;
33 and to love him
with all the heart,
and with all the understanding,
and with all the strength,
and to love one's neighbor
as oneself,
is much more than all whole
burnt offerings and sacrifices."
34 And when Jesus saw
that he answered wisely,
he said to him,

"You are not far from the
kingdom of God."
And after that no one dared
to ask him any question.

27 And he answered,

"You shall love the Lord
your God
with all your heart,
and with all your soul
and with all your strength,
and with all your mind;

and your neighbor
as yourself."

28 And he said to him,
You have answered right;
do this, and you will live."

Jesus' reaction, "You have answered right" (Lk 10:28) is reminiscent of Mk 12:34, "And when Jesus saw that he answered wisely, . . ." But there is something further. In Lk 10:27 it is the lawyer who answers, quoting the double commandment of love of God and neighbor; in Mk 12:29–31 it is Jesus who does so. In Mk the two commandments are neatly distinguished into the first (cf. Mk 12:28–29; vv. 29–30 cite Deut 6:4–5) and the second (cf. Mk 12:31; here Lev 19:18 is quoted). These two facts—that in Luke's text the two Old Testament quotations are fused into a single sentence and that it is the lawyer and not Jesus who makes the daring equation of the two commandments—strongly suggest that the Lucan text is less original than its Marcan parallel. Luke has introduced redactional changes. Why did he do so?

(b) A second example of literary dependence leads us further. In 10:25 Luke writes, "Teacher, what shall I do to inherit eternal life?" The formulation of this question is verbally almost the same as that of Lk 18:18 "(Good) Teacher, what shall I do to inherit eternal life?" (= Mk 10:17). Just as in the Good Samaritan, Jesus refers here in the pericope of the Rich Man to the commandments (Lk 18:20: "You know the commandments"; cf. 10:26: "What is written in the law? How do you read?"). One can hardly avoid the impression that in his editing of 10:25–28 Luke not only used the Marcan pericope of the Great Commandment (Mk 12:28–34), but was also influenced by the pericope which he incorporated in 18:18–30. This too is an indication of important Lucan editorial activity in the Good Samaritan.

A Q-version of the Great Commandment?

It would, however, be wrong to conclude from the literary data just mentioned that Luke merely transposed and rewrote Mk 12:28–34 with a view to using it in his gospel as an introduction to the parable of the Good Samaritan. A comparison with Mt 22:34–40 seems to indicate that Luke had access to a second source for the Great Commandment pericope which was more or less similar to the version known to him from Mark's gospel. The reason for postulating this second source is that Matthew and Luke exhibit a number of remarkable agreements in this passage against the Marcan parallel text which can only be explained in terms of a second common source (= Q).

Mt 22:34–40 reads as follows:

34 But when the Pharisees heard that he had silenced the Sadducees, they came together.
35 And one of them, a lawyer, asked him a question, to test him.
36 "Teacher, which is the great commandment in the law?"
37 And he said to him, "You shall love the Lord your God with all your heart, and with all your soul, and with all your mind.
38 This is the great and first commandment.
39 And a second is like it, You shall love your neighbor as yourself.
40 On these two commandments depend all the law and the prophets."

The points on which Matthew and Luke agree with one another and at the same time differ from Mark are the following: both Matthew and Luke offer a much shorter version (they have no parallel to Mk 12:32–34); unlike Mk 12:29, their quotation of the first commandment does not begin with "Hear, Israel, the Lord our God, the Lord is one"; Jesus is initially addressed as "Teacher," a title not found at the beginning of the Marcan pericope but only subsequently in v. 32; the question is asked by a "lawyer," whereas in Mk it is posed by "one of the scribes"; by his question the lawyer intends to put Jesus to the test, while Mark's scribe questions Jesus "seeing that he answered them (= the Sadducees) well" (v. 28).

Apparently, then, Luke must have also known, in addition to Mk 12:28–34, a Q-version of the Great Commandment. He realized that both accounts dealt with the same incident and therefore narrated it only once in his gospel. In his redaction, however, he drew upon both sources.

Dialogue and Parable

Should we thus assume that in Q, Luke's second source, the dialogue and the parable already stood together? Two considerations militate against such a supposition:

(a) We have already seen that Jesus' reaction, "You have answered right," in 10:28 is probably literally dependent on Mk 12:34. Luke presents Jesus as reacting favorably here, although in

10:25 he follows the Q-version which emphasizes the hostile behavior of the scribe: "in order to test him." It is unlikely that the original narrator would have placed a negative question and a positive response so close to one another. The rest of v. 28 (*"do* this, and you will *live"*) constitutes a striking inclusion with 10:25 (". . . what shall I *do* to inherit eternal *life?"*) It has already been indicated that in his redaction of 10:25 Luke was clearly inspired by 18:18: "Good Teacher, what shall I do to inherit eternal life?" (= Mk 10:17). This leads us to the conclusion that the whole verse in Lk 10:28 is redactional.

(b) Lk 10:29 also appears very Lucan. First of all, there is the striking fact that the idea of the lawyer's "desiring to justify himself" occurs in the gospels only here and in another Lucan text, Lk 16:15, where it is said the Pharisees justify themselves before men. What is decisive, however, in leading us to view this transitional v. 29 as a purely Lucan creation is the question which it contains: "And who is my neighbor?" As stated above, this question stands in a certain tension with that of 10:36: "Which of these three became neighbor to the man . . . ?" Verse 29 is evidently formulated by the same redactor who had just previously written at the end of v. 27, "(Love) your neighbor as yourself," and who, with this commandment in mind, reads the parable and wishes to use it as a commentary on that commandment. Luke makes the lawyer ask, Who, concretely, is my neighbor? (cf. v. 29). The answer is, the wounded traveler! Later, at the end (v. 36), comes the other question, Jesus' question: Who became a neighbor?

What can be concluded from all this? Since 10:28 and 10:29 are redactional Lucan transitions from dialogue to parable, since v. 28 constitutes a redactional inclusion with v. 25 and the editorial v. 29 stands in a certain tension with v. 36, and since v. 30 contains the phrase "a certain man" with which many other originally independent parables begin, it seems best to ascribe the connection between dialogue and parable to Luke himself. The evangelist realized that he could explain and illustrate the commandment of love of neighbor with the parable of the Good Samaritan. Perhaps this idea came to him from reading Mk 12:33b: "And to love one's neighbor as oneself, is much more than all burnt offerings and sacrifices." As he wrote, however, he may not have realized that his parable commentary actually explains only the second commandment and not the first concerning the love of God.

The Final Dialogue

With vv. 36–37 the dialogue resumes. Jesus questions the lawyer: "Which of these three, do you think, proved neighbor to the
man who fell among the robbers?" (v. 36). The lawyer replies:
"The one who showed mercy on him" (v. 37a). Then in v. 37b
follows Jesus' command: "Go and do likewise."

Commentators do not agree as to which parts of this dialogue
belonged to the pre–Lucan parable. In view of the shift in meaning
with respect to the term "neighbor" one might be inclined to consider the whole of v. 36 as traditional. On the other hand, we note
that the second person singular in this verse refers to the lawyer
mentioned in the dialogue (vv. 25–29) with which Luke prefaces
the parable. Moreover, the word "neighbor" used in this verse
does not occur in the parable itself; it is found in vv. 27 and 29,
but with a different meaning. Finally, there is also one or another
word here which could be considered as typically Lucan. If we
suppose that the original parable ended with a more neutral question (e.g., "Which of these three showed mercy to the man who
fell among the robbers?"), then it becomes quite probable that
Luke introduced the second person and the term "neighbor" here
in v. 36 in order to adapt its original concluding question to his
introductory dialogue. By so doing, Luke would have brought the
parable to a climax with the theme of "becoming a neighbor." That
Luke here in v. 36 speaks about "becoming oneself a neighbor,"
and not as in v. 29 about passively "being a neighbor," is thus due
to the influence of the preceding parable which concerns the active
expression of compassion. Although Luke has written or, better,
rewritten v. 36, the tension between this verse and v. 29 was already present in the tradition. And, it is in any case improbable
that Luke experienced this tension as strongly as we do today.

If the present v. 36 is a product of Lucan rewriting, what is then
to be said about v. 37a? Does it derive in its entirety from Luke?
Did the pre–Lucan parable end with a rhetorical question (v. 36)
or did it already contain an answer of some sort (cf. v. 37a)? We
hesitate to choose between these two alternatives. It is said that
the phrase "to do mercy with someone" (literal translation) in v.
37a reflects a Semitic idiom, but this does not prove that the verse
is pre–Lucan since the evangelist might have formulated this
expression on the basis of the original concluding rhetorical question (cf. above).

It is even more uncertain that v. 37b was part of Luke's source. The thematic word, "to do," recalls the Lucan inclusion of vv. 25 and 28: "doing" as the way to obtain life. Verse 37b is therefore most probably an element of the redactional framework composed by Luke.

Conclusion

The results of our literary investigation can be summarized as follows. Luke wrote a concrete introduction to the parable with the help of a traditional discussion concerning the Great Commandment of which he possessed a double version, i.e., Q and Mk 12:28–34. In Luke's mind the parable of the Good Samaritan constitutes a commentary on the commandment of love of neighbor. Luke created the transitional vv. 28 and 29. Through his insertion of these verses the tension with respect to the double meaning of the term "neighbor" arose. That tension was, therefore, not introduced or intended by Jesus. Although Luke perhaps gave v. 36 its present form, he himself may not have noticed the tension, and thus it would not have been intended by him either as the real point of the story. Instead, it is a tension occasioned by the juxtaposition of redaction and tradition, caused by an editor who used the parable (tradition) for his own redactional purposes in a rather awkward fashion.

A second important conclusion from all of this is that whoever wishes to investigate Jesus' intention in the parable of the Good Samaritan must view it apart from its redactional framework. The parable probably came to Luke without any specific indications as to the occasion on which it was spoken by Jesus. In any case, the situation depicted by Luke is secondary. This conclusion leads us to a consideration of Jesus and the Good Samaritan parable.

III. The Message of Jesus

An Authentic Parable?

Is it so certain after all that the Good Samaritan came from Jesus himself? Even recently this has been strongly denied by G. Sellin. Although he admits that 10:25–28 depends on Mk 12:28–34 and a Q-pericope, Sellin regards the whole of 10:29–37 as a purely Lucan creation. His main arguments are the following: (1) The style

Lambert agrees with Sellin.

and vocabulary are typical of Luke. (2) There is no tension whatsoever between v. 29 and vv. 36–37a. (3) The theology of the parable concerns the Samaritan's observance of the Law; cultic Judaism is a thing of the past; the Samaritan shows that the ethical and religious precepts of the Torah remain in force even for non–Jews. In Sellin's opinion this theology can only be explained in terms of the conceptions of a Hellenistic Jew like Luke.

With some reservation, the argument regarding style and vocabulary can be accepted, but Sellin's second assertion concerning the absence of tension between v. 29 and vv. 36–37a seems incorrect (cf. above). As for the theology of the pericope, it can be admitted that Luke's own theological understanding is present throughout. But the question is, leaving aside the whole problem of the identity of Luke, whether Sellin has correctly characterized that theology, and whether Luke has not used a preexistent parable in order to express his own viewpoint. And in fact, given the tension in the use of the term "neighbor," we cannot but conclude that Luke did possess an already existing parable.

In making the step back from this preexisting tradition to Jesus himself, the observations made on p. 45 can be recalled. Further, it is not a priori excluded (although also difficult to prove) that Jesus, the original narrator, could have been inspired by a story such as that in 2 Chr 28:8–15:

> The men of Israel [i.e. the northern kingdom] took captive two hundred thousand of their kinsfolk, women, sons, and daughters; they also took much spoil from them and brought the spoil to Samaria.
>
> But a prophet of the Lord was there, whose name was Oded; and he went out to meet the army that came to Samaria, and said to them, "Behold, because the Lord, the God of your fathers, was angry with Judah, he gave them into your hand, but you have slain them in a rage which has reached up to heaven. And now you intend to subjugate the people of Judah and Jerusalem, male and female, as your slaves. Have you not sins of your own against the Lord your God? Now hear me, and send back the captives from your kinsfolk whom you have taken, for the fierce wrath of the Lord is upon you.
>
> Certain chiefs also of the men of Ephraim, Azariah the son of Johanam, Berechiah the son of Meshillemoth, Jehizkiah the son of Shallum, and Amasa the son of Hadlai, stood up against those who were coming from the war, and said to them, "You

shall not bring the captives in here, for you propose to bring us
guilt against the Lord in addition to our present sins and guilt.
For our guilt is already great, and there is fierce wrath against
Israel."
So the armed men left the captives and the spoil before the
princes and all the assembly. And the men who have been
mentioned by name rose and took the captives, and with the
spoil they clothed all that were naked among them; they
clothed them, gave them sandals, provided them with food and
drink, and anointed them; and carrying all the feeble among
them on asses, they brought them to their kinsfolk at Jericho,
the city of palm trees. Then they returned to Samaria.

Compassion

Our first reaction when we attempt to find out what Jesus originally intended with the parable of the Good Samaritan is one of
bewilderment. Luke is the only evangelist who preserves the parable. He places it at the beginning of Jesus' long journey from
Galilee to Jerusalem. He rather extensively depicts a particular
encounter between Jesus and a lawyer. The lawyer's question
about how one is to inherit eternal life furnishes Jesus with the
occasion to tell the parable of the Good Samaritan. Our analysis,
however, indicates that this background to Jesus' telling the parable is probably not historical but rather a secondary Lucan creation. If this is true, does it then make sense to ask further about
Jesus' original intention?

Would not the maximal admissible reconstruction or hypothesis
be that Jesus with this parable simply wanted to illustrate what
real compassion means? With this story of the compassionate Samaritan Jesus would have deliberately intended to shock his hearers since the Jews normally would have expected their priests and
Levites to excel in an active love of neighbor. Or, could an anti-
clerical mentality be assumed on the part of his hearers? In that
case they would get a chuckle out of the negative portrayal of the
priest and the Levite and would look forward eagerly to the contrast to follow in which the layman acts otherwise and better than
the clergy! Jesus, however, springs a surprise: he wants to scandalize. Instead of the good layman whom they expect, he brings a
compassionate Samaritan into the story. The shock among his dis-
appointed hearers must have been all the greater.

However it may be with this last hypothesis, we should not too

easily accept the idea that Jesus' hearers would have excused their
clergy in the name of ritual purity. In other words it should not be
assumed that the hearers would know from the story that both the
priest and the Levite thought that the half-dead (cf. v. 30) traveler
was perhaps really dead, and that contact with the dead body
would make the priest unclean (cf. Lev 21:1–4, 11) and the Levite
unfit for temple service. This sort of reconstruction is unconvincing. No, Jesus deliberately intended to provoke his hearers, for it
is not an "elected one" of their people but a despised half–Jew, a
Samaritan, who is presented as an example in the parable. Jesus
hopes that through its shock value the intended lesson will have a
greater impact. He wants his Jewish hearers to recognize that the
Samaritan of the story indeed proved "neighbor" to the man who
fell among robbers.

In what precedes we have used the terms "example" and "lesson" rather freely. Does this mean then that Jesus told a genuine
exemplary story in this case? We think so. Whoever supposes that
an exemplary story would necessarily involve Jesus explicitly com-
mending the example narrated for imitation, as happens in the
(Lucan) addition of v. 37b ("go and do likewise"), might hesitate
on this point in light of the conclusions of our literary analysis.
Nevertheless, it would be wrong to do so, for even without this
addition the summons to imitation is implicitly present.

Teaching, Apology, Appeal

The problem of whether or not we may call the Good Samaritan
an exemplary story is however not settled by the mere distinction
between an implicit and an explicit command. It must be further
asked, Why did Jesus narrate his parable? What was his real intention?

(a) In an exemplary story, in contrast to many other types of
parables, it is impossible to distinguish between the image (the
comparison, e.g., a pearl, a seed) and the reality intended (e.g.,
the kingdom of God). From this point of view then, it can at least
provisionally be maintained that the Good Samaritan is more an
example than an image, and is thus a real exemplary story. There
is no need for a transposition from image to intended reality. The
example is an integral part, a "sample" of the reality. Man's response (the exercise of compassion) is demanded and made possi-

ble by God's eschatological envoy Jesus. Announcement and exhortation, kerygma and parenesis are the two fundamental aspects of Jesus' proclamation of the kingdom of God. Consequently, we can affirm that Jesus told this parable because compassion belongs essentially to his message. God reigns where people act like the Samaritan. To do as the Samaritan does always and everywhere witnesses to the breakthrough of God's reign.

It must be noted, however, that Jesus' first concern with this parable is clearly insight. He teaches here and instructs, revealing an essential feature of the kingdom of God. He provides information with his story. The concluding rhetorical question of v. 36 implicitly asks for assent to what the Samaritan has done. Agreement with his action must come first. The person who intellectually accepts the teaching of the parable as true will inevitably have to proceed to the personal application. He who approves the example will have to follow it. But, as was shown above, the application was probably not formulated in so many words by Jesus himself.

(b) We are familiar with the parable of the Prodigal Son. We find more in this simile today than a moving lesson about God's love for the repentant sinner. The Christological dimension of this parable is now emphasized, i.e., it is stressed that Jesus also narrated the Prodigal Son in order to defend himself against charges and objections raised by the Jews against his way of acting. Just as the father welcomes the sinful younger son notwithstanding the unwillingness of the older son, so Jesus deals mercifully with sinners and tax collectors in spite of the indignant murmuring of the Pharisees and scribes (cf. 15:1–2). In this parable Jesus points to the attitude of God, his Father. This is his justification: God is like that and he wills that Jesus should act the same way on earth

It is not impossible that the Good Samaritan comes from a similar historical situation of opposition and self-defence. And if this is the case, then the parable shows us not only the teacher who explains and illustrates a lesson with a moving example, but also the prophet sent by God, who is criticized and attacked because he helps the wounded traveler and by his behavior unmasks the hypocrisy of the temple functionaries.

Everything we know from other authentic gospel passages about Jesus' attitude towards outcasts strongly supports the Christological character of our parable. Although this "typical" situation, i.e., Jesus' *constant* way of acting in a given set of circumstances, the *Sitz im Leben Jesu* (cf. pp. 44–45), is more than sufficient as an explanation for his telling this parable, H. Zimmermann even ventures to postulate a concrete occasion: One day Jesus conveyed God's mercy to someone in need, perhaps a sinner. Because of this action he was criticized and so justified himself by telling this story. The exemplary story is thus at the same time an apologetic parable! The image of the Samaritan and his deed must be transposed to Jesus and his conduct. The image is in the service of the reality intended—a reality which has to be defended.

The Good Samaritan involves then more than information about an important moral implication of the preaching of the kingdom of God. It is also a true-to-life apology by means of which Jesus defends himself and justifies his mission. With the help of this parable Jesus formulates and sustains his messianic claims. Jesus identifies himself with the Samaritan!

(c) But is this all? It seems to us that the parable of the Good Samaritan also participates in the power of language as word-event. Time and again Jesus' way of acting led to a conflict situation. His opponents resented and rejected his authority and his concern for the "little people" of his time. They demanded his credentials and made accusations: Not by the spirit of God, but by the prince of demons he casts out dreams (cf. Mk 3:22). In the midst of Jesus' mighty deeds the Pharisees demand a clear, convincing, heavenly sign from him (cf. Mk 8:11).

This conflict situation forced Jesus to defend himself. He did so, among other ways, in parables. This is, however, a risky business. Jesus certainly tries to justify himself, but at the same time he wants to convince his opponents, to win them over. For the moment he condemns no one. He tries to make them recognize that he is from God. What is asked of them is not purely intellectual assent or rational agreement. A decision involving the deepest existential level is at stake: He who is not with me is against me (cf. Lk 11:23). What Jesus aims for is conversion, a real self-surrender accompanied by insight, repentance, and a change of life. Through his speaking in parables something has to happen in the hearts of his hearers. The opponents who hear the parables cannot remain unmoved, on the sidelines. They must make a decision for or against Jesus. They must either reject him yet again or accept him in surrendering themselves. All this shows that Jesus told the story of the Good Samaritan intending to place his hearers before an inescapable existential call to conversion. The Good Samaritan is thus ultimately a missionary parable. He who accepts its message is led to follow the example of the Samaritan in his personal life (cf. a). All who hear it are themselves invited to become "Samaritans." For Jewish listeners this concretely meant abandoning their nationalistic feelings of religious superiority, reversing value judgments, and radically changing their attitudes towards their "neighbor." Notwithstanding the second messianic function pointed out above (cf. b), it must be repeated, then, that for Jesus, too, the parable of the Good Samaritan remains essentially an exemplary story (cf. a).

Our discussion concludes here. The precise occasion, the wording of the accusation, the particular group of opponents, the exact time and place—all these details are irrevocably lost to us. Indeed, it could hardly be otherwise. Yet, we are helped by the whole context of Jesus' earthly life as known to us through his usual conduct, many of his words and deeds, and through the historical course of his existence. The Good Samaritan can be situated against this background. Originally as told by Jesus the Good Samaritan was an exemplary story. It would be a one-sided and faulty image of Jesus, however, to see him here only as a teacher who in God's name explains the moral implications of his message and who wishes to evoke insight. Without denying this element of Jesus' teaching, by referring to his habitual way of acting we have discovered a second function. As an apology for Jesus' claims, the parable also involves a Christological dimension. But, Jesus' speaking is above all a word-event. The ultimate aim which Jesus pursues in his speaking is human salvation. More than insight, even more than self-defence, the Good Samaritan issues an existential call to all Jesus' hearers, including his opponents.

If this many-sided interpretation is correct, it can safely be concluded without danger of an artificial, exaggerated allegorizing that Jesus intended the Samaritan in the story to stand as an apology for himself, but that at the same time, he told the parable as a call to imitation by his hearers. Such an imitation, especially when it is done in a radical way, is often challenged by the world and even some Christians. In the face of that challenge, we ask why a modern follower of Jesus—whether a prophet or priest, a social worker, catechist, or simple convinced Christian—could not justify himself before the world and his own conscience by means of this parable of the Good Samaritan?

IV. A Plea for Luke

Many a Christian has (metaphorically) wept like Mary Magdalene at the tomb. The work of exegetes they say is so often destructive. All that remains of the gospel texts, formerly so full of life, seems many times to be nothing but an arid, desolate desert. An empty tomb! "They have taken away my Lord!" (cf. Jn 20:11–13). But after the foregoing analysis, can we not identify even a little with Mary Magdalene's joy as we see Jesus rediscovered, "rising" in this parable to his own defense? We recognize him in the Good Samaritan: "Rabboni!"

At this point we may feel hesitant about returning to Luke. What has Luke done with the original intention of Jesus? Has he buried the living Lord once again? Has he unconsciously mutilated the image of Jesus beyond recognition?

The Lucan Reworking

With a fair degree of certainty Lucan editorial activity within 10:25–37 can be pinpointed:

(a) Mk 12:28–34 is not, stylistically speaking, a pure controversy, since in it Jesus praises the scribe because he answered wisely: "You are not far from the kingdom of God" (v. 34). In the Q-version, on the contrary, the intention of the lawyer was decidedly hostile. He asked his question in order to test Jesus. Luke in his redaction has followed Q for the most part (cf. 10:25; but note the Marcan influence in 10:28).

It is, however, of greater importance to carefully observe how Luke rewrites the introductory discussion in view of the following parable. As long as the pericope of the Great Commandment stood alone, it was, logically speaking, Jesus himself who in his answer should have made the connection between the two commandments and thus created a challenging new viewpoint. Luke's attention was, however, so exclusively focused on what he wanted to illustrate by the following parable that in his introductory presentation he did not hesitate to place that connection in the mouth of the lawyer (see 10:27).

(b) The parable which he was about to present no doubt affected Luke's editing of vv. 25–28. The converse, however, is also true—perhaps even more so. The discussion leading up to the parable orientates our understanding of the parable in a particular direction. For Luke, Jesus' parable is an illustrative example, no longer concerning "doing mercy" in general, but specifically about love of neighbor, with reference to the question in v. 29. It is a commentary on what "love of neighbor" involves. Jesus is no longer defending himself. He is now the authoritative, competent teacher who first quickly approves the lawyer's answer and then goes on to explain, by using an image, who the neighbor is, or better, how one becomes a neighbor. One becomes a neighbor by showing compassion and thus fulfilling God's commandment of love for one's fellow humans.

(c) The whole pericope 10:25–37 is, moreover, characterized by a typical Lucan emphasis. The central theme here is "doing": "doing" as the only way to inherit eternal life. Luke strongly accentuates this idea of doing by means of his redactional phrases: "What shall I *do* . . . ?" (v. 25); "*do* this" (v. 28); "*do* likewise" (v. 37b); and possibly also "to *do* mercy" (v. 37a). In this way the whole passage becomes an exhortation to act in order to inherit life. We noted above that it was precisely in this accentuation that Luke's redaction was influenced by the pericope of the Rich Man (Lk 18:18–30 = Mk 10:17–31).

The Lucan Exemplary Story

As told by Jesus, the Good Samaritan parable probably was simultaneously teaching, apology, and appeal. In the concrete conflict (that day, that place) which was the occasion for the parable, the whole Jesus with his unique claims and extraordinary authority was present in his speaking. From this viewpoint, it can be said that every gospel passage and even every saying of Jesus contains the whole Christ and the complete gospel message. This, however, is no longer true in the case of Luke's gospel, a written document, since the pericope occupies a definite place therein and cannot simply be removed from the whole in which it stands.

In transforming Jesus' many-sided parable into *his* illustrative exemplary story, Luke was undoubtedly influenced by the post-paschal, ecclesiastical situation with its own needs and problems. Jesus' message had to be adapted to different and urgent circumstances. That is the law of every effort at actualization. But for this reason we are entitled to ask whether Luke's rendering of the Good Samaritan has not resulted in a reduction of its original intention. It must be conceded that the Christological dimension of Jesus' convinced and convincing self-justification has almost completely disappeared in Luke's presentation of a Jesus giving authoritative instruction on genuine Christian love of neighbor. This Lucan Christ is no longer the complete and true-to-life earthly Jesus.

These observations may be somewhat disturbing, but they are so only if the pericope is isolated from the rest of the gospel. It should be recalled that each of the four evangelists sketches his own picture of Jesus with the help of many traditions. Inevitably, the parts function differently in the literary whole of the gospel than they did within the context of Jesus' earthly life. Each part contributes to the whole, but every part does not contain the whole, certainly not in the same rich way as the earthly Jesus did in his concrete confrontation with disciples, crowds, and opponents. Each part points to some aspect and illustrates some facet of the total Jesus Christ whom the written document as a whole presents to the reader. We must keep in mind the literary genre "gospel" if we are not to do an injustice to the actualizing, rewriting evangelist.

Samaria

Luke has placed the pericope 10:25–37 near the beginning of his travel narrative in 9:51–19:46: Jesus' going up to Jerusalem (cf. pp. 25–26). After stating that Jesus had set his face to go to Jerusalem and had sent messengers ahead of him, he immediately adds:

> [The messengers] went and entered a village of the Samaritans, to make ready for him; but the people would not receive him, because his face was set toward Jerusalem. And when his disciples James and John saw it, they said, "Lord, do you want us to bid fire come down from heaven and consume them?" But he turned and rebuked them. And they went on to another village. (9:52b–56)

It is striking that in both of the two other passages of his gospel where Luke mentions a Samaritan the person in question is portrayed in a favorable light: the parable of the Good Samaritan (10:30–35) and the Samaritan leper who returns to thank Jesus after being cured (17:11–19). Further, from Acts 1:8 we learn that there was to be missionary activity also in Samaria: "But you shall receive power when the Holy Spirit has come upon you; and you shall be my witnesses in Jerusalem and in all Judea and *Samaria* and to the end of the earth." This missionary activity in Samaria is described in Acts 8:1–25. Those who had dispersed on account of the violent persecution against the church in Jerusalem went about and preached the good news not only in the plains of Judea but also in many villages of Samaria. In a generalizing way it is said that the Samaritans accepted the word of God: cf. Acts 8:14 and 9:31 (see also 15:3).

One cannot avoid the impression that Luke did not place the story of the Good Samaritan in such close proximity to the pericope 9:52b–56, in which Jesus strongly rebukes James and John for wanting to call down fire upon the Samaritan village, by mere chance. From 10:30–35 on Luke begins to refer to the openness which the Samaritans will manifest towards Jesus' message. It is a Samaritan and not a Jewish priest or Levite who fulfills the foremost commandment of the Law (Lk 10:26–27). Were the Samaritans, those half–Jews for whom the Torah was also binding, in Luke's judgment perhaps those who formed a bridge to the Gentile mission?

Theory and Practice

With the parable of the Good Samaritan Luke intends to exhort his local church community. He actualizes the parable for the benefit of his fellow Christians. That is why he de-emphasizes the authority of the Law, which after all was sufficiently known since the lawyer answers his own question. In place of the authority of the Law, Luke's actualization brings Jesus to the fore. He first authoritatively commands, ". . . do this, and you shall live" (v. 28), and then concretely elucidates the all-encompassing Law with an exemplary story, and finally once again commands, "Go and do likewise" (v. 37).

It was suggested above that Luke did not create the shift in the concept "neighbor" with conscious emphasis. The tension between neighbor seen as an object of action and neighbor as a subject was probably the accidental result of Luke's inattentiveness. Nevertheless, Luke does seem to have accentuated the opposition between theory and praxis in the parable. Initially the lawyer asks in a very intellectual way, cautiously, and as it were at a distance, the theoretical question "And who is my neighbor?". Jesus does not answer with a conceptual definition or in a notional paraphrase. He uses an example taken from life. In his story the initial intellectual question becomes an existential appeal: we ourselves must act and become neighbors to the other. And in the context of this opposition between theory and praxis, the above-mentioned shift does not function all that badly. Why, therefore, should the contemporary preacher not use it in explaining and actualizing the text? "Neighbor" is not a static designation of the person next to me, but an appeal to me. Further, I am not a neighbor by nature; I have to become a neighbor by showing mercy.

Doing Mercy

Thus, Luke stresses one particular point in his presentation of the Good Samaritan. Attention is focused, not on what Jesus historically did, but on what Christians of his time should do. "To do" is the key word here, emphasized by its repeated use. The same theme of "doing" is also prominent elsewhere in Luke's gospel: cf. e.g., Lk 3:10–14 where three different groups of people each ask in turn, "What shall we *do*?"; or 8:21, "My mother and my brothers are those who hear the word of God and *do* it!"; or Acts 2:37, "What shall we *do*?".

"To do mercy" in 10:37 sums up in a comprehensive expression what had been worked out in detail throughout the story: to have compassion at the sight of the half-dead man; to go to him; to bind up his wounds, pouring on oil and wine; to set him on his own beast; to bring him to an inn; to care for him and to make provisions for his continued care by others, just as the Samaritan gave money to the innkeeper.

Luke must have welcomed this story which he found in the tradition. It depicts his favorite theme, his conviction that in Christian communities there should no longer be poor, needy people. To realize this goal, he thought everything should be owned in common and those who had possessions should sell them and lay the profits at the feet of the apostles so that the money might be distributed to those in need (cf. Acts 4:32, 34–37; 2:44–45). In his gospel Luke underlines the opposition between rich and poor: see e.g., "blessed are you poor" and "woe to you that are rich" (6:20 and 24), or the parable of the Rich Man and Lazarus (16:19–31). The rich man is accused because he did not help the poor in an effective way. Luke illustrates the manner in which such help should be given: Zacchaeus gives half of his goods to the poor (cf. 19:8) and the "ruler" is commanded by Jesus to distribute to the poor all that he has (cf. 18:22). That is the way to have treasure in heaven (cf. 18:22; 12:33–34: "Sell your possessions, and give alms; provide yourselves with purses that do not grow old, with a treasure in the heavens that does not fail, where no thief approaches and no moth destroys. For where your treasure is, there will your heart be also"). The rich man who lays up treasure for himself and is not rich toward God is a fool (cf. 12:20–21). We should make friends for ourselves by means of this world's goods so that those friends will someday receive us into the eternal habitations (cf. 16:9). Radical renunciation of riches and possessions is a condition for following Jesus (cf. 18:22; see also 5:11: Peter and the sons of Zebedee leave everything and follow him; 5:28: Levi leaves everything, rises, and follows him). For "whoever of you does not renounce all that he has cannot be my disciple" (14:33).

Love of neighbor, showing mercy, having compassion, helping the poor in an effective way by a renunciation of possessions: all these are elements of a central theme of Luke's parenesis. It is obvious that these exhortations emerge from a world with different social structures and situations than our own. No one, however, can doubt the enduring relevance of this Lucan thematic.

V. Fruitful Exegesis

We must love our neighbor: this is indeed the self-evident lesson of the story of the Good Samaritan for all readers or hearers, past and present. In this connection it has been suggested that the parable's message is that the neighbor is not the person who needs my help, but the one who helps me. In its own way this all too subtle explanation tends to emphasize the shift within the use of the term "neighbor," already discussed above. This explanation is hardly convincing, however, and would be even less so if it were to imply the further extravagant claim that we should love only those who as a matter of fact help us, as in the so-called "tax collector morality" (cf. Mt 5:46).

Insight into the Genesis of the Pericope

Nevertheless, it was our intention in this investigation to account for the manifest tension between the questions: Who is my neighbor? and Who became a neighbor? How did this unevenness originate? Should it be compared to a dissonant chord deliberately struck in order to please the ear by its very resolution? Our analysis has led to a different view. In his editing of 10:25–37 Luke was dependent on many elements. The parable itself came to him from the tradition. In the introductory dialogue, vv. 25–28, literary influence from Mk 12:28–34 and a Q-version, which probably contained a more or less similar Great Commandment pericope, can be noted.

We saw that it is not advisable to assume that Luke possessed a source where dialogue and parable were already combined since the transitional vv. 28 and 29 are thoroughly Lucan. It was Luke himself, then, who staged and dramatized the parable. Varied tradition and far-reaching redaction: these are the two mutually complementary factors which were discovered in our literary analysis. The recognition that Luke in his editorial work did not bother to iron out all the wrinkles in his overlapping traditions should hardly come as a surprise. The so-called tension in the use of the word "neighbor" should probably be explained along the lines of this recognition.

Jesus and Luke

Literary analysis is not an end in itself. The results of such an analysis make it possible to determine the point of the pericope under consideration with a greater degree of certainty, both within its written Lucan context and in the preaching of Jesus.

In order to determine Jesus' intention in telling the parable of the Good Samaritan, we had to abstract from the introductory dialogue (vv. 25–28), because it was Luke who placed the parable in its present context. We also succeeded in reconstructing a typical—although general!—situation in the setting of Jesus' life in which this parable could have been told as an exemplary story and also in self-defence and appeal. For Jesus, the Good Samaritan was thus a Christological, apologetic, and missionary exemplary story. For Luke, on the other hand, the Good Samaritan has become primarily an explanation, an illustration of what it means to love our neighbor and what is involved in becoming a neighbor to a person in need. The Lucan Jesus urges the faithful to act ("to do") in the same way as the Samaritan in order to inherit eternal life. The parable has become an explicit exemplary story (cf. vv. 25, 29, 37b); it is an authoritative commentary given by Jesus on the commandment of love of neighbor as quoted by the lawyer (cf. v. 27).

Actualizing

The fruit of such critical study should not be underestimated. Besides giving the intellectual satisfaction of understanding more fully the origin and the various layers of tradition within the gospel text, such analysis also shows us more clearly that the distinction between tradition and redaction and especially between Jesus and the evangelist is indeed justified. With the Good Samaritan parable Jesus taught the crowds, defended himself, and challenged his hearers. Luke regarded the parable as a moving example of truly Christian assistance shown to one in need. Our investigation was neither destructive nor sterile, even if much attention had to be given to the complexities of the rewritten, compiled, adapted, and actualized traditions which make up a gospel.

The Spirit inspired Luke in his editing and actualizing, the same Spirit who so clearly manifested the uniqueness of Jesus of Nazareth and who also continues to inspire the contemporary preacher. Whether today's preacher uses the Good Samaritan to explain and defend his own "scandalous" way of life as Jesus did, or like Luke uses it as a parenetical, authoritative, exemplary word of Jesus with an eye to the actual demands of effective love, is a choice which is a matter of personal freedom. That choice is ultimately of secondary importance as long as the preacher allows himself to be guided by the Spirit in union with the church.

BIBLIOGRAPHY

Binder, H., "Das Gleichnis vom barmherzigen Samariter," *TZ* 15 (1959) 176–94.

Crespy, G., "La parabole dite: 'Le bon Samaritain': Recherches structurales," *ETR* 48 (1973) 61–79.

Crossan, J. D., "Parable and Example in the Teaching of Jesus," *NTS* 18 (1971–1972) 285–307.

Daniel, C., "Les Esséniens et l'arrière-fond historique de la parabole du Bon Samaritain," *NovT* 11 (1969) 71–104.

Derrett, J. D. M., "Law in the New Testament: Fresh Light on the Parable of the Good Samaritan," *NTS* 11 (1964–1965) 22–37; also in Derrett, *Law in the New Testament*, London, 1970, pp. 208–27.

Eulenstein, R., " 'Und wer ist mein Nächster?' Lk 10,25–37 in der Sicht eines klassischen Philologen," *Theologie und Glaube* 67 (1977) 127–45.

Fuchs, E., "Was heisst: 'Du sollst deinen Nächsten lieben wie dich selbst'?," in Fuchs, *Zur Frage nach dem historischen Jesus*, Tübingen, 1960, pp. 1–20.

————, "Gott und Mensch im Text und als Text," *ZThK* 67 (1970) 321–34.

Funk, R. W., "The Old Testament in Parable: A Study of Luke 10:25–37,"*Encounter* 26 (1965) 251–67; also in Funk, *Language, Hermeneutic and Word of God*, New York, 1966, pp. 199–222.

Gerhardsson, B., *The Good Samaritan—The Good Shepherd?*, Coniectanea neotestamentica 16, Lund–Copenhagen, 1958.

Gewalt, D., "Der 'Barmherzige Samariter'. Zu Lukas 10,25–37," *EvT* 38 (1978) 403–17.

Hermann, I., "Wem ich der Nächste bin. Auslegung von Lk 10,25–37," *BibLeb* 2 (1961) 17–24.

Kieffer, R., "Analyse sémiotique et commentaire. Quelques réflexions à propos d'études de Luc 10,25–37," *NTS* 25 (1978–79) 454–68.

Klemm, H. G., *Das Gleichnis vom Barmherzigen Samariter. Grundzuge der Auslegung im 16./17. Jahrhundert*, BWANT 103, Stuttgart, 1973.

Lambrecht, J., "The Message of the Good Samaritan (Lk 10:25–37), *Louvain Studies* 5 (1974–1975) 121–35.

Leenhardt, F. J., "La Parabole du Samaritain (Schéma d'une exégèse existentialiste), in *Aux sources de la tradition chrétienne. Mélanges offerts à M. Goguel*, Bibliothèque théologique, Neuchâtel-Paris, 1950, pp. 132–38.

Légasse, S., "L'étendue de l'amour interhumain d'après le Nouveau Testament: limites et promesse," *RTL* 8 (1977) 283–304.

Lindijer, C. H., "Oude en nieuwe visies op de gelijkenis van de barmhartige Samaritaan," *NThTij* 15 (1960–1961) 11–23.

Monselewski, W., *Der barmherzige Samariter. Eine auslegungsgeschichtliche Untersuchung zu Lukas 10,25–37*, Beiträge zur Geschichte der biblischen Exegese 5, Tübingen, 1967.

Mussner, F., "Der Begriff des 'Nächsten' in der Verkündigung Jesu. Dargelegt am Gleichnis vom barmherzigen Samariter," in Mussner, *Praesentia Salutis. Gesammelte Studien zu Fragen und Themen des Neuen Testamentes*, KuBANT, Düsseldorf, 1967, pp. 125–32.

Patte, D., "Structural Network in Narrative: The Good Samaritan," *Soundings* 58 (1975) 221–42.

Ramaroson, L., "Comme 'le Bon Samaritain', ne chercher qu'à aimer (Lc 10,29–37)," *Bib* 56 (1975) 533–36.

Reicke, B., "Der barmherzige Samariter," in *Verborum Veritas. Festschrift für G. Stählin*, ed. O. Böcher and K. Haacker, Wuppertal, 1970, pp. 103–9.

Sellin, G., "Lukas als Gleichniserzähler: die Erzählung vom barmherzigen Samariter (Lk 10, 25–37)," *ZNW* 65 (1974) 166–89; 66 (1975) 19–60.

Seven, F., "Hermeneutische Erwägungen zur poetischen Realisation eines neutestamentlichen Textes ('Sprachereignis' bei E. Jüngel und E. Güttgemanns)," *LB* (1973) no. 29/30, pp. 52–55.

Ternant, P., "Le bon Samaritain. Luc 10,25–37," *AssSeign II* (1974) no. 46, pp. 66–77.

Trudinger, L. P., "Once Again, Now, 'Who is my Neighbour?'," *EvQ* 48 (1976) 160–63.

Young, N. H., "Once Again, Now, 'Who is my Neighbour?' A Comment," *EvQ* 49 (1977) 178–79.

Zimmermann, H., "Das Gleichnis vom barmherzigen Samariter: Lk 10, 25–37," in *Die Zeit Jesu. Festschrift für H. Schlier*, ed. G. Bornkamm and K. Rahner, Freiburg, 1970, pp. 58–69.

In the above-cited article Crossan defends the thesis that the Good Samaritan is not an exemplary story but a parable in the strict sense. On this question a structuralist discussion arose, a number of the contributions to which have appeared in the new experimental American journal *Semeia* (1974) no. 1 (with contributions of J. D. Crossan, D. O. Via, N. R. Petersen, and R. W. Funk) and (1974) no. 2 (with contributions of D. Patte, G. Crespy—Crespy's article being a translation of that cited above—R. W. Funk, J. D. Crossan, R. C. Tannehill, and D. O. Via). See also *LB* (1974) no. 31 (with a response by G. Sellin to Crossan and Via).

Four

Parables in Mark 4

In this chapter devoted to Mk 4:1–34 the evangelist Mark stands in the foreground. The question of the original or traditional meaning of the parables which occur in this chapter—the Sower, the Seed Growing by Itself, and the Mustard Seed—cannot be avoided, but the redactional work of the evangelist is in many respects quite striking and worthy of note. The most remarkable feature in this parable chapter is Jesus' statement addressed to "those who were about him with the Twelve": "To you has been given the secret of the kingdom of God, but for those outside everything is in parables; so that they may indeed see but not perceive, and may indeed hear but not understand; lest they should turn again, and be forgiven" (Mk 4:11–12). In this text we are confronted with the famous obduracy theory: Jesus does not use parables in order to illumine his teaching, but rather to make it obscure. His intention is not to evoke insight or to summon people to decision, but rather to prevent them from understanding, to harden their hearts, and make it impossible for them to change their ways and thus obtain forgiveness for their sins. Was this really Jesus' conception? If not, how did this "theory" arise? To whom is it to be attributed? Can we understand, and accept it? And what is the meaning of the privilege enjoyed by the Twelve and the bystanders, namely their being given the secret of the kingdom of God?

Our exposition proceeds in five steps. First, the problems involved in this fourth chapter are outlined (I). A sound methodological procedure requires that thereafter an attempt be made to determine the redactional contribution of the evangelist within this chapter (II). The way in which the parable of the Sower in 4:14–

20 has been allegorized is discussed (III), followed by an analysis of the chapter's component parables and similitudes (IV). Finally, the discussion returns to the evangelist Mark and asks what exactly he had in mind when he had Jesus solemnly declare to the bystanders with the Twelve, "To you has been given the secret of the kingdom of God" (4:11) (V).

I. Defining the Problem

Temporarily setting aside the introduction (vv. 1–2) and the conclusion (vv. 33–34), we find three different literary forms in this fourth chapter of Mk: (a) first the parables, or rather one parable (the Sower: vv. 3–9) and two similitudes (the Seed Growing by Itself, vv. 26–29, and the Mustard Seed, vv. 30–32); (b) the explanation of the Sower in vv. 13–20; (c) various utterances: the logion about obduracy (vv. 11–12) which gives an answer to the question concerning the purpose of the parables (in v. 10), and a series of four sayings which at first seem rather unrelated (vv. 21–25), namely the Lamp, "that which is hidden and will be revealed," the Measure, and "those who have and those who do not have."

Cyclic Structure

On closer inspection, however, it becomes clear that Mk 4:1–34 is not a hopelessly heterogeneous accumulation of disjointed units. Rather, it appears that Mark has taken up elements of different origin and divergent character and worked them into a fairly harmonious whole. The cyclic character of the structure of the chapter is quite clear:

A   Introduction: vv. 1–2
B   Parable of the Sower: vv. 3–20
    a   Sower (vv. 3–9)
    b   Obduracy (vv. 10–12)
    a' Explanation of the Sower (vv. 13–20)
C   Sayings: vv. 21–25
    a   Lamp and its explanation (vv. 21–22)
    b   Double summons to hear (vv. 23–24b)
    a' Measure and its explanation (vv. 24c–25)

B' Seed Similitudes: vv. 26–32
   a Seed Growing by Itself (vv. 26–29)
   a' Mustard Seed (vv. 30–32)
A' Conclusion: vv. 33–34

We have proposed this concentric structure in a previous study "Redaction and Theology in Mk 4" (see bibliography). Although some details may not be acceptable to all, our proposed structuring of verses 21–25, e.g., seems incontestable:

21 And he said to them,
  a "Is a lamp brought in to be put under a bushel,
      or under a bed, and not on a stand?
22   *For* there is nothing hid, except to be made manifest;
      nor is anything secret, except to come to light.
23 *b* If any one has ears to hear, let him hear."
24   And he said to them,
      "Take heed what you hear;
  a' the measure you give will be the measure you get,
      and still more will be given to you.
25   *For* to him who has will more be given;
      and from him who has not, even what he has will be taken
      away."

The two metaphors of the Lamp (v. 21) and the Measure (v. 24c) are both followed by a short proverbial explanation, each introduced by "for" (v. 22 and v. 25). The resulting units are linked by a concluding (v. 23) and an introductory (v. 24b) summons to hear. This double summons is the hinge on which this remarkable group of sayings turns.

The typically Marcan "sandwich" structure in *B* (Sower, Obduracy, and Explanation of the Sower) is as equally incontestable as is Mark's intention of forming a framework by means of the summons to hear in vv. 3 and 9, and with the introduction (vv. 1–2) and conclusion (vv. 33–34).

There is also an undeniable parallelism in the construction of the two seed similitudes (vv. 26–32):

26 And he said,
"The kingdom of God is

as if a man should scatter
seed
upon the ground,

27 and should sleep and rise
night and day,
and the seed should sprout and
grow, he knows not how.
28 The earth produces of itself,
first the blade, then the ear,
then the full grain in the ear.
29 But when the grain is ripe,
'at once he puts in the sickle,
because the harvest has
come.' "

30 And he said,
"With what can we compare the
kingdom of God, or what
parable
shall we use for it?
31 It is like a grain of
mustard seed, which,
when sown upon the ground,
is the smallest of all the
seeds of the earth:

32 yet when it is sown it
grows up
and becomes the greatest of
all shrubs, and puts forth
large branches,
so that 'the birds of the air
can make nests in its shade.' "

Both similitudes are introduced by a reference to the kingdom of God. In both the comparison itself has to do with the germinating and growing of the seed and with the harvest or the full stature of the shrub. The words and expressions correspond. Both similitudes end with an allusion to an Old Testament passage.

It can, therefore, hardly be denied that Mark did intend to give a definite structure to this chapter. However, our interest here is focused more on the contents than the form as such.

Some Questions

Mark concludes his parable chapter with the following statement, "With many such parables, he spoke the word to them, as they were able to hear it; he did not speak to them without a parable, but privately to his own disciples he explained everything" (vv. 33–34). From this it can be inferred that Mark selected only a few representative parables for inclusion in his gospel. According to Mark Jesus' speaking in parables was the rule, not the exception. Spontaneously one might think that his parable speaking was intended as an illustration, an aid to better understanding, as an adaptation to the mentality of the hearers. His metaphorical language does not, however, make everything transparent. Explanation to an "inner circle" is necessary.

On the other hand, in an earlier passage in the same chapter it is said that speaking in parables was intended to induce a hardening of heart (see vv. 11–12). How are we to understand these verses? Can we reconcile this intention with what must be supposed to have been the motivation behind Jesus' preaching, i.e., his wish to be understood? When we look at the expressions in vv. 33b–34a, "in as far as they were able to understand," and "he did not speak to them except in parables," do they not seem to express the same restrictive and negative intention as vv. 11–12?

In addition, there is some unevenness in the presentation. Why is the explanation of the Sower separated from the parable itself by the saying concerning hardening? What are the series of utterances (vv. 21–25) doing between the Sower and the seed similitudes? Why in v. 10 do "those who were about him with the Twelve" ask Jesus about the parables (in the plural) even though only one parable had been narrated hitherto? Finally, questions might also be raised about the abrupt shift from the crowd around the boat (vv. 1–2) to Jesus' suddenly being alone with "those who were about him with the Twelve" (v. 10), and then again to the crowd and the boat (vv. 33–36).

These various inconsistencies in thought and presentation stand in sharp contrast to the attractive structural unity of the chapter as presented above. Is there an explanation for this state of affairs?

II. Mark's Redactional Role

In our preceding survey of the content of Mk 4:1–34 we noted that the chapter is made up of varied material including a parable, similitudes, an explanation of the parable, added sayings, and framework elements. To throw some light on the problems to which we have just alluded, the most appropriate method is to start with an investigation of Mark's redactional work. How did he proceed? What was his contribution as the final redactor of the chapter? Once the latest redactional layer has been delimited, the way will be clear to work back to the preexistent elements of Mark's tradition. There is a possibility of discovering major activity on the part of the evangelist especially in three sections: the framework, the insertion of the obduracy statement, and the addition of the various sayings.

The Framework (vv. 1–2 and 33–34)

1 Again he began to teach beside the sea. And a very large crowd gathered about him, so that he got into a boat and sat in it on the sea; and the whole crowd was beside the sea on the land.
2 And he taught them many things in parables, and in his teaching he said to them. . . .

33 With many such parables he spoke the word to them, as they were able to hear it;
34 he did not speak to them without a parable, but privately to his own disciples he explained everything.

Most exegetes agree that it was almost certainly Mark himself who wrote the introductory vv. 1–2. Without going into detail, the most important arguments in favor of this view can be noted. It is not just a matter of a typically Marcan choice of words and style here. Several of Mark's favorite motifs are also found: e.g., to teach, the presence of large crowds pressing around Jesus, "in parables," a boat to keep the multitude at a distance. In this connection, reference can further be made to the story line which relates chap. 4 to its wider context. Thus, the boat mentioned in v. 1 was already introduced in 3:9: "He told his disciples to have a boat ready for him because of the crowd, lest they should crush him." It reappears in 4:36: "Leaving the crowd, they took him with them, just as he was, in the boat." Again the multitude referred to in the introduction (4:1–2) was present in 3:7–12 and 3:31–35, and is mentioned again in 4:36 (perhaps already in 4:26). In all likelihood then, it was the evangelist himself who by means of these framework elements attempted to introduce a certain unity and movement into his extended gospel story. All these considerations taken cumulatively justify the conclusion that these introductory vv. 1–2, almost in their entirety, are to be attributed to Mark.
There is less agreement concerning vv. 33–34. These verses

round off the parable chapter and form an obvious inclusion with vv. 1–2, almost in their entirety, are to be attributed to Mark. repetition. We shall refer below to the Marcan character of the motif of the lack of understanding implicit in v. 34 (in this case on the part of the people). Also, notwithstanding certain *hapaxlego-mena* (terms or expressions used only once), e.g., "without," "his own disciples," and "to explain," the vocabulary of v. 34 appears to be characteristically Marcan. And as for the content of the verse, that Jesus speaks in parables and teaches his disciples within a closed circle is also quite in accordance with Mark's conceptions. It is therefore not so evident that this verse could have functioned as the conclusion of the so-called pre–Marcan parable collection, as is frequently affirmed by exegetes.

Verse 34 is often considered traditional because of its alleged opposition to the previous verse. It is argued that the same author would not have formulated these two mutually contradictory statements unless he were dependent on a preexistent source. It can, however, immediately be asked if it is not rather v. 33 which seems to go against Mark's line of thought and which must therefore be regarded as traditional. It is true that the phrase, "with many such parables he spoke the word to them" (v. 33a), is reminiscent of the Marcan v. 2a: "He taught them many things in parables." Nevertheless, v. 33b, "as they were able to hear it," taken in isolation from its context in chap. 4, can be understood in a positive way as expressing Jesus' desire to adapt himself to the capacities of his hearers (which would be an indication of its possibly traditional character). The use of parables would then be a form of accomodation, an aid to understanding. The initial particle *kathōs* in v. 33b would then mean "as much as (they could understand)." But within its present Marcan context, as will become clearer in what follows, the term must be interpreted in a more negative and restrictive sense, i.e., "only in the way (they could understand)." And so it would seem that the redactor composed v. 34 precisely in order to clarify his somewhat ambiguous statement in v. 33, in accordance with his real point regarding Jesus' use of the parables. Furthermore, it would be very strange if the expression in v. 33b were to have, in opposition to the emphatic theme in v. 34, a positive meaning in its present context. This is all the more so since the whole of v. 33, as we have shown in

"Redaction and Theology in Mk 4" (see bibliography), is thoroughly Marcan in its choice of words and expressions. We are therefore led to the conclusion that not only the beginning (vv. 1–2) but most probably also the concluding verses (33–34) of the section are to be attributed in their entirety to Mark. If this view is correct, vv. 33–34, precisely because of their redactional character, can no longer be used either wholly or in part as a kind of proof for the existence of a so-called parable source in which different parables would already have been combined prior to Mark.

The Insertion (vv. [10], 11–12, [13])

10 And when he was alone, those who were about him with the Twelve asked him concerning the parables.
11 And he said to them, "To you has been given the secret of the kingdom of God, but for those outside everything is in parables;
12 so that they may indeed see but not perceive, and may indeed hear but not understand; lest they should turn again, and be forgiven.
13 And he said to them, "Do you understand this parable? How then will you understand all the parables?"

The introductory formula "and he said to them" in v. 11 is one of Mark's typical linking phrases, an *Anreihungsformel*, as the Germans say. In vv. 10–12 the boat mentioned in vv. 1–2 and vv. 35–36 seems to be forgotten. In content, the explanation of the Sower (vv. 14–20) connects very well with the parable of vv. 3–9. One gets the impression that the evangelist has rewritten v. 10 (cf. the motif of "being alone" and the reference to parables, although hitherto only one parable has been narrated) and v. 13 (theme of incomprehension) in view of the saying of vv. 11–12 which he inserted between them. Originally v. 10 must have been a simple request for an explanation of the Sower, and v. 13 a rather neutral formula introducing the immediately following explanation. We also know that Mark favors the motif, found in v. 10, of private teaching by Jesus to the disciples (cf. e.g., 7:17–23 and 13:3–37). Taking all this varied data into account and considering that the idea of speaking in parables in order to induce obduracy is contrary both to Jesus' own conception of the parables and to that of the early church, we are led to conclude that vv. 11–12 are a secondary insertion placed here by the evangelist himself. But this inserted material is not, as such, necessarily Mark's own creation. As is well known, the reputable exegete J. Jeremias tries to minimize the intention of hardening in vv. 11–12. After the *hina* ("in order that") in v. 12 one should, in his view, supply, "(in order that they), as stands written, (may see . . .)." According to this interpretation v. 12 expresses God's intention, not (directly) that of Jesus. The *mēpote* ("lest") at the end of the same verse would be the rendering of an Aramaic conjunction which can also mean "unless" (a meaning which the Greek *mēpote*, however, does not possess): "unless they come to better insight and God forgive them." Moreover, Jeremias affirms that the saying originally had a much wider significance. The Hebrew term *mashal* (or its Aramaic equivalent) means not only "parable" but also proverb, witty saying, example, pseudonym, riddle, etc. The pre–Marcan form of the saying could therefore be reconstructed as follows, "To you is given the secret of the kingdom of God, but to those who are outside all things become riddles" (so J. Gnilka). In this case it is presupposed that Jesus did not come to the awareness expressed in this saying right from the beginning of his public life, nor was the saying specifically connected with his preaching in parables. It was only after experiencing the culpable ill will of "those outside" that he spoke of their hostile attitude towards his whole message as the fulfillment of Isaiah's threatening announcement (Is 6:9–10). Subsequently, the translation of *mashal* by *parabole* very much restricted the significance of the term and moreover misled the redactor Mark, for it was in view of this Greek term *parabolē* that the evangelist was led to insert this logion into his parable chapter. Thus arose the famous theory of using the parables for the purpose of hardening. According to Mark, Jesus spoke in parables in public with the intention of inducing obduracy in his hearers. The metaphorical language of the parables now becomes a calculated obscuring of his message in order that, in fulfillment of Isaiah's prophecy, "outsiders" would indeed hear but not understand. Explanation is given only within a closed circle.

It cannot be doubted that it was Mark himself who, by his rewriting of v. 10 and v. 13 and the insertion of vv. 11–12, created the parable theory. The hardening theory is definitely Marcan, although it is true that already before Mark the primitive church had wrestled with the problem of Israel's obduracy (cf. e.g., Rom 9–11). This reflection by the Christian community may very well have influenced the evangelist on this point. On the other hand, Jeremias' whole argumentation from the terms *mēpote* and *mashal-parabolē* loses its basis if it can be demonstrated that vv. 11–12 as such—the saying about the secret of the kingdom and the so-called Isaiah quotation—did not form a fixed literary unit before the redaction of Mark, to say nothing of being authentic sayings of Jesus. The detailed analysis of vocabulary and thematic which we have made in "Redaction and Theology in Mk 4" would seem to indicate that this is the case.

Mark knew that Jesus' parables were not always understood. In his sources he possessed the Sower together with its explanation, the addition of which had already been deemed necessary at the pre–Marcan stage. He himself often stresses the motifs of withdrawal and selection. He was also familiar with the ill will and obduracy of, among others, the Pharisees and the scribes (cf. e.g., 3:6 and 3:22–30). What he knew of the continuing hostility of the Jews must have also spurred him to reflect on the mystery of their hardening. He was probably familiar with the threatening word of Isaiah in its Aramaic paraphrase. Finally, his Christian background had acquainted him with the apocalyptic themes of secrecy and the privilege of a special group. All this, together with the preexisting reflection of the primitive church about the obduracy of the Jews which was often attributed in a predestinarian way to God's activity, seems to us to constitute an adequate explanation of the origin of Mk 4:11–12 at the redactional level. Mark ascribes to Jesus' use of parables the intention of hardening. This theory as such is new. It is not found or attested to in the primitive church, and neither the Jewish traditions of the time nor the Old Testament speak of such a use of parables. That Mark consciously formulated this radical statement is, to a certain extent, confirmed by other related and very redactional passages in his gospel, cf. e.g., 4:33 and 7:14–18. In our next chapter we shall return to Mark's theory on the parables and try to see whether it is maintained throughout his gospel.

The Added Sayings (vv. 21–25)
21 And he said to them, "Is a lamp brought in to be put under a bushel, or under a bed, and not on a stand?
22 For there is nothing hid, except to be made manifest; nor is anything secret, except to come to light.
23 If any man has ears to hear, let him hear."
24 And he said to them, "Take heed what you hear; the measure you give will be the measure you get, and still more will be given to you.
25 For to him who has will more be given; and from him who has not, even what he has will be taken away."

The preceding investigation has shown that there are no positive arguments indicating that the similitudes of the Seed Growing by Itself and the Mustard Seed formed a pre-Marcan literary unit with the parable of the Sower. It therefore seems better to speak of the sayings of vv. 21–25 not as an insertion (understanding by "insertion" here the introduction of further material *within* a preexisting context), but rather as an addition. The material which Mark brings together in these verses also appears in Matthew and Luke but in different positions, outside their respective parable chapters and mostly in a Q-context:

Compare:

Mk		Lk		Mt
4:21	with	11:33	and	5.15
4:22		12:2	=	10:26
4:24c		6:38	=	7:2
4:24d		12:31b	=	6:33b
4:25		19:26	=	25:29

It thus appears that Mark used preexisting material in these verses and that his main redactional work consists in a partial rewriting of that material and in the addition of the two summons to hear in vv. 23 and 24ab. The parallel and concentric structure of this short unit has already been discussed.

Why did Mark place this group of sayings in the middle of his parable chapter? What is the significance of his doing so? Perhaps by means of the following paraphrase we can clarify Mark's line of thought in these verses. The lamp (v. 21) is the Word spoken of in the explanation of the Sower. Did this lamp come to remain hidden? No! Its being hidden, i.e., its being revealed only in a closed circle (v. 11), is only temporary. The ultimate aim is to make it known to all (vv. 21–22). Just as the seed growing by itself and the mustard seed, which irresistibly grew into a rich harvest or a large impressive shrub, so also the Word presses toward its full revelation. (This dynamism is expressed by the four clauses in vv. 21–22 introduced by *hina* = "in order that"). The disciples should understand this well (v. 23). Verses 21–23 are thus complementary to v. 11: the privilege of the closed circle together with the Twelve (vv. 11–12) ultimately gives rise to their task of proclaiming the Word (vv. 21–23).

The way in which the privileged ones listen, i.e., the extent to which they accept the Word, will be the measure by which they themselves will be measured on the day of judgment; they can count on an abundant reward for every effort made (v. 24). For, to him who possesses, more will be given, but from him who does not possess, even what he has will be taken away (v. 25). With the summons to hear (v. 24b) a subtle shift of thought occurs: vv. 21–23 connect with vv. 10–11 and prepare for vv. 26–32; but, vv. 24–25 exhort and speak in a warning tone. This second section thus seems to develop the exhortation found in vv. 14–20.

Conclusion

At this stage we interrupt our investigation of Mark's personal contribution to the composition of 4:1–34, a question to be reconsidered later in this chapter when we deal with the two similitudes. A complete redactional analysis of the chapter would require an investigation of the extent to which Mark has rewritten the remaining traditional material, the parable of the Sower with its explanation, and the Mustard Seed. What has been indicated above may suffice to give an idea of how Mark has collected and selected, structured and rewritten, and has also not hesitated to add whole sentences to his traditional material. We now turn to the explanation of the Sower.

III. The Explanation of the Sower (vv. 14–20)

14 "The sower sows the word.

15 And these are the ones along the path, where the word is sown; when they hear, Satan immediately comes and takes away the word which is sown in them.

16 And these in like manner are the ones sown upon rocky ground, who, when they hear the word, immediately receive it with joy;

17 and they have no root in themselves, but endure for a while; then, when tribulation or persecution arises on account of the word, immediately they fall away.

18 And others are the ones sown among thorns; they are those who hear the word,

19 but the cares of the world, and the delight in riches, and the desire for other things, enter in and choke the word, and it proves unfruitful.

20 But those that were sown upon the good soil are the ones who hear the word and accept and bear fruit, thirtyfold and sixtyfold and a hundredfold."

This passage explains the parable of the Sower in an allegorical way, even though every element is not interpreted (the sower himself, e.g., is not identified). The seed is the Word (v. 14; also vv. 15–20), but the hearers are also the seed which is sown (vv. 16–20). The birds who devour the seed are identified with Satan (v. 15); the rocky ground with oppression and persecution (v. 17); the thorns with earthly cares, the allurement of riches, and covetousness for every sort of thing (v. 19). The falling on fertile soil and bearing abundant fruit refers to people who hear and accept the Word and yield much fruit (v. 20).

The Author

This allegorizing explanation of vv. 14–20 does not go back to Jesus himself. J. Jeremias has shown that not only the language but also the conceptions of this section are typical rather of the early church and the postpaschal period. Indeed, one can point to certain possible shifts of thought from parable to explanation in the line of church interests. The original parable was strongly escha-

tological, developing the contrast between initial failure (represented by the first three types of seed taken together) and final
successful harvest. In the allegory this eschatological character of
the narrative gives way to a descriptive psychology. Attention is
no longer focused on the above-mentioned opposition. Rather, the
four kinds of seed each receive a separate and independent treatment. Instead of proclamation there is now a developed ecclesial
parenesis, an admonition. Through its contrast the parable articu-
lates a clear message, while the allegorical explanation becomes a
kind of warning, an elaborated exhortation to the Christian community.

If it can then be assumed that Jesus did not add this allegory to
his parable of the Sower, neither can it however be attributed to
Mark. It is hardly conceivable that Mark himself would have created this explanation which forms a literary unity with the preceding parable only to disrupt this unity by his insertion of the sayings
about obduracy in vv. 11–12. Furthermore, a number of commentators, in particular J. Jeremias, have shown that the style, vocabulary, and main ideas of this explanation are far more typical of the
early church than of Mark. Nevertheless, Mark has taken over the
text and made it his own. We shall therefore eventually have to
pose the question of how this explanation of the parable functions
within Mark's line of thought in this chapter.

The Intention

What did the anonymous pre–Marcan author intend with this
explanation? To whom did he address it? Was he primarily thinking of preachers, "sowers of the Word," whom he wished to exhort
to persevere and not lose courage, notwithstanding the apparent
fruitlessness of their efforts?

More probably, in his admonition the author had the faithful of
his church in mind. He wanted to remind his own people that it is
not sufficient to hear the Word. They must see that it bears fruit.
Satan should not steal it away; they should not be undone by their
own inconstancy; worldly cares should not "choke" the Word. The
unknown pre–Marcan writer thus exhorts and admonishes, warns
and encourages. He speaks from a concrete church situation. The
style of his allegorical interpretation of the Sower is certainly typical of early Christian pareness.

IV. The Similitudes and the Parable

Three more passages remain to be examined: the parable of the Sower (vv. 3–9) and the two similitudes, the Seed Growing by Itself (vv. 26–29) and the Mustard Seed (vv. 30–32). The two similitudes describe typical, natural phenomena that recur regularly and can easily be observed. With the exception of the aorists "scatter (seed)" in v. 26 and "sow" in vv. 31–32, which both logically express actions which have already taken place, the verbs of vv. 26–28 and v. 32 are in the present tense or its equivalent. At the very beginning the point of comparison is explicitly stated: "The kingdom of God is as if . . ." (v. 26) and, "With what can we compare the kingdom of God, or what comparison shall we use for it? It is like . . ." (vv. 30–31). Both are thus similitudes about the kingdom. The hearers know how the figurative parts are to be interpreted since the introductory formulas give guidelines according to which their applications are to be thought out.

The parable of the Sower is quite different. It is a story narrated in the past tense: "Listen! A sower went out to sow. . . ." This narrative undoubtedly contains some strange and fictive elements, e.g., the fourfold sowing, the various fortunes that befall the seed that is sown. Nevertheless, the story remains plausible since its material is taken from the everyday life and work of a small farmer in the Palestine of Jesus' time. Still, when heard for the first time it must have sounded somewhat strange. What is the Sower up to here?

But the most important question for our purpose is whether or not these similitudes and this parable go back to Jesus, and, if so, what exactly he wished to convey by using them.

The Seed Growing by Itself and the Mustard Seed

From Mt and Lk it can be concluded that the Q-tradition also preserved a twin-similitude, that of the Mustard Seed and the Leaven:

> He said therefore, "What is the kingdom of God like? And to what shall I compare it? It is like a grain of mustard seed which a man took and sowed in his garden; and it grew and became a tree, and the birds of the air made nests in its branches." (Lk 13:18–19; cf. Mt 13:31–32)

And again he said, "To what shall I compare the kingdom of God? It is like leaven which a woman took and hid in three measures of meal, till it was all leavened." (Lk 13:20–21; cf. Mt 13:33)

In Mark's gospel, this twin-similitude has become that of the Seed Growing by Itself and the Mustard Seed:

26 And he said, "The kingdom of God is as if a man should scatter seed upon the ground.
27 and should sleep and rise night and day, and the seed should sprout and grow, he knows not how.
28 The earth produces of itself, first the blade, then the ear, then the full grain in the ear.
29 But when the grain is ripe, at once he puts in the sickle, because the harvest has come."

30 And he said, "With what can we compare the kingdom of God, or what parable shall we use for it?
31 It is like a grain of mustard seed, which, when sown upon the ground, is the smallest of all the seeds on earth;
32 yet when it is sown it grows up and becomes the greatest of all shrubs, so that the birds of the air can make nests in its shade."

The similitude of the Seed Growing by Itself is only in Mark's gospel. One might wonder where the evangelist found it and why he replaced the traditional twin-similitude by a new one. His intention was certainly to present his own "twins." As already noted, Mark made the two similitudes conform to one another in form and vocabulary. In "Redaction and Theology in Mk 4" (see bibliography), we have made a detailed analysis of Mark's rewriting and redactional composition of this text. In view of the sustained parallel construction carried through both similitudes and in view of the fact that the first one is proper to Mark while the other was combined with the similitude of the Leaven in the pre–Marcan tradition, some uncertainty prevails—rightly in our opinion—as to the origin of the Seed Growing by Itself. Does this similitude really go back to Jesus? Or must it be ascribed either to Mark or to an anonymous church author? All things considered, the arguments in favor of a Marcan origin do not seem sufficiently convincing, and the hypothesis of a pre–Marcan postpaschal origin is also rather gratuitous. As for the Mustard Seed, there is no reason at all to doubt that this ancient traditional similitude goes back to Jesus himself.

With similitudes like the Mustard Seed and the Leaven, Jesus revealed the nature of the kingdom of God, God's imminent kingly rule. The idea of a process of growth is not altogether absent here, but the focus is much more on the contrast between small beginnings and a great fulfillment. Jesus used this type of similitude to express his firm conviction that, notwithstanding the small inconspicuous beginnings of God's dominion, a great unexpected result is assured. It is God's work. The seed is already sown; Jesus' public appearance inaugurates the coming kingdom. This message encouraged the disciples and exhorted them to persevere in joy since they knew that they were involved in the realization of God's plan.

In the context of Mark's gospel the point of the Seed Growing by Itself is not quite the same as that of the Mustard Seed. Both emphasize the final outcome, the assurance of a rich harvest and the large shrub with many branches that give abundant shade. But the figurative part of the Seed Growing by Itself further states that the sower remains inactive during the growth process and that the seed brings forth fruit by itself. In this way special emphasis is placed on the fact that the coming of the kingdom is effected by God, in a miraculous way, without any visible cause. The Mustard Seed, on the other hand, focuses more exclusively on the contrast between large and small, i.e., the plant's unexpected growth. Nevertheless, it is above all the similarity of theme between the two similitudes which is most striking. Both are seed similitudes and both witness to the certain coming of the kingdom and its far-reaching extension. The secret of the kingdom stands at the center of Mk 4, i.e., in v. 11. Prior to the twin-similitude, this secret is compared to a seed that is sown, to a word, and to a lamp. Thereafter, the Seed Growing by Itself and the Mustard Seed both give assurance that the glorious, final stage of the kingdom will come. The former similitude shows that after the sowing the farmer remains inactive until the harvest and emphasizes that the seed which has been sown bears fruit by itself. The latter strongly develops the contrast between a small beginning and an abundant result; it stresses both the smallness of the seed and the huge size of the full-grown shrub.

The Sower

3 "Listen! A sower went out to sow.

4 And as he sowed, some seed fell along the path, and the birds came and devoured it.

5 Other seed fell on rocky ground, where it had not much soil, and immediately it sprang up, since it had no depth of soil;

6 and when the sun rose it was scorched, and since it had no root it withered away.

7 Other seed fell among the thorns and the thorns grew up and choked it, and it yielded no grain.

8 And other seed fell into good soil and brought forth grain, growing up and increasing and yielding thirtyfold and sixtyfold and a hundredfold."

9 And he said, "He who has ears to hear, let him hear!"

The summons to hear in v. 3a and the whole of v. 9 apparently derive from Mark. But the parable of the Sower (vv. 3b–8) lies on the firm ground of the Jesus tradition. Here too there is no reason to doubt the authenticity of the text.

We know the speaker Jesus, at least to a certain extent. But we are ignorant both of the identity of the hearers and the concrete circumstances in which the Sower was told. This makes it difficult to discover its original meaning. Still, there is nothing extraordinary about comparing the work of a sower with all types of human labor and exertion. Nor is there anything exceptional about contrasting the wearisome and tedious activity of sowing with the joy of reaping an abundant harvest (cf. e.g., Ps 126:5–6). To determine the original meaning of the parable, what is known about the general pattern, content, and purpose of Jesus' way of life must be kept in mind. Although the exact time and place of each event cannot be pinpointed, there is some incontrovertible data: Jesus' speaking about the coming of God's kingdom, his authority, his signs and wonders, his resolute advocacy of God's will, and his determined search for people who were on the verge of being lost.

An investigation of the meaning of the Sower should not be determined by the later allegorical explanation given to it by the early church and now found in vv. 14–20. Nor should we be misled by what is said in v. 11: "To you has been given the secret of the kingdom of God." This latter statement might lead us to suppose that from the very beginning the Sower had to do with the kingdom, and therefore to conclude that the Sower is one of the parables about the kingdom of God. But v. 11, as we have shown, with its notion of obduracy, is a redactional product and an insertion by the evangelist. Still, it might be objected that the parable does appear alongside two similitudes of the kingdom. But this situating of the parable is to be ascribed to Mark himself. The conclusion of our literary analysis was that a pre–Marcan parable collection behind Mk 4 cannot be accepted. It was Mark who combined the parable and similitudes in view of their common theme—sower, sowing, seed. Since the introductory formulas of vv. 26 and 30, which he found in the similitudes, refer to the kingdom of God, Mark spontaneously also connected the parable of the Sower with the kingdom of God. By so doing he could easily proceed to the addition of v. 11 which speaks about the secret of the kingdom. However, taking the Sower as originally narrated by Jesus, there is nothing to indicate that it was already a parable about the kingdom of God.

It has become fashionable of late to assert that Jesus had little or nothing to say about himself and only spoke of God and his kingdom. In this connection reference can be made to the discussion concerning the use of Christological titles by Jesus and the negative conclusions of that discussion. Jesus did not explicitly call himself Son of God, Lord, the Christ, perhaps not even Son of man. Nevertheless, it is necessary to postulate some kind of implicit or indirect, existential, and nonthematic Christology on the part of Jesus, a Christology which comes to expression in his whole way of life. Otherwise, it is said, one could not explain his unique claims and authority.

But is this sufficient? Some scholars, such as H. Frankemölle, do not think so. In the case of the Sower, in any event, it is very probable that Jesus did speak about himself and his work using metaphorical terms. With the figure of the sower he refers to himself, with the sowing to his own eschatological preaching. At first the hearers must have been disconcerted, asking themselves why this story was told. But after their initial surprise and incomprehension, they understood and at last realized that this parable placed them once again with a choice; they saw themselves compelled to make an existential decision, i.e., for or against the person of Jesus.

Jesus thus speaks about himself and his messianic work in the Sower. The contrast motif stands in the foreground here just as in the similitudes of the kingdom. Notwithstanding many failures and apparently hopeless situations, Jesus gives assurance of an ultimate abundant harvest. He expresses his firm confidence that in spite of opposition and setbacks, he will succeed in his eschatological mission as God's envoy. The Sower is therefore a parable of contrast and of confidence. Jesus speaks about himself with what perhaps seems to be a strange image—a sower. But whoever listens closely enough cannot fail to grasp the message and the challenge it contains. Just as he did elsewhere with other images (e.g., the son of the owner of the vineyard, cf. Mk 12:6–8; the bridegroom, cf. Mk 2.19–20; the stronger man, cf. Mk 3:27; and perhaps also the Son of man), here also, Jesus identifies himself. In this way he justifies his claims and his authority, he defends his work: He is the expectant and hopeful sower.

Conclusion

In the two similitudes of the Seed Growing by Itself and the Mustard Seed, Jesus spoke about the kingdom of God in an objective and didactic way. In the parable of the Sower he speaks in a much more personal way about himself and his work. Although their specific points and literary forms (parable or similitude) do thus differ, these three pericopes are nonetheless closely related. Jesus is no less than God's ultimate, definitive messenger because in him God's imminent rule is already inaugurated: "If it is by the Spirit of God that I cast out demons, then the kingdom of God has come upon you!" (Mt 12:28).

V. The Secret of the Kingdom of God

Now that we have tried to explain Jesus' intention, i.e., what he wanted to achieve by speaking in the similitudes and parable of chap. 4, we might consider our task accomplished. Nevertheless,

we wish to take one more look at Mk 4:1–34 in its present form
and to ask what Mark as the final redactor had in mind with this
parable section. Our starting point is 4:11: "To you has been given
the secret of the kingdom of God." Those who receive this secret
are the ones belonging to his inner circle together with the Twelve
(cf. v. 10). What is the content of this secret? This question, it
should be realized, no longer concerns what Jesus himself intended at the prepaschal level, but what Mark the evangelist
understood as the content of the secret.

The Current Interpretation

Most exegetes relate this secret of the kingdom (and thus also
Mark's obduracy theory) to what the famous German exegete,
W. Wrede, at the turn of the century called the "messianic secret." Mk 8:27–30 states that Jesus does not want his identity (cf.
the title "Christ") to be made known outside the circle of the
Twelve. In strong terms he forbids the unclean spirits who know
who he is (cf. the title "Son of God") to declare this in public (3:11–
12; 1:24–25: "the Holy One of God"). If the "secret of the kingdom
of God" spoken of in 4:11 is to be understood in terms of the above
passages concerning the messianic secret, then it refers to Jesus'
real identity and must be interpreted in relation to the hidden
presence of God's kingly rule in Jesus' person and way of life.

Is this however precisely the insight which according to Mark
was communicated to the inner circle around Jesus together with
the Twelve? Is knowledge of who Jesus is the content of the secret?

Objections

Not long ago, S. Brown compiled a number of objections which
militate against the idea that Mark's motif of secrecy in 4:11 is used
later in the gospel in an identical sense: (a) The messianic secret
(8:27–30; cf. also 3:11–12, and 1:24–25) primarily concerns Jesus'
person, whereas Mk 4:11 explicitly states that the secret has to do
with the kingdom of God. (b) Furthermore, it is evident from
4:35–41; 6:45–52; and 8:17–21 that the disciples still do not understand even after the secret is said to be revealed to them (4:11).
In these texts their ignorance precisely concerns the identity of
Jesus. In fact it is not until 8:29 that Peter, in the name of the

Twelve, confesses that Jesus is the Christ. The cure of the blind man (narrated in 8:22–26) symbolizes the gradual, difficult opening of their eyes. On the other hand, Mk 4:11 very clearly states that the "secret has been given" to the disciples. On the assumption that 4:11 thematically corresponds to the passages mentioned above, the explicit affirmation of this verse makes the disciples' later lack of understanding inexplicable. No, the secret *is* already given. Or, consider 4:13: "Do you not understand this parable? How then will you understand all the (other) parables?" This suggests it will be given immediately, i.e., in the appended explanation of the parable (vv. 14–20). (c) Mk 4:14–20 gives the interpretation of the Sower. According to the evangelist, the meaning of this parable was not immediately evident to all its hearers since those who were about Jesus together with the Twelve ask for an explanation. Must we, then, not consider the explanation of the parable in vv. 14–20 precisely as that "giving of the secret" of which v. 11 in the immediately preceding context speaks?

Secret Teaching

It is probable then that Mark did not conceive of v. 11 as referring to restricted knowledge about Jesus' identity which is freely imparted only to a select group. What he affirms is rather that only a privileged group received a special explanation and that this explanation concerns the kingdom of God. The explanation announced in v. 11 follows in vv. 14–20: The seed is the Word of the gospel. Undoubtedly Mark refers here to the historical situation of Jesus' public ministry, but—through this situation—he also has his own contemporaries in mind. The disciples are the future preachers of the gospel. From the explanation of the parable (vv. 14–20), they know that Jesus had to face many difficulties during his public life. They too should be prepared to meet the same fate in their own apostolic activity. Nevertheless, they are assured of ultimate success. Mark does not, of course, differentiate between parable, similitude, and allegory. For him the Sower is a parable of the kingdom just as are the similitudes of the Seed Growing by Itself and the Mustard Seed. The whole section, 4:1–34, contains secret instructions about the kingdom. With this parable chapter, which informs and exhorts, Mark addresses himself to the preachers of his time.

In other places in the gospel, the Jesus of Mark also gives secret instructions reserved for the disciples. In 7:17–22 he explains to them, privately and inside the house, the real cause of uncleanness. In 9:28–29, again indoors and within the closed circle of disciples, he speaks about the necessity of prayer. Similarly in 10:10–12, when they are indoors by themselves, Jesus answers the disciples' questions about divorce. And in 13:3–37 Peter, together with James, John, and Andrew, hears what the future and the endtime will bring: "And what I say to you I say to all (the Twelve and future Christians): Watch" (13:37). Obviously then Mk 4 is not an isolated case. This literary motif of secret teaching is typical of Mark's entire gospel.

It is possible that for Mark the messianic secret was, among other things, a means to suggest the discontinuity between the periods before and after Easter. It may witness to the fact that the clarity, the transparency of the Christological confessions and titles did not exist prior to Easter. Might not then the same Mark, by means of the literary fiction of secret instruction, have wished to express his awareness that these clear instructions, attuned as they were to the postpaschal church situation, were not all words actually spoken by Jesus himself?

Whether or not we accept this last supposition, it would seem better to distinguish between the messianic secret and the secret of the kingdom of God. The former has a kerygmatic, Christological content and refers to the person of Jesus. The latter has to do with church instructions, communicated as didactic explanation in the form of a secret teaching. The reader will not fail to notice that this distinction between the messianic secret and the secret of the kingdom of God at the level of Marcan redaction is reminiscent of our findings concerning Jesus' speaking in parables and similitudes. There too Jesus speaks of himself (the Sower; cf. the messianic secret) and of the kingdom of God (the Seed Growing by Itself and the Mustard Seed; cf. the secret of the kingdom of God). But, after all, can Jesus' person and God's work in him be altogether separated from one another?

BIBLIOGRAPHY

Brown, S., " 'The Secret of the Kingdom of God' (Mark 4:11)," *JBL* 92 (1973) 60–74.

Bultmann, R., "Die Interpretation von Mk 4,3–9 seit Jülicher," in *Jesus und Paulus. Festschrift für W. G. Kümmel*, ed. E. E. Ellis and E. Grässer, Göttingen, 1975, pp. 30–34.

Casalegno, A., "La parabola del granello di senape (Mc. 4,30–32)," *Rivista biblica* 26 (1978) 139–61.

Crossan, J. D., "The Seed Parables of Jesus," *JBL* 92 (1973) 244–66.

Dietzfelbinger, C., "Das Gleichnis vom ausgestreuten Samen," in *Der Ruf Jesu und die Antwort der Gemeinde. Exegetische Untersuchungen J. Jeremias zum 70. Geburtstag gewidmet*, ed. E. Lohse, Göttingen, 1970, pp. 80–93.

Dupont, J., "La parabole du Semeur," *Foi et Vie* 66:5 (1967) (=Cahiers bibliques 5) 3–25.

———, "La parabole de la semence qui pousse toute seule (Marc 4,26–29)," *RScR* 55 (1967) 367–92.

———, "Le chapitre des paraboles," *NRT* 79 (1967) 800–820.

———, "Les paraboles du sénevé et du levain," *NRT* 79 (1967) 897–913.

———, "Le couple parabolique du sénevé et du levain. Mt 13,31–33; Lc 13,18–21," in *Jesus Christus in Historie und Theologie. Neutestamentliche Festschrift für H. Conzelmann*, ed. G. Strecker, Tübingen, 1975, pp. 331–45.

Frankemölle, H., "Hat Jesus sich selbst verkündet? Christologische Implikationen in den vormarkinischen Parabeln," *BibLeb* 13 (1972) 184–207.

Funk, R. W., "The Looking-Glass Tree Is for the Birds: Ezekiel 17:22–24; Mark 4:30–32," *Interpr* 27 (1973) 3–9.

Geischer, H. J., "Verschwenderische Güte. Versuch über Markus 4,3–9," *EvT* 38 (1978) 418–27.

Gnilka, J., *Die Verstockung Israels. Isaias 6,9–10 in der Theologie der Synoptiker*, StANT 3, Munich, 1961.

Hahn, F., "Das Gleichnis von der ausgestreuten Saat und seine Deutung (Mk iv.3–8,14–20)," in *Text and Interpretation. Studies in the New Testament presented to M. Black*, ed. E. Best and R. McL. Wilson, Cambridge, 1979, pp. 133–42.

Hubaut, M., "Le 'mystère' révélé dans les paraboles (Mc 4,11–12)," *RTL* 5 (1974) 454–61.

Jeremias, J., "Palästinakundliches zum Gleichnis vom Sämann," *NTS* 13 (1966–1967) 48–53.

Kümmel, W. G., "Noch einmal: Das Gleichnis von der selbstwachsenden Saat: Bemerkungen zur neuesten Diskussion um die Auslegung der Gleichnisse Jesu," in *Orientierung an Jesus. Zur Theologie der Synoptiker. Für J. Schmid*, ed. P. Hoffmann, Freiburg, 1973, pp. 220–37.

Kuhn, H.-W., *Ältere Sammlungen im Markusevangelium*, Studien zur Umwelt des Neuen Testaments 8, Göttingen, 1971 (see especially pp. 99–146).

Kuss, O., "Zum Sinngehalt des Doppelgleichnisses vom Senfkorn und Sauerteig," *Bib* 40 (1959) 641–53.

Lambrecht, J., "De vijf parabels van Mc. 4. Structuur en theologie van de parabelrede," *Bijdragen* 29 (1968) 25–53; also in Lambrecht, *Marcus interpretator. Stijl en boodschap in Mc. 3,20–4,34*, Bruges–Utrecht, 1969, pp. 99–128, 133–34.

——, "Redaction and Theology in Mk., IV," in *L'Evangile selon Marc. Tradition et rédaction*, BETL 34, ed. M. Sabbe, Louvain–Gembloux, 1974, pp. 269–307.

——, "Parabels in Mc. 4," *TT* 15 (1975) 26–43.

Lampe, P., "Die markinische Deutung des Gleichnisses vom Sämann: Markus 4,10–12," *ZNW* 65 (1974) 140–50.

Laufen, R., "*Basileia* und *Ekklēsia*. Eine traditions- und redaktionsgeschichtliche Untersuchung des Gleichnisses vom Senfkorn," in *Begegnung mit dem Wort. Festschrift für Heinrich Zimmermann*, Bonner Biblische Beiträge 53, ed. J. Zmijewski and E. Nellessen, Bonn, 1980, pp. 105–40.

Lemcio, E. E., "External Evidence for the Structure and Function of Mark iv 1–20, vii 14–23 and viii 14–21," *JTS* 29 (1978) 323–38.

Léon–Dufour, X., "La parabole du Semeur," in Léon–Dufour, *Etudes d'Evangile*, Paris, 1965, pp. 255–301.

McArthur, H. K., "The Parable of the Mustard Seed," *CBQ* 33 (1971) 198–210.

Minette de Tillesse, G., *Le secret messianique dans l'Evangile de Marc*, Lectio Divina 47, Paris, 1968 (see especially pp. 165–221).

Payne, P. B., "The Order of Sowing and Ploughing in the Parable of the Sower," *NTS* 25 (1978–79) 123–29.

Räisänen, H., *Die Parabeltheorie im Markusevangelium*, Schriften der Finnischen Exegetischen Gesellschaft 26, Helsinki, 1973.

Schelkle, K. H., "Der Zweck der Gleichnisreden (Mk 4,10–12)," in *Neues Testament und Kirche. Für R. Schnackenburg*, ed. J. Gnilka, Freiburg 1974, pp. 71–75.

Stuhlmann, R., "Beobachtungen und Überlegungen zu Markus IV.26–29," *NTS* 19 (1972–1973) 153–62.

Trocmé, E., "Why Parables? A Study of Mark IV," *BJRL* 59 (1977) 458–71.

Wilder, A. N., "The Parable of the Sower: Naiveté and Method in Interpretation," *Semeia* (1974) no. 2, pp. 134–51.

Wilson, R. R., "The Hardening of Pharaoh's Heart," *CBQ* 41 (1979) 18–36.

Five

Parables Elsewhere
in Mark's Gospel

The intention of hardening, as expressed in Mk 4:11–12, seems so unnatural that every reader must spontaneously think that this could not really have been Jesus' intention in using the parables. On the other hand, it cannot simply be assumed without further proof that Mark created the theory. Did he really believe that Jesus spoke in parables in order to keep outsiders in ignorance and to prevent their conversion? Can he have maintained this position in a consistent way? Such questions are not easily answered. The statements of Mk 4 regarding the use of the parables are, as we have seen, somewhat obscure and difficult to interpret. Perhaps something further concerning Mark's conception about Jesus' speaking in parables can be learned from the remainder of the gospel. We shall, therefore, in this chapter examine the parable material outside 4:1–34. Our first concern here is with Mark's conception, not that of Jesus, the tradition, or the other evangelists.

In the survey at the conclusion of our first chapter (pp. 18–20), we listed six Marcan parables: the Sower (4:3–9), the Seed Growing by Itself (4:26–29); the Mustard Seed (4:30–32); the Wicked Tenants (12:1–11), the Budding Fig Tree (13:28–29), and the Doorkeeper (13:34–36). This limited number of six parables is due to our decision to include only passages of a certain length and with at least the beginning of a narrative. Mark himself, however, certainly had a much broader concept of what constitutes a parable.

The following survey of Marcan passages which are related at least in some way to the parable material represents a supplement to our previous list. Within these passages symbolic acts, similes, and metaphors are distinguished. Among the symbolic acts in Mark are the baptism performed by John (1:5), shaking the dust from one's feet (6:11, a command), the appointment of the Twelve (3:13–19), the cursing of the fig tree (11:12–14, 20–21), the cleansing of the temple (11:15–19), and the Last Supper (14:22–25).

Mark's gospel also contains a number of similes. Jesus sees the Spirit descend upon him "like a dove" (1:10). He teaches in the synagogue of Capernaum "as one who has authority and not like the scribes" (1:22). At the multiplication of the loaves he has compassion on the multitude, because they were "like sheep without a shepherd" (6:34). The blind man who had been cured by Jesus initially only sees people who "look like trees walking" (8:24). When the spirit left the boy who was possessed, he appeared "like a corpse" (9:26). "Whoever does not receive the kingdom of God like a child shall not enter it" (10:15). When people "rise from the dead, they neither marry nor are given in marriage, but are like angels in heaven" (12:25). The second commandment is this, "You shall love your neighbor as yourself" (12:31). And Jesus said to those who came to arrest him, "You have come out as against a robber . . ." (14:48).

Metaphors are even more numerous than similes in Mk: John's task is to prepare the way of the Lord and make straight his paths (1:2–3). The first disciples called will become fishers of men (1:17). Jesus is the bridegroom (2:19–20). The messianic age is new cloth and new wine (2:21–22). Revelation is a lamp (4:21), the manner in which it is handed on is the measure one gives (4:24). The Jews are children; the Gentiles are dogs (7:27–28). What the Pharisees and Herod do is leaven (8:15). Jesus' Passion, in which James and John are called to share, is a cup or baptism (10:38). The temple has become a den of robbers (11:17). Jesus is the cornerstone which the builders rejected (12:10). In the garden of Olives, Jesus prays, "Abba, Father, . . . remove this cup (i.e., the Passion) from me" (14:36).

Mark uses the term *parabolē* as such only thirteen times. Although it is not likely that he would have applied the term to all of the above-mentioned symbolic acts, similes, and metaphors, he could certainly have employed it for a number of them. Therefore, we should pay close attention to the passages where he actually does use the term *parabolē* as having a wider significance for the understanding of Mark's conception of Jesus' speaking in parables. In 3:23; 4:2, 11, and 12:1 we find the expression "in parables," i.e., "with the help of, by way of parables, in parable language." Apparently this phrase had become somewhat stereotyped since, despite the plural in 12:1a, only a single parable follows in 12:1b–11.

Mark himself characterizes the following passages as parables: the similitudes and parable of Mk 4 (cf. vv. 2, 10, 13, 30, 33, 34); the Wicked Tenants (cf. 12:1, 12); the Budding Fig Tree (cf. 13:28); but also the short comparisons with a kingdom and a house (3:23–25); what is said in 3:27 about plundering the house of the strong man (cf. 3:23); and finally, the proverb in 7:15: "There is nothing outside a man which by going into him can defile him; but the things which come out of a man are what defile him" (cf. 7:17).

In 3:23–27 Jesus narrates his parable—or parables—before the antagonistic scribes from Jerusalem; in 12:1–11, before the hostile chief priests, scribes, and elders (cf. 11, 27); in 13:28–29, before the disciples. All these different groups of hearers seem to grasp the meaning of his parables. In chaps. 4 and 7, where the parables are intended for the people, only the disciples receive an explanation.

How does all this data relate to Mark's conception about Jesus' use of parables? Our investigation of this point is restricted to the passages in connection with which the evangelist himself uses the term "parable." This chapter will consist of five parts: the parables of chaps. 3 (I), 7 (II), 12 (III), and 13 (IV) are successively examined; in a fifth section some general conclusions concerning Mark's vision of the parables are drawn (V).

I. Discussion about Beelzebul (Mk 3:22–30)

22 And the scribes who came down from Jerusalem said, "He is possessed by Beelzebul, and by the prince of demons he casts out the demons."

23 And he called them to him, and said to them in parables, "How can Satan cast out Satan?

24 If a kingdom is divided against itself, that kingdom cannot stand.

25 And if a house is divided against itself, that house will not be able to stand.
26 And if Satan has risen up against himself and is divided, he cannot stand, but is coming to an end.
27 But no one can enter a strong man's house and plunder his goods, unless he first binds the strong man; then indeed he may plunder his house.
28 Truly, I say to you, all sins will be forgiven the sons of men, and whatever blasphemies they utter;
29 but whoever blasphemes against the Holy Spirit never has forgiveness, but is guilty of an eternal sin"—
30 for they had said, "He has an unclean spirit."

The comparison with a kingdom and a house (family) (vv. 24–25) and the statement about plundering the strong man's house (v. 27) stand within the discussion concerning Beelzebul which Jesus holds with the scribes who had come from Jerusalem (3:23b–29). This discussion in turn cannot be separated from the situation which leads up to it (cf. 3:22 and 30), and the whole of 3:22–30 has been framed by Mark with the pericope of the true relatives of Jesus (3:20–21 and 31–35).

True Kinship and Eternal Sin
After the appointment of the Twelve (3:13–19), a new narrative begins. Jesus enters a house and the crowd once more gathers around him in such great numbers that Jesus and his disciples do not even find time to eat (cf. 3:20). When his family heard this they set out to seize him, for they said, "He is beside himself" (v. 21). Subsequently the scribes also express their opinion concerning Jesus. They make a grave accusation: "He is possessed by Beelzebul" (3:22; cf. also 3:30). Then follows Jesus' self-defence (vv. 23b–29). In 3:31 the relatives appear once again: his mother and his brothers, i.e., obviously those who had set out in v. 21. They remain outside but send someone to call Jesus who is seated in the house with the crowd around him. Jesus answers the message sent in to him with the words, "Who are my mother and my brothers?" Thereupon he looks at the people sitting around him and says, "Here are my mother and my brothers! Whoever does the will of God is my brother and sister and mother!" (cf. 3:31–35).
The same scene is found in 3:20–21 and 3:31–35. Jesus is in the

house surrounded by a crowd. It is said in v. 21 that his "relatives" (literally "those from him," but in the *Koine* Greek this expression refers to persons intimately linked to someone, e.g., his friends, his family) set out, and they are said to arrive in v. 31. In the latter verse they are also explicitly identified as his mother and his brothers. In 3:21 they set out "to seize him." From this we can infer why they call him in v. 31. The statement of the scribes (v. 22) is clearly placed in parallel to what the relatives are said to be thinking in v. 21, and this statement is the occasion for the lengthy insertion within the pericope about the relatives.

The whole pericope 3:20–35 is constructed according to a pattern in which the parts correspond to one another in a concentric way, like circles around a central core:

A Jesus' busy activity and the setting out of the relatives
        (vv. 20–21)
B Accusation by the scribes (v. 22)
C Jesus' self-defense (vv. 23–29)
   a refutation (vv. 23b–26)
   b need of exorcism (plundering, v. 27)
   a' judgment logion (vv. 28–29)
B' Repetition of the scribes' accusation (v. 30)
A' Arrival of the relatives; true kinship (vv. 31–35).

In A the relatives themselves take the initiative (they set out); in A' this becomes a reaction by Jesus (his statement about true kinship). With this saying he dissociates himself from a kinship understood in a purely natural way. This does not necessarily imply an actual hostility, but there is a certain separation and distance. A' is a response by Jesus and also as such it forms a counterpart to A which concerns the attitude of the relatives. They claimed, but obviously without much understanding of the meaning of his activity, that he "was beside himself." A and A' thus correspond, and most probably did in the conception and intention of the redactor, in content and composition and to a certain extent also as regards vocabulary. With them Mark created a framework, a narrative which functions as an inclusion.

Obviously the accusation repeated in B' is materially the same as that in v. 22, i.e., B—an indication that Mark has purposely constructed this schema. Not only is the content identical, but the speakers are also the same. And, in both cases the verbs "say" and "have" are used. On the other hand, v. 30 is shorter and instead of "Beelzebul" or "prince of the demons" Mark simply speaks of an "unclean spirit."

Jesus' self-defense, the central section *C*, is thus embedded within two inclusive circles *A, A'* (appearance of the relatives) and *B, B'* (accusation of the scribes). *B* and *B'* obviously provide the occasion for the discourse (*C*). Within Jesus' self-defense itself there seems to also be a concentric pattern *a b a'*. *b* (v. 27) is shorter and comprises only a single sentence, whereas *a* (vv. 23b–26) and *a'* (vv. 28–29) are longer. However, we cannot conclude to the inclusive character of *a* and *a'* from the identity of content between them, for the judgment logion (vv. 28–29) cannot be called a parallel in content to the refutation (vv. 23b–26). Our reason for, nevertheless, describing this central section as *a b a'* rather than *a b c* is the remarkable structural similarity between *a* and *a'*, a similarity which cannot be a mere coincidence. Both passages are approximately the same length and both manifest a similar (though not fully identical) *1 2 2' 1'* pattern:

vv. 23b–26:
1   How can Satan cast out Satan?
2   If a kingdom is divided against itself,
    that kingdom cannot stand.
2' And if a house is divided against itself,
    that house will not be able to stand.
1' And if Satan has risen up against himself and is divided,
    he cannot stand,
    but is coming to an end.

vv. 28–29:
1   Truly, I say to you,
    all sins will be forgiven the sons of men,
2   and whatever blasphemies they utter;
2' but whoever blasphemes against the Holy Spirit
1' never has forgiveness,
    but is guilty of an eternal sin.

A factor which complicates the study of any concentric structure is the content of the discourse or narrative in which it is employed. The material of the discourse or narrative does not completely lend itself to the static schema of a central core surrounded by inclusive elements. There is a progression, a development in the line of thought or in the recounting of an event. As long as the inclusion remains completely extrinsic, e.g., restricted to a short call for attention as is the case in Mk 4 ("listen" and "he who has ears to hear, let him hear," vv. 3, 9), there is no problem. The "included" core receives full attention and is not affected by the inclusion. But when the concentric sections are complex and moreover serve to structure the discourse or the narrative itself, one has to keep in mind the basic law of a cyclic pattern: the central core is the most important element and deserves more attention, a fact to which the structure itself bears witness. In the case of a discourse or a narrative which is constructed in a concentric way, the static, restful character of the structural pattern and the dynamic particularity of the discourse or narrative necessarily go together, and many times tension arises between emphasis on the central core and movement towards the final climax. When applied to Mk 3:20–35, these considerations can explain a great deal.

(1) There is a definite progression from A to A', from action to reaction. The initiative of the relatives in A and at the beginning of A' is seen by Jesus as a kind of challenge. With his question and answer he makes a countermove which, with its demonstrative "see" (v. 34), gives the real point of the saying about true kinship and constitutes the climax of the narrative. It is not by accident that Mark twice notes that Jesus' relatives stood *outside* (vv. 31 and 32) and likewise twice mentions that his "new" relatives are sitting *around him* in the house (vv. 32 and 34). The distinction between the two groups of people is more than a matter of mere local separation. In Mark's conception the separation is theologically qualified by Jesus' word (vv. 34b–35).

(2) The accusation of the scribes introduces the discourse and frames the central passage. Practically no progression can be observed from B to B'. Verse 30 simply reiterates the charge of v. 22. Nevertheless, it must be said that the intervening refutation parables and above all the judgment saying in C make it possible

for Mark to call the "Beelzebul" of v. 22 an "unclean spirit" (cf. v. 29: the Holy Spirit) in v. 30.

(3) The center of the pericope is *C*. According to the logic of the cyclic structure, it is here that the main point, the basic idea, or the chief event should be found. And, to a certain extent, this is the case here. The fact that Jesus speaks, the importance of what he says, the length of the discourse, and the conciseness of the argument confirm this. In this central section in turn, *b* (v. 27) constitutes the core. After the rather abstract and logical refutation in vv. 23b–26, this verse illustrates what exorcism means, i.e., to bind the strong man, and what is thereby intended, i.e., plundering and regaining possession of the man. Although it is in elusive parable language, we nevertheless learn something concerning the necessity of exorcism and of a kind of mysterious struggle between a strong man and a stronger one. But this central verse, around which everything is concentrically structured in a cyclic and static way, itself functions as a part of a discourse which progresses towards a climax. There are noteworthy differences between *a* (vv. 23b–26) and *a'* (vv. 28–29): *a* is an indignant, but not very aggressive, outburst (cf. the "how?" in v. 23b), *a'* contains threatening and condemning language; *a* uses comparisons, *a'* is purely an utterance; *a* is addressed to the scribes in order to refute them, *a'* is introduced by "Truly I say to you!" and must have been understood by the hearers as a definitive word, directly relating to their own persons and deeds. The solemnity of this introductory formula elevates *a'* to a climax which is both the conclusion and the culmination of the discourse.

(4) *A A'* is not merely a framework vis à vis *B C B'*. Just as the relatives' point of view is censured and corrected by Jesus' statement in *A A'* so in *B C B'* the accusation of the scribes is refuted; the scribes are told what happens in an exorcism and are made aware of the sinfulness of their insinuations against Jesus. But all this is rather negative and defensive. Actually, the entire controversy begins and ends with Jesus' more positive words and deeds. He is busy with his disciples and the people. He recruits followers and summons them to fulfill God's will. He lets the people sit around him and by his preaching creates a relationship which must be called a new community, a new family. While *C* ends with an

allusion to the negative and sinful self-exclusion of the scribes, A' opens the perspective of a discipleship which is devoted, pleasing to God, and obedient. Over against the blaspheming of the Holy Spirit stands the doing of God's will.

The Q-Version

There is another and longer version of the Beelzebul discussion in Lk 11:14–26:

14 Now he [Jesus] was casting out a demon that was dumb; when the demon had gone out, the dumb man spoke, and the people marvelled.

15 But some of them said, "He casts out demons by Beelzebul, the prince of demons";

16 while others, to test him, sought from him a sign from heaven.

17 But he, knowing their thoughts, said to them, "Every kingdom divided against itself is laid waste, and house falls upon house.

18 And if Satan also is divided against himself, how will his kingdom stand? For you say that I cast out demons by Beelzebul.

19 And if I cast out demons by Beelzebul, by whom do your sons cast them out? Therefore they shall be your judges.

20 But if it is by the finger of God that I cast out demons, then the kingdom of God has come upon you.

21 When a strong man, fully armed, guards his own palace, his goods are in peace;

22 but when one stronger than he assails him and overcomes him, he takes away his armor in which he trusted, and divides his spoil.

23 He who is not with me is against me, and he who does not gather with me scatters.

24 When the unclean spirit has gone out of a man, he passes through waterless places seeking rest; and finding none he says, 'I will return to my house from which I came.'

25 And when he comes he finds it swept and put in order.

26 Then he goes and brings seven other spirits more evil than himself, and they enter and dwell there; and the last state of that man becomes worse than the first."

Luke omits the Beelzebul controversy before his parable discourse in 8:4–18 (cf. the position of Mk 3:20–30 with respect to the parable chapter of Mk 4), although he does include the passage which is joined to that controversy in Mk, i.e., the appearance of the relatives, in its Marcan place (8:19–21 = Mk 3:31–35). The Beelzebul controversy itself comes later in Lk, at the beginning of his travel narrative (11:14–26). It is preceded by a series of sayings and pericopes about prayer (11:1–13). With 11:14 a new section, the Beelzebul controversy, clearly begins, introduced by the specific incident of the exorcism (11:14). This is followed by the account of the woman praising Jesus and his reaction (11:27–28). Then comes Jesus' answer to the demand for a sign which was made in 11:16 (11:29–32).

Matthew's version (Mt 12:22–45) agrees for the most part with Luke's, often against Mk 3:22–30. The following elements found in Mt and Lk are absent in Mark:

Mt		Lk	
12:22	=	11:14ab	concrete case of exorcism
12:23a	=	11:14c	astonishment of the crowds
12:27	=	11:19	"If I cast out demons by Beelzebul . . ."
12:28	=	11:20	"but if by the spirit (finger) of God . . ."
12:30	=	11:23	"He who is not with me . . ."
12:43–45	=	11:24–26	return of the unclean spirit

Moreover, the Marcan parallels to Mt 12:38 = Lk 11:16 and Mt 12:39–42 – Lk 11:29–32 stand in another context (cf. Mk 8:11–12).

The Q-tradition obviously had its own version of the Beelzebul controversy. In line with his usual procedure, Matthew conflated this Q-version with that of Mark. Luke places the controversy in his travel narrative. It is not to be excluded that Luke in some way used Mk 3:20–30 in his text 11:14–26. Moreover, he has probably rewritten the Q-text to a certain extent. But all in all, it does seem reasonable to suppose that, as far as content goes, Lk 11:14–26 offers a rather faithful rendering of the Q-version.

What are the implications of this for the Marcan text? Did Mark in 3:20–30 use a source which already differed from Q? It seems unnecessary to assume this. Consequently, it is of interest to indicate the possible Marcan redactional reworking of the Q-version:

(1) Mark's version omits many elements: the exorcism (Lk 11:14ab), the astonishment of the crowd (Lk 11:14c), the application (Lk 11:19–20), the saying "He who is not with me . . ." (Lk 11:23), and the return of the unclean spirit (Lk 11:24–26).

(2) Mark places the pericope concerning the request for a sign at a later point in his gospel (8:11–12).

(3) In Mk Jesus' accusers are scribes who had come from Jerusalem (cf. 3:22).

(4) Mark explicitly mentions Jesus' indirect way of answering: "He said 'in parables' " (3:23a).

(5) Mark duplicates the comparison. In Lk 11:17 the house is part of the kingdom, the divided houses which fall illustrate the laying waste of the kingdom. In Mk 3:24–25 there are two distinct images: a divided kingdom and a divided house (family).

(6) Mark makes the expression "to bind the strong man" serve as the single positive, allegorical explanation of what an exorcism is. In the Q version (cf. Lk 11:21–22) this statement was an element of a short parable illustrating Lk 11:20. In this parable the meaning of exorcism by Jesus is explicated.

(7) In 3:28–29 Mark adds the anthithetical judgment saying concerning guilt and forgiveness. This saying is also found in Q (cf. Mt 12:31–32 = Lk 12:10), but Mark has altered it considerably.

(8) Through his redactional work Mark formed a concentric, well-structured unit of text. The creative freedom which he allowed himself in so doing is amazing.

"In Parables"

In Mk 3:23a it is explicitly stated that Jesus answers the accusation of the scribes "in parables." With comparisons and images he refutes their charge that he works with the power of the prince of demons. The two comparisons in 3:24–25 are interpreted in v. 26, but the symbolic language in v. 27 is not further explained. It is certain that with the expression "in parables" (v. 23a) Mark announces the rewriting which he carries out in 3:24–27. Although the plural form in this stereotyped formula should probably not be emphasized, it is nevertheless striking that the following apology of Jesus does contain several "parables" or "images." Mark builds up a double comparison with two images (vv. 24–25). He wants the expression "in parables" to also refer to 3:27. In the Q-version (cf. Lk 11:21–22) this statement had the character of a narrative, but Mark has condensed the elements of that narrative into a solemn declaration whose metaphors must be interpreted by the reader: the strong man is Satan and the one who breaks in and plunders is Jesus, the speaker.

There is no indication that in Mark's view this speaking "in parables" would have been unintelligible to the scribes. On the contrary, the comparisons of vv. 24–25 are interpreted in v. 23b and v. 26. And although the indirect character of the symbolic language used in v. 27 demands a careful listening, reflection, and application, the whole context nevertheless suggests that the scribes did understand it—even if Mark does not say so explicitly. Nothing is said here about an intention of hardening on the part of Jesus as is mentioned in Mk 4:11–12, and it would be wrong to presuppose it in this context.

In connection with Mk 4, it should be pointed out that in 3:20–35 not only the scribes, but also Jesus' relatives are depicted in a negative way. The relatives remain outside while the people sit inside around Jesus. In Mk 4 the separation is made along somewhat different lines: those outside (here meaning some of the people) do not understand, while to "those around him" (*hoi peri auton*), together with the Twelve, the secret of the kingdom of God is given.

II. Clean and Unclean (Mk 7:1–23)

If it were not for the redactional transition in 7:17, no one would ever suspect that there is a parable in chap. 7. As it is however, the disciples in this verse ask "about the parable," referring to Jesus' statement in v. 15: "There is nothing outside a man which by going into him can defile him; but the things which come out of a man are what defile him." These verses (15 and 17) are part of the pericope 7:14–23 which itself belongs to the larger whole of the discourse concerning clean and unclean (7:1–23).

We first cite the text of Mk 7:14–23:

14 And he called the people to him again, and said to them, "Hear me all of you, and understand:

15 there is nothing outside a man which by going into him can defile him; but the things which come out of a man are what defile him."

(16 If any man has ears to hear, let him hear.)

17 And when he had entered the house, and left the people, his disciples asked him about the parable.

18 And he said to them, "Then are you also without understanding? Do you not see that whatever goes into a man from outside cannot defile him,

19 since it enters, not his heart but his stomach, and so passes on?" Thus he declared all foods clean.

20 And he said, "What comes out of a man is what defiles a man.

21 For from within, out of the heart of man, come evil thoughts, fornication, theft, murder, adultery,

22 coveting, wickedness, deceit, licentiousness, envy, slander, pride, foolishness.

23 All these evil things come from within, and they defile a man."

Tradition of the Elders and True Uncleanness

Mark 7:1–23, by Marcan standards, is a long pericope. The Pharisees and the scribes who had come from Jerusalem ask Jesus why his disciples eat with unwashed hands (vv. 1–5). Jesus answers with a series of statements: (a) He reproaches his questioners for neglecting God's commandment while holding fast to man-made traditions (vv. 6–8). To illustrate this general reproach he refers to the directives they lay down which make it impossible for someone who makes an offering to God to help his parents in their need (vv. 9–13). Jesus' answer could end here. His hearers have to draw the conclusion from what has been said that Jesus condemns their concern for cleanliness, dismissing it as one of "many such things." (b) But thereafter Jesus calls the people around him and affirms by way of conclusion: It is not what comes from outside that defiles a man but the things which come out of a man are what defile him (vv. 14–15). (c) After Jesus has withdrawn from the crowd, his disciples question him about the meaning of this saying (v. 17, "the parable"). A rather long explanation by Jesus follows. He first negatively states that food which is taken in does not defile a man (vv. 18–19), and then positively affirms that a man is defiled instead by all the evil things which come forth from his heart (vv. 20–23).

The structure of Mk 7:1–23 could be presented in this schematic way:

A. Introduction and question (vv. 1–5)
  1. Pharisees and scribes criticize the negligence of the disciples (vv. 1–2; explanatory note in vv. 3–4)
  2. Question concerning
     a) tradition (in general, v. 5b)
     b) unwashed hands (particular case, v. 5c)
B. Jesus' answer (vv. 6–23)
  1. Tradition (not a real answer as such to the Pharisees and scribes)
     a) vv. 6–8: counter-accusation (Isaiah-quotation)
     b) vv. 9–13: concrete example (Corban case)
  2. Defilement
     a) vv. 14–15: answer to the people
        v. 15a: what does not defile
        v. 15b: what does defile
     b) vv. 17–23: explanation to the disciples of foregoing answer
        vv. 18c–19: what does not defile
        vv. 20–23: what does defile

This discussion about clean and unclean probably underwent a long process of development before reaching its final Marcan formulation. It would seem that three pre–Marcan layers can be distinguished: (a) The oldest kernel is the authentic saying in v. 15. (b) This statement was, on the basis of a well-defined ecclesial situation, expanded into an apophthegm (a short narration of an incident which leads to a saying) in vv. 1, 5, 15, this sort of "biographical" narrative being one of many such controversies with the Pharisees in Mark's gospel. (c) In a third, but still pre–Marcan, stage a catechetical commentary would have been added (vv. 1, 5, 15, 18–19b, 20–23).

Subsequently, Mark's own redactional activity was very extensive in 7:1–23. He specifies that the scribes came from Jerusalem (v. 1; cf. 3:22). He inserts an explanation in vv. 3–4: washing one's hands before meals is one of the many prescriptions found in the tradition of the elders which are binding for all Jews. By rewriting v. 5 Mark makes the question a matter of principle. That the disciples neglect to wash their hands becomes for the Pharisees and the scribes a proof that they are not guided in their way of life by the tradition of the elders. By his addition of vv. 6–13, Mark has Jesus first answer this question of principle regarding tradition. The Pharisees and scribes themselves are taken to task by Jesus in these verses.

Mark's Redactional Work in 7:14–23

For this section Mark used a source which contained the saying in v. 15 (Jesus' answer to the pre–Marcan question of v. 5: "Why do your disciples eat with unwashed hands?") and the explanation to the disciples in vv. 18c–19b, 20–23. Before Mark this explanation must have been combined with the saying and its setting (vv. 1, 5), but it is quite possible that in Mark's source the explanation was directly joined to the saying of v. 15, without a change of scene and without a transitional request for such an explanation on the part of the disciples.

Apart from the addition of the small, parenthetical note in v. 19c, "Thus he [Jesus] declared all food clean" (and the new introduction in v. 20, "And he said"), and the rewriting of v. 23, Mark radically reworked his source in three ways: (1) In Mark's presentation the logion of v. 15 is addressed to the people whom Jesus had called together in v. 14, while the explanation of vv. 18–23 is given to the disciples inside the house. After v. 14 the Pharisees and scribes are no longer mentioned in the pericope. Our impression is that for this change of scene Mark very closely follows the structure of chap. 4.

Compare:

Mk 4	Mk 7
1 the crowd	14a the people around Jesus
2 "he said to them"	14a "he said to them"
3a "listen!"	14b "hear me, all of you, and understand"
3b–8 parable (the Sower)	15 parable (logion on cleanness)
9 "he who has ears to hear . . ."	(16 "if any man has ears to hear . . .")
10a withdrawal	17 withdrawal
13a "and he said to them"	18a "and he said to them"
13bc reproachful questions	18bc reproachful questions
14–20 explanation of the parable	19–23 explanation of the parable

For chap. 4, as we have seen, Mark already had in his source, in addition to the parable and explanation, a request for an explanation of the parable (i.e., an earlier form of v. 10; cf. p. 92). Given the thoroughly redactional character of vv. 14 and 17–18, it is improbable that an analogous request for an explanation was in Mark's source for chap. 7. Mark himself is most likely responsible for both the request and the change of scene here.

(2) The double question in v. 18, "Then are you also without understanding? Do you not see . . . ?" is a reproach addressed to the disciples which is clearly reminiscent of the equally reproachful question directed to them in 4:13, "Do you not understand this parable? How then will you understand all the parables?" Furthermore the remark after the storm at sea, "And they [the disciples] were utterly astounded, for they did not understand about the loaves, but their hearts were hardened" (6:51b–52) is anything but flattering to the disciples. And, in 8:17–21 Jesus chides them in strong language for their lack of understanding, for they had entirely misunderstood his warning against the Pharisees and Herod (8:15):

> And being aware of it, Jesus said to them, "Why do you discuss the fact that you have no bread? Do you not yet perceive or understand? Are your hearts hardened? Having eyes do you not see, and having ears do you not hear? And do you not remember? When I broke the five loaves for the five thousand, how many baskets full of broken pieces did you take up?" They said to him, "Twelve." "And the seven for the four thousand, how many baskets full of broken pieces did you take up?" And they said to him, "Seven." And he said to them, "Do you not yet understand?" (Mk 8:17–21)

All these reproaches addressed to the disciples are obviously connected with one another, and all derive from Mark. In chap. 7 it is thus the redactor Mark who, with the two questions of v. 18, once again underscores the disciples' lack of understanding.

(3) Finally, the term "parable" in v. 17 probably also stems from Mark. With this term Mark refers to the saying of v. 15. Actually the entire v. 17 has a Marcan character: going into the house, Jesus and the disciples alone by themselves, the typically Marcan verb *eperōtaō* ("to question"). The very Marcan character of the verse is an indication that its designation of the logion of v. 15 as a "parable" also derives from Mark. Apparently Mark uses this

term because the saying of v. 15 was not understood; it is an obscure and mysterious statement that needs to be explained, i.e., a parable.

The Parable

How in Mark's conception does the "parable" (i.e., the saying of v. 15) function within the whole of 7:14–23? Did Jesus intend to blind the people with this parable? The answer to these questions is not simple. If it is correct to suppose that Mark is dependent on Mk 4 for the three above-mentioned redactional interventions in 7:14–23, then it could logically be expected that the hardening theory in 4:11–12 would also make its influence felt here. If the disciples ask for an explanation of the saying in v. 15, it is because even they did not understand it; *a fortiori* neither did the people. And moreover, just like the parables of Mk 4, the statement or parable in 7:15 is obscure.

But, notwithstanding this logical explanation, no mention is found in Mk 7:14–23 of an intention of hardening on the part of Jesus as is expressed in Mk 4:11–12. In chap. 4 the people around Jesus, together with the Twelve (4:10), are placed over against "those outside"; but in chap. 7 the real enemies are the Pharisees and the scribes who had come from Jerusalem. Furthermore, after reading 7:1–13 one would suppose that the people who are called together by Jesus in v. 14 would be better disposed than the Pharisees and scribes. As such, there is nothing negative in the formulation of the summons in v. 14b: "Hear me, all of you, and understand." When Jesus thereafter says to the disciples, "are *you also* without understanding?" (v. 18b), it is not so certain that he is comparing them with the people rather than with the Pharisees and scribes. Moreover, seeing that it is not explicitly said that the people remained uncomprehending, the full force of the reproach in 7:14–23 falls on the disciples.

What can be concluded from all this? It seems that Mark is not consistent in his conception of Jesus' use of parables. In 3:23–27 the scribes do understand the parables. In 4:10–34 Jesus speaks in figurative parable language to prevent outsiders from grasping his message; only the disciples are given a further explanation. In 7:14–23 the disciples also receive an explanation in private. We have to suppose then that in Mk 7 the parable is not immediately understandable, also not to the people. That the people are uncomprehending or hardened is, however, not expressly said, and there is not even an allusion to an intention of hardening by Jesus here. Further, more than in Mk 4, the disciples are placed in a negative light in 7:14–23 because they should have understood but did not. All this indicates that Mark did not consistently maintain the theory that Jesus' parables had the (deliberately intended) effect of hardening his hearers.

III. The Wicked Tenants (Mk 12:1–12)

1 And he began to speak to them in parables. "A man planted a vineyard, and set a hedge around it, and dug a pit for the wine press, and built a tower, and let it out to tenants, and went into another country.
2 When the time came, he sent a servant to the tenants, to get from them some of the fruit of the vineyard.
3 And they took him and beat him, and sent him away empty-handed.
4 Again he sent to them another servant, and they wounded him in the head, and treated him shamefully.
5 And he sent another, and him they killed; and so with many others; some they beat and some they killed.
6 He had still one other, a beloved son; finally he sent him to them, saying, 'They will respect my son.'
7 But those tenants said to one another, 'This is the heir; come, let us kill him, and the inheritance will be ours.'
8 And they took him and killed him, and cast him out of the vineyard.
9 What will the owner of the vineyard do? He will come and destroy the tenants, and give the vineyard to others.
10 Have you not read this scripture: 'The very stone which the builders rejected has become the head of the corner;
11 this was the Lord's doing, and it is marvelous in our eyes'?"
12 And they tried to arrest him, but feared the multitude, for they perceived that he had told the parable against them; so they left him and went away.

The word "parable" occurs twice in connection with the story of the Wicked Tenants. The introduction contains the formula "to speak in parables" with which we are already familiar (cf. 3:23; 4:2,

11) and in the concluding v. 12 we read "the parable" in the sense of "the just narrated parable." Before proceeding to examine how, according to Mark, Jesus used this parable and whether it would have been understandable to his hearers, we must first situate the narrative within its context and consider its pre–Marcan form.

The Question Concerning Authority (Mk 11:27–12:12)

Mk 11:1–11 describes Jesus' solemn entry into Jerusalem. Sitting on a colt and proceeding through the jubilant crowds, Jesus "entered Jerusalem, and went into the temple; and when he had looked round at everything, as it was already late, he went out to Bethany with the Twelve" (11:11). The next day he returns to Jerusalem, enters the temple, and cleanses it (cf. 11:16–17). "The chief priests and the scribes heard it and sought a way to destroy him; for they feared him, because all the multitude was astonished at his teaching" (11:18). In the evening Jesus and the Twelve leave the city once more (cf. 11:19) and on the third day they return to Jerusalem (cf. 11:20–27a). In the courtyard of the temple the chief priests, the scribes, and the elders come up to Jesus and ask him by what authority he had done "these things." Jesus poses a counter-question concerning the baptism of John: Did it come from heaven or from men? After considering the implications of the two possible answers, they reply, "We do not know." To this answer Jesus responds, "Neither will I tell you by what authority I do these things!" (cf. 11:27–33). Instead of replying to their question, Jesus speaks in parabolic form about their attitude towards God's envoys, towards his Son, and about their future condemnation. Thus, the parable of the Wicked Tenants is intimately linked with the question concerning authority.

In Mk 11:18 it is stated for the first time that the chief priests and scribes were seeking an opportunity to destroy Jesus. They had to proceed cautiously out of fear of the people who sympathized with him. In 12:12 after the unsuccessful discussion and after Jesus' parable of judgment, we read again that they were trying to find a way to get him into their power, but here too it is stated that they were afraid of the people (cf. also 11:32bc: "They were afraid of the people, for all held that John was a real prophet"). They withdraw, but send some Pharisees and Herodians to entrap Jesus (cf. 12:12–13), and they ask him whether it is lawful to pay taxes to Caesar. Jesus sees through their hypocrisy and replies, "Render to Caesar what is Caesar's, and to God the things that are God's" (cf. 12:14–17). This second, indirect attack also ends in failure. Jesus remains in the temple giving instructions on various subjects (cf. 12:18–44). In chap. 13 as he leaves the temple he predicts the destruction of its buildings, and on the Mount of Olives he delivers his apocalyptic discourse. But then in chap. 14 the authorities reappear on the scene: "It was now two days before the Passover and the feast of the Unleavened Bread. And the chief priests and the scribes were seeking how to arrest him by stealth, and kill him; for they said, 'Not during the feast, lest there be a tumult of the people' " (14:1–2). Judas finally broke the deadlock and the third attempt was successful.

In Mark's gospel the parable of the Wicked Tenants is part of the first attempt. The authorities accost Jesus when he appears in the courtyard of the temple the morning after he had cleansed it. They ask him for his credentials, for the source of his authority. Jesus, however, is in full control of the situation. This first attempt ends with his announcement of the condemnation of his opponents and, at the same time, with an allusion to his own future glorification.

Authenticity of the Parable

There is a fundamental disagreement among scholars on the question of whether the parable in Mk 12:1–12 goes back to the earthly Jesus. According to some, the allegorizing is so inherent to the narrative and so postpaschal in its content that the only reasonable position is to admit that this parable originated after Easter and was an allegory from the beginning. Others try to reconstruct the original form of the parable by eliminating elements which are clearly secondary. But even this possibly older form would not necessarily derive from Jesus himself.

The following indicates what in the parable could be secondary and what original:

(1) Verse 1a undoubtedly stems from Mark as does v. 12, at least in its present form. Mark's source might have mentioned that the hearers realized that the parable was aimed at them and that they withdrew, but the rest of v. 12 is clearly Marcan.

(2) It is generally admitted that the quotation from Ps 118:22–

23 in vv. 10–11 is an addition. Whether the insertion was made by the evangelist or at the pre–Marcan level is uncertain. With these verses attention is again directed to the son.

(3) Many authors think that v. 5 ("And he sent another and him they killed; and so with many others, some they beat and some they killed") cannot have belonged to the original form of the parable. For, according to the usual narrative style of the parables, only three missions would be expected: a servant who is ill-treated, a second who is wounded in the head, and the son who is killed.

(4) According to some exegetes, the Isaiah quotation in v. 1 would also be secondary. In the Old Testament passage the vineyard is Israel, whereas in the supposedly original parable the vineyard is the property which is entrusted to the tenants and will be taken from them. If the quotation did not belong to the original parable, then v. 9 which takes up motifs from the quotation of v. 1 must also be secondary, at least in part. Some scholars think that the parable ended prior to v. 9 with the murder of the son.

(5) Perhaps there is a secondary influence in v. 7 from the Joseph story in Genesis: "Come, let us kill him" (cf. Gen 37:20).

What remains after the excision of these possibly secondary elements is the story of a man who leases his vineyard to vinedressers and, at the appointed time, sends a servant to them to collect his part of the produce. This servant is ill-treated. A second servant is wounded in the head. Finally the owner sends his own son, but he is murdered (the uncertain conclusion: on his return the owner punishes the tenants).

There is no reason to doubt the authenticity of the reconstructed parable. It is a "parable in the strict sense," an imaginary story which fits the social and agricultural situation of Palestine in Jesus' time, but nevertheless contains enough fictitious, strange features so that the hearer is obliged to reflect. The hearers must have perceived that with the figure of the son Jesus was referring to himself and that with the sending of the servants and the son he was pointing to God's salvific initiatives. They must further have realized that in the crisis announced by Jesus they themselves were also confronted with a choice: to do as the tenants did or to accept Jesus. By means of such parables Jesus spoke about himself and his work (cf. the Sower!). He was conscious of the fact that, as

God's son, he was the final envoy; he also knew that he thus belonged to the company of the prophets who were rejected and killed by Israel (already in Jesus' own parable the servants represented God's envoys). Towards the end of his life Jesus must have reckoned with this prophetic fate which was coming ever closer. The parable about the murder of the son reflects all these concerns.

After Easter the early church proceeded to allegorize the already allegorical parable of Jesus to a much greater extent. (1) By appending the Psalm quotation in vv. 10–11, the allegory became explicitly Christological. To say nothing about the ultimate status of the son was no longer tolerable in the postpaschal situation. Accordingly this quotation with its allusion to Jesus' resurrection and exaltation was added. (2) Thanks to the Isaiah quotation in v. 1, the parable became an allegorical survey of the history of God's dealings with Israel: God chose Israel; Israel rejected the prophets and put Jesus to death; God will come in judgment to punish Israel. (3) By the addition of v. 5 (many sendings, many servants persecuted and executed) Jesus' fate was emphatically paralleled with that of the prophets who were persecuted and violently put to death.

The Allegory in the Marcan Gospel

One gets the impression that Mark must have had 12:1b–11 in his source in approximately its present form (minus v. 5 and perhaps also v. 7). He takes over the Christological, salvation-historical, and prophetic-theological allegorizing of the early church. At the same time his attention is clearly focused above all on the function which the allegory has to fulfill in the context of his gospel.

For Mark the allegory is part of the question concerning authority. The audience to which it is addressed consists of the chief priests, scribes, and elders. It is they who understand the parable and realize that their first attempt against Jesus has failed. Despite their fear of the people, however, they keep trying to find a way to get Jesus into their power. According to Mark, Jesus intends this allegory first and foremost as a judgment on the tenants. And the leaders to whom he addresses himself understand that the story is aimed at them.

In 11:33 Jesus refuses to answer the demand for his credentials and then in 12:1 begins to "speak in parables" to his opponents. By means of this expression Mark wishes to indicate that Jesus will not speak openly, i.e., in clear and direct words, but rather in figurative language. The expression using the plural form "parables" seems stereotyped and surely does not mean that vv. 1–9 and vv. 10–11 should be viewed as two separate "parables." In fact, v. 12 speaks of "the (one) parable."

In 12:12 Mark notes that Jesus' opponents perceived that the parable was directed against them. This implies that they had fully grasped its meaning. An understanding by the hearers also had to be presupposed in 3:23–27. Once more, then, there is something here quite different from Mk 4 with its statement about hardening and also from Mk 7 where the people apparently understand the parable. In both chaps. 4 and 7 the disciples must first be given a special explanation so they can understand; and in both they are reproached for their lack of comprehension. In Mk 12 the opponents catch the point at once; no explanation is needed! Here it is again apparent that Mark's conception of Jesus' use of parables is not univocal.

IV. The Budding Fig Tree and the Doorkeeper
(Mk 13:28–29 and 34–36)

In Mk 13:28a we read, "From the fig tree learn its lesson [*parabolē*]." The similitude of the Budding Fig Tree follows with its application (vv. 28bc–29). In 13:34 there is a sentence introduced by the formula "it is like": "It is like a man going on a journey, when he leaves home and puts his servants in charge, each with his work, and commands the doorkeeper to be on the watch. . . ." The application is given in vv. 35–36. These two parables must also be considered in forming an accurate view of the way in which Mark represents Jesus as using the parables. An analysis of Mark's apocalyptic discourse in which the two similitudes have a well-defined place and function is our starting point.

The Apocalyptic Discourse of Mk 13
The discourse of Mk 13 clearly has something of a final address by Jesus, a farewell speech, a last will and testament about it. The long day with its discussions in the temple has come to an end.

Jesus had given an answer to the many questions of several groups of people: the chief priests, scribes, and elders, but also the Pharisees and Herodians, and the Sadducees, all of them persons of authority. They were amazed at him (12:17) and, finally, no one dared ask him any further questions (12:34). But this did not alter the firm resolution of the leaders: they continued to seek to destroy him (cf. 11:18; 12:12; and 14:1–2). After all the questions put to him by others, Jesus poses a question of his own about his identity: "David himself calls him [the Messiah] Lord; so how is he his son?" (12:37). He also again gives a warning against the scribes (12:38–40). Then, leaving the temple he predicts, "There will not be left here one stone upon another, that will not be thrown down" (13:2). Seated opposite the temple, on the Mount of Olives, Jesus pronounces his last discourse. After the definitive break with the leaders of his people and before his Passion begins, to four of his disciples he speaks of the future: the coming persecution, the destruction of Jerusalem, and the coming of the Son of man. He instructs his disciples, he warns and exhorts them. All of this was included by the evangelist in his thirteenth chapter which is known to us as the apocalyptic discourse.

We could dwell at length on the ingenious, concentric structure of Mk 13:5b–37 which has the following plan:

Introduction (vv. 1–4)
Discourse (vv. 5–37):
A   Oppression: information and warning (vv. 5b–23)
   a   deceivers (vv. 5b–6): "'Take heed . . .'"
   b   wars (vv. 7–8): "When you hear . . ."
   c   persecutions (vv. 9–13): ". . . take heed . . ."
   b' war (vv. 14–20): ". . . when you see . . ."
   a' deceivers (vv. 21–23): ". . . take heed . . ."
B   Coming: announcement (vv. 24–27)
A' The Day and the Hour: information and warning (vv. 28–36)
   a   parable of the Budding Fig Tree (vv. 28–29)
   b   logion about the certain and imminent return (v. 30)
   c   confirmation logion (v. 31)
   b' logion about the sudden, unexpected return (v. 32)
   a' parable of the Doorkeeper (vv. 33–36)
Concluding verse (v. 37)

The most remarkable feature of this structure is undoubtedly its concentric character. The first and the third sections of the discourse run parallel to one another. Both announce and give information; both warn and exhort. In the middle section stands the text concerning the coming of the Son of man. Each of the three sections has its own character. In A we find: Look out, don't be deceived, persevere, flee as soon as the final crisis breaks in, don't be unduly preoccupied. The calamity is announced; an oppressive atmosphere reigns which necessitates counsel and strengthening. Section A', on the other hand, because of the parables it contains, seems more serene: Look out, be ready for the coming of the Lord. The atmosphere here is pervaded by a sense of hope, although the exhortations still make it very serious. This part is, as it were, illuminated by the Parousia which is treated in the central section B. The coming of the Son of man with great power and glory stands at the center here. His coming is directed to the assembling of the elect.

On the basis of the line of thought and the linking phrases, the *first section* (A) has been further subdivided into five paragraphs. The first and the last concern "deceivers." They correspond precisely to one another and frame the remaining parts. The second and fourth paragraphs are also formulated as parallels, as is evident from the introductory temporal clauses "when . . ." (vv. 7 and 14), as well as from their respective contents which deal with wars and the great oppression. Persecution is the subject of the central paragraph, the heart of section A, which as such is the most strongly emphasized element within it. The *third section* (A') with its two parables, one at the beginning and one at the end, may also have a fivefold structure. If this is the case, vv. 30 and 32 also belong together; both have to do with the time when all this will take place. On the other hand, there is a sharp contrast between them. Verse 30 concerns a happening which is certain and can be expected imminently; "this generation" will still witness it. Verse 32, in contrast, treats of the exact moment and says that it is unknown. Nevertheless, this does not imply a real contradiction. The two time specifications complement one another. This third section deals specifically with the question of the time and alertness, whereas the first section focuses more on the threatening oppression, persecution and confusion. The coming of the Son of man which is seen as imminent will certainly happen during this generation. It will be preceded by wars and disasters, by a period of persecution, by the proclamation of the gospel to all nations, by the destruction of Jerusalem and by the great oppression. Meanwhile there will be the activity of false Christs and prophets who will try to deceive. In the *central section* (B) the Parousia stands isolated without a single accompanying exhortation. The Parousia certainly motivates the tense expectation and it demands great alertness. For, after the oppression of those days, the Son of man will come and he will have the initiative. Humanity will only be a witness to that coming when the elect will be assembled by the angels.

Many scholars are sceptical about the idea of such a concentric structure. Admittedly, in many cases in Mk the linking of sentences and pericopes is rather clumsy. On the other hand, if the structure suggested above is present in Mk 13, then it would be necessary to recognize this as an instance of Mark's ability to produce a tightly structured composition. It would not, however, be necessary to conclude from this that everything in chap. 13 is a pure creation of Mark. He has undoubtedly so radically rewritten, reordered, and expanded his source material with redactional additions in function of his intended structure that it is practically impossible to isolate the pre–Marcan elements within the present discourse. But, at the same time, Mark has certainly integrated into this discourse sayings of Jesus and elements of parables which were known to him from the tradition and parts of which are also preserved in Lk 17. Moreover, it is not excluded that Mark used preexisting elements of a midrash-like commentary on Daniel. In his discourse Mark combats an anxious expectation of an immediate Parousia and an exaggerated apocalyptic mentality which tries to interpret particular happenings as signs that the end has come. He does not, however, restrict himself to a merely negative stance; his main objective is admonition and exhortation. He calls for alertness because the Lord is certainly coming, although the day of his coming is not known.

The Two Parables

28 *a* From the fig tree learn its lesson [*parabolē*]:
as soon as its branch becomes tender and puts forth its leaves, you know that summer is near.

29   So also,
       when you see these things taking place,
       know that he [or: it] is near, at the very gates.
30 *b*   Truly, I say to you, this generation will not pass away
       before all these things take place.
31 *c*   Heaven and earth will pass away,
       but my words will not pass away.
32 *b'* But of that day or that hour no one knows,
       not even the angels in heaven, nor the Son,
       but only the Father.
33 *a'* Take heed, watch,
       for you do not know when the time will come.
34   It is like a man going on a journey, when he leaves home
       and puts his servants in charge, each with his work, and
       commands the doorkeeper to be on the watch.
35   Watch therefore—for you do not know when the master of
       the house will come, in the evening, or at midnight, or at
       cockcrow, or in the morning—
36   lest he come suddenly and find you asleep.
37 *concluding verse:* And what I say to you I say to all: Watch.

The two parables (*a* and *a'*) must now be examined since the parallelism between them is not limited to their parable form. The repetition "you know that . . ." (v. 28) and "know that . . ." (v. 29) in the Fig Tree has clearly been composed by Mark in function of the similar repetition in the Doorkeeper, i.e., "you do not know when . . ." (vv. 33 and 35). The phrase "at the very gates" (literally: at the very *door*) which "lags behind" a bit at the end of v. 29 was apparently inserted into *a* in order to reinforce the parallelism with *a'*: cf. the "*door*keeper" in v. 34. One can also readily suppose that "learn" (v. 28) and "take heed" (v. 33) are, in view of their initial position in their respective sentences and their imperative form, intended to be symmetrical and to function as connectives. But this symmetry is strongly antithetical: two aspects of the coming are illustrated: the one (in *a*) is known, the other (in *a'*) is hidden; in *a* the budding fig tree is a sign which announces the Parousia in unambiguous terms, in *a'* the absent master returns unexpectedly; in *a* attention is focused principally on the first part of the discourse (A) (not completely, however, since "he is near,"

v. 29), and indeed on a period which presupposes a definite duration, where in *a'*, on the contrary, the concern is with the sudden coming, thus more with the second section (*B*).

It is possible that the Budding Fig Tree is a pre–Marcan, authentic parable. But v. 28a is a transitional phrase created by Mark, and the application (v. 29) in its present form never existed apart from the actual Marcan discourse. Perhaps the pre–Marcan application ran, "When you see . . . , know that *the kingdom of God* is near." We shall, however, not seek further for a hypothetical earlier form.

As for the Doorkeeper, it seems very doubtful that it existed before Mark. The long sentence in v. 34 is certainly awkward and, grammatically speaking, even incorrect. There is, moreover, a certain tension between the many servants and the one doorkeeper in that the application in vv. 35–36 focuses simply on the doorkeeper's watching and neglects the servants. It is not excluded that Mark himself composed the parable of the Doorkeeper out of fragments and elements of traditional Parousia parables which were known to him. The man going on a journey reminds us of the Talents or the Pounds (Mt 25:14–30 = Lk 19:12–27); the delegation of authority and the distribution of tasks recall that same parable and also the Faithful or Wicked Servant (Mt 24:45–51 = Lk 12:42–46); the doorkeeper, keeping watch, and the various nightwatches are all reminiscent of the Watchful Servants (Lk 12:35–38) while the return of the master at an unexpected hour is a motif that recurs in each of the parables just mentioned. It would seem then that Mark himself composed the Doorkeeper for his apocalyptic discourse, making use of fragments of preexisting parables.

Clarifying Similitudes

The two parables found in the third section of the apocalyptic discourse each have their own character and distinct function. The Budding Fig Tree is announced as a *parabolē* in v. 28a. This similitude consists of a comparison with a natural happening, i.e., the yearly budding of the fig tree (v. 28b), and an application introduced by "so also" (v. 29). The subject of the phrase "is near" (v. 29) is not expressed as such, but in light of v. 26 (cf. "They will see the Son of man coming in clouds . . .") it is probable that it is "he" (the Son of man). Because the Budding Fig Tree is a similitude it requires reasoning. The hearers must know, i.e., be able to see the connection between certain happenings which are signs and the imminence of the Son of man, just as there is an observable temporal connection between the budding of the fig tree and the beginning of summer. The similitude is intended to evoke insight.

The point of the Doorkeeper is different. It serves as an exhortation to vigilance, to staying awake. The exhortation is present already in v. 33, prior to the parable ("take heed and watch"), and a similar injunction follows immediately after the image ("watch therefore," v. 35; cf. v. 37: "Watch"). The motivation is given twice: you do not know when the time will come or when the master of the house will return (cf. vv. 33 and 35). The comparison is introduced by "it is like," but there is no corresponding "so also" in vv. 35–36: comparison and reality are fused. In these verses there is still talk of the master of the house, nightwatches, and sleeping (the image) but the hearers are summoned to (spiritual, moral) vigilance (the reality). In light of this reality, the images "master of the house" and "to be asleep" cannot but be interpreted in an allegorical sense. The comparison is not derived from a natural happening but from figures known in social life, a master and his servants.

The two parables are addressed, like the entire discourse, to the group of four disciples (Peter, James, John, and Andrew; cf. 13:3); but in v. 37 we read, "What I say to you I say to all." In the most matter of fact way, in this discourse Mark represents Jesus as using similitudes to clarify something (cf. 13:28a: "From the fig tree learn its lesson"). These comparisons are meant to help the listeners to understand and to draw them into a new insight. Since the discourse is addressed to the disciples there is no need for a later interpretation given elsewhere in a closed circle. The disciples do not even ask for an explanation; Jesus makes the application spontaneously and at once. The two similitudes function as illustrations. In chap. 13 there is thus a presentation very different from that of Mk 4 with its reference to an intention of hardening and from both Mk 4 and 7 with their reproaches addressed to the disciples. While in chaps. 3 and 12 Mark stresses the fact that Jesus expresses his accusation or condemnation "in parables," i.e., in a veiled way, here in chap. 13 he seems to regard the parables simply as clarifying. Jesus uses them spontaneously with no ulterior motive.

V. A Marcan Parable Theory?

At the end of this long analysis our findings must now be synthesized and compared. The conclusions of the previous chapter on the parables in Mk 4 must also be taken into account. In the light of all these considerations, is it possible to describe more precisely Mark's vision of Jesus' use of parables? Is there such a thing as a Marcan parable theory?

Parables in Mark's Gospel

Mark obviously considers very different literary genres to be "parables." The Sower (4:3–8) and the Wicked Tenants (12:1–11) are relatively long narratives which are understood allegorically by the author. The Seed Growing by Itself (4:26–29) and the Mustard Seed (4:30–32) are introduced as "similitudes of the kingdom." Both of these similitudes, and also the Doorkeeper (13:34–36), are introduced by *hōs* ("as if"). The Doorkeeper does not have an introductory verse indicating the point, but in vv. 35–36 the intended exhortation emerges from the parable itself. The Budding Fig Tree (13:28–29) consists of two elements, an image and an application. In 3:24–25 there are two short comparisons of the "kingdom" and the "house"; v. 23b announces the intended point and v. 26 makes the application, but there is no particle of comparison at the beginning. If the plundering of the strong man's house (3:27) is a parable, as affirmed earlier, then there is here an allegorical saying which explains what exorcism implies. Finally, 7:15 is nothing more than an enigmatic double saying about defilement. However, for Mark these are all equally parables. In some cases Mark's redactional contribution within the "parables" is rather extensive (e.g., 3:24–27; 4:26–29; 13:28–29, and 34–36), in others his editorial activity is minimal (e.g., 4:3–8, 14–20; 7:15, 18–22; 12:1–11).

Mark knows that speaking in parables is a type of indirect speech, a use of figurative language. He uses "in parables" four times (3:23a; 4:2, 11; 12:1) and each time by means of this expression he underscores the symbolic character, the hidden and indirect aspect of this manner of speaking. The metaphor needs to be explained for it is not always immediately clear. The Sower is interpreted in 4:14–20, the saying about cleanness in 7:18–23 and the Budding Fig Tree in 13:29.

According to Mark, Jesus told his parables in public (to the people and the disciples) (cf. Mk 4 and 7). Jesus also used parables to answer his opponents (cf. Mk 3 and 12). Finally, the parables appear in a discourse heard by only four of his disciples (cf. Mk 13).

Are the parables understandable according to Mark? Only a very nuanced answer can be given to this question: (1) In Mk 4 and 7 an explanation is needed, otherwise the parables remain unintelligible to the hearers; this explanation is given only to the Twelve (and to those "around him"). (2) Moreover, according to Mk 4:11–12, Jesus uses parables so that outsiders might not understand and so be converted. (3) Elsewhere in Mk when Jesus uses parables, both before his opponents (in chaps. 3 and 12) and before the four disciples (in chap. 13), the listeners seem to understand him quite well. That they do so is explicitly stated in 12:12. (4) While in chaps. 3 and 12 Mark, with the expression "in parables," still focuses attention on the figurative language as such, the use of parables in the discourse of chap. 13 seems to happen in a more spontaneous way, as it were, with no ulterior motive. Here the parables are an aid to understanding; they are clarifying images whose meaning is readily understandable to the disciples with or without an application.

No Strict Theory

Our investigation has shown that one cannot speak of a parable theory in the strict sense in Mk, i.e., a theory which is held throughout the entire gospel and consciously maintained. The hardening theory is indeed present in Mk 4:11–12; it seems probable that it is Mark's own creation. Yet even for Mark himself this is not the whole truth. The theory is formulated explicitly only once, in chap. 4. In chap. 7 it still makes its influence felt (in the disciples' incomprehension), although the theory itself is no longer mentioned as such. Elsewhere in Mark's gospel the parables are understood. This is true in chaps. 3 and 12 where Jesus does not use them in order to leave his opponents in the dark.

Must this duality of perspective in Mark be explained by supposing that the hardening theory existed before Mark? In our view certain distinctions also have to be made here: (1) Before Mark, the primitive church was already confronted with the unbelief of Israel. To understand this problem, certain Old Testament statements about a hardening worked by God (cf. Isaiah, but also other texts) were reflected upon and these statements were regarded as having been realized. (2) From Mark 4:12 it appears that Mark must have known the Targum version of Is 6:9–10. (3) Mark has reflected on the obscure and indirect character of figurative speech. This enigmatic quality of parable language seems to have been more a Semitic than a Greek conception. The apocalypses or revelations (dreams, parables) require an interpreter. All this is pre–Marcan. (4) The biblical themes of election, privilege, and initiation are also traditional.

Nevertheless, it seems improbable that Mk 4:11–12 already constituted a unit of text before Mark. That v. 11 existed before Mark appears very doubtful to us. Just as Mark uses the phrase "those who are around him" in 4:10 to refer to 3:32, 34 (the people seated round Jesus), so it seems that with "those who are outside" in v. 11 he consciously alludes to 3:31–32 (the relatives who stand outside). The two expressions in 4:10–11 definitely express a religious opposition and the intentionally contrasted groups in Mk 3:31–35 and 4:10–12 are thus not completely identical. This does not however negate the fact that Mark seems to have created the expressions in 4:10–11 on the basis of 3:31–35. We are therefore of the opinion that Mark himself is responsible for relating the obscure parable language to the intention of hardening (and the Isaiah paraphrase) in chap. 4: hardening through parables. This parable theory, in our view, derives from Mark. But, even for Mark it is anything but a theory in the "strict" sense—something which would have dominated all of Jesus' speaking in parables.

Is Mark Inconsistent?

Perhaps it is wrong to presuppose too great a consistency in Mark. In 4:34 we read, "He [Jesus] did not speak to them [the people] without a parable." Nevertheless, it can be concluded from the gospel that Mark did not intend this statement as literally as we are inclined to think, cf. e.g., 12:35–40 where Jesus gives instruction without parables.

How does Mark view the people? Are they for him the sympathetic hearers who are feared by the authorities (cf. 11:18; 12:12; 14:2)? Or are they, for the most part, "outsiders" (cf. 4:11)? Or, are they those who sit around Jesus and also do the will of God (cf. 3:31–35)? Obviously, Mark's vision on this point is not as unified as we might wish. Something similar is to be said concerning the image of the disciples given by Mark's gospel. The Twelve are called, appointed, and sent out; they are certainly privileged (cf. 4:11). Yet in many cases they are very uncomprehending (cf. 4:13; 6:51; 7:17–18; 8:17–21, 32–33; 9:32–34; 10:35–45).

Already in chap. 4 Mark does not seem very happy with his hardening theory. He seems to have difficulty maintaining it consistently even here. In any case, in v. 13 attention is diverted to the disciples' lack of understanding. And perhaps Mark, in view of the theory of v. 11, had to correct in v. 34 what he had spontaneously written in v. 33 ("as they were able to hear it," i.e., "in the way in which they could understand it"). Similarly, Mark initially could hardly have understood the summons to hear in vv. 3 and 9 otherwise than as a sincere invitation to understand and accept the gospel message. Does this not presuppose the intelligibility of the parable, an intelligibility which immediately afterwards in vv. 11–12 is denied with respect to the outsiders? And as for the disciples, Mark says in 4:21–22 that their privilege (v. 11) must lead to their later proclamation. It seems, therefore, that in chap. 4, in the very place where he formulates the theory, Mark must have been aware of its unnatural character. That he nevertheless did formulate it perhaps ultimately has to do with the mystery of Israel's infidelity, a mystery which the early church and Mark were trying to explain.

Thus Mk 4, but above all Jesus' use of parables elsewhere in Mark's gospel, shows us that for Mark, too, the parables have more than one function. They can be a means of hardening, but Jesus also used them to accuse and condemn, to instruct and to exhort.

Hardening

This study of Jesus' use of parables in Mark's gospel has shown that the intention of hardening cannot be attributed to Jesus himself. But Mark also, who in his chap. 4 apparently formulated this intention as a parable theory for the first time, did not limit his view of the parables to the idea that Jesus used parables to blind certain people, the outsiders, so that they would not be converted. Nevertheless, these statements about hardening must lead us to reflect. It would be a sign of narrow-mindedness if we had no understanding of the efforts of the primitive church and of Mark to find an explanation for the mystery of human infidelity and blindness. In the explanation to which they came, it was affirmed that even this infidelity and blindness was part of God's plan: it was foreseen; God had foretold it; in this way he had, already in history, punished sin. Neither the first Christians nor Mark thereby denied human freedom in the least—hardening by God was only a sealing and confirmation of man's guilt and freedom.

In the last analysis, these sayings concerning hardening confront us with the seriousness of man's answer to God's call. Through the repeated summons to hear in Mark, this existential seriousness is underlined again and again. In our time, too, man cannot neglect God's offer of salvation with impunity. He will ultimately harden himself. Mk 4:11–12 is intended not only as a reflection, but also as a warning. What the evangelist writes in admonition to his fellow believers in 13:37 holds for every Christian and also for us: "What I say to you [the four disciples] I say to all," i.e., to all disciples and all Christians.

BIBLIOGRAPHY

Cf. also Bibliography for chap. 4.

Banks, R., *Jesus and the Law in the Synoptic Tradition*, Society for New Testament Studies, Monograph Series 28, Cambridge, 1975.

Berger, K., *Die Gesetzesauslegung Jesu. Ihr historischer Hintergrund im Judentum und im Alten Testament*. Teil I: *Markus und Parallelen*, WMzANT 40, Neukirchen, 1972.

Blank, J., "Die Sendung des Sohnes. Zur christologischen Bedeutung des Gleichnisses von den bösen Winzern Mk 12,1–12," in *Neues Testament und Kirche. Für R. Schnackenburg*, ed. J. Gnilka, Freiburg, 1974, pp. 11–41.

Carlston, C. E., "The Things that Defile (Mark VII.14) and the Law in Matthew and Mark," *NTS* 15 (1968–1969) 75–96.

Cothenet, E., "Pureté et impureté. III: Nouveau Testament," *Dictionnaire de la Bible. Supplément* 9 (1975) cols. 528–54.

Crossan, J. D., "The Parable of the Wicked Husbandmen," *JBL* 90 (1971) 451–65.

Dupont, J., "La parabole du figuier qui bourgeonne (Mc, XIII,28–29 et Par.)," *RB* 75 (1968) 526–78.

———, "La parabole du maître qui rentre dans la nuit (Mc 13,34–36)," in *Mélanges bibliques en hommage au R. P. B. Rigaux*, ed. A. Descamps and A. de Halleux, Gembloux, 1970, pp. 89–116.

Hahn, F., "Die Rede von der Parusie des Menschensohnes Markus 13," in *Jesus und der Menschensohn. Für A. Vögtle*, ed. R. Pesch and R. Schnackenburg, Freiburg, 1975, pp. 240–66.

Hartman, L. *Prophecy Interpreted: The Formation of Some Jewish Apocalyptic Texts and of the Eschatological Discourse Mark 13 par.*, Coniectanea Biblica, New Testament Series 1, Lund, 1966.

Hengel, M., "Das Gleichnis von den Weingärtnern Mc 12,1–12 im Lichte der Zenonpapyri und der rabbinischen Gleichnisse," *ZNW* 59 (1968) 1–39.

Hubaut, M., "La parabole des vignerons homicides: son authenticité, sa visée première," *RTL* 6 (1975) 51–61.

———, *La parabole des vignerons homicides*, Cahiers *RB* 16, Paris, 1976.

———, "Jesus et la Loi de Moïse," *RTL* 7 (1976) 401–25.

Hübner, H., "Mark VII.1–23 und das 'jüdisch hellenistische' Gesetzesverständnis," *NTS* 22 (1975–1976) 319–45.

Jane, E. and R. E. Newell, "The Parable of the Wicked Tenants," *NovT* 14 (1972) 226–37.

Klauck, H. J., "Das Gleichnis vom Mord im Weinberg (Mk 12,1–12; Mt 21,33–46; Lk 20,9–19)," *BibLeb* 11 (1970) 118–45.

Kümmel, W. G., "Äussere und innere Reinheit des Menschen bei Jesus," in *Das Wort und die Wörter. Festschrift G. Friedrich*, ed. H. Balz and S. Schulz, Stuttgart, 1973, pp. 35–46.

Lambrecht, J., *Die Redaktion der Markus–Apokalypse. Literarische Analyse und Strukturuntersuchung*, AnBib 28, Rome, 1967.

———, "Ware verwantschap en eeuwige zonde. Ontstaan en structuur van Mc 3,20–35," *Bijdragen* 29 (1968) 114–50, 234–58, 369–93; also in Lambrecht, *Marcus interpretator. Stijl en boodschap in Mc. 3,20–4,34*, Bruges–Utrecht, 1969, pp. 15–97, 131–33.

———, "Jesus and the Law. An Investigation of Mk 7,1–23," *ETL* 53 (1977) 24–82.

Léon-Dufour, X., "La parabole des vignerons homicides," *ScEccl* 17 (1965) 365–96; also in Léon-Dufour, *Etudes d'Evangile*, Paris, 1965, pp. 308–27.

Lövestam, E., "Le portier qui veille la nuit. Mc 13,33–37," *AssSeign II* (1969) no. 5, pp. 44–53.

McEleney, N. J., "Authenticating Criteria and Mk 7:1–23," *CBQ* 34 (1972) 431–60.

Merkel, H., "Markus 7,15—Das Jesuswort über die innere Verunreinigung," *ZRGG* 20 (1968) 340–68.

Paschen, W., *Rein und Unrein. Untersuchung zur biblischen Wortge-schichte*, StANT 24, Munich, 1970.

Pesch, R., *Naherwartungen. Tradition und Redaktion in Mk 13*, KuBANT, Düsseldorf, 1968.

———, "Pur et impur: précepte humain et commandement divin. Mc 7,1–8.14–15.21–23," *AssSeign II* (1970) no. 53, pp. 50–63.

Robinson, J. A. T., "The Parable of the Wicked Husbandmen: A Test of Synoptic Relationships," *NTS* 21 (1974–1975) 443–61.

Trilling, W., "Les vignerons homicides. Mt 21,33–43," *AssSeign II* (1974) no. 58, pp. 16–23.

von der Osten–Sacken, P., "Streitgespräche und Parabel als Formen mar-kinischer Christologie," in *Jesus Christus in Historie und Theologie. Neutestamentliche Festschrift für H. Conzelmann*, ed. G. Strecker, Tübingen, 1975, pp. 375–94.

Weiser, A., "Von der Predigt Jesu zur Erwartung der Parusie. Überlie-ferungsgeschichtliches zum Gleichnis vom Türhüter," *BibLeb* 12 (1971) 25–31.

Six

The Wise and Foolish Virgins

(Mt 25:1–13)

The last three chapters of this book are once again devoted to individual parables. The three parables treated are taken from Matthew's eschatological discourse (chaps. 24–25): the Wise and Foolish Virgins (Mt 25:1–13), the Talents (Mt 25:14–30), and the Last Judgment (Mt 25:31–46). Together these three parables form a continuous narrative which concludes Jesus' last discourse and which Matthew uses to bring the public ministry to an end. With the following chapter, Mt 26, the passion narrative begins.

Mt 24–25 is also called the Parousia discourse since in it Jesus announces his Parousia, his second coming. Each of the three parables in this discourse concerns Jesus' coming again. It is well-known that the critics have their reservations about the authenticity of such announcements of the Parousia. Did Jesus during his public life ever speak of his return as the glorified Son of man? This question is, for the most part, answered in the negative in modern exegesis. But then the problem of the authenticity of the Parousia parables also arises and this raises a further question: Even if these parables do go back to Jesus, what was their original meaning?

Related to the doubts concerning the authenticity of the Parousia announcement is the problem of the *Naherwartung*, i.e., the imminent expectation. The early Christians awaited Jesus' return soon within their own life time. Did their expectation of the Lord's imminent return have its roots in Jesus' own preaching? Did Jesus proclaim the coming of God's kingly rule in categories of temporal imminence? How did the primitive church react when the delay of the Parousia was experienced time and again? Do the evangelists witness to such an experience? In our discussion of three of the Parousia parables we shall be confronted with these and similar questions.

This chapter contains five sections. Matthew's eschatological discourse must be briefly discussed as a whole in order to situate the Wise and Foolish Virgins as well as the Talents and the Last Judgment in their wider context (I). In our analysis of the Ten Virgins the problems connected with this parable are first sketched (II). This in turn leads to an investigation of the relation between redaction and tradition within the parable (III). After this investigation, the question concerning the original meaning of the Wise and Foolish Virgins can then be posed (IV). Finally, in the last section the parable is considered in its allegorized form as it now lies before us in Matthew's gospel (V).

I. Matthew's Eschatological Discourse (Mt 24–25)

Mt 24–25 comprise the Matthean version of the eschatological discourse, or the "little apocalypse" as it is often called. This long text forms the last discourse in Matthew's gospel; it is the conclusion of Jesus' public life. Following it we read in 26:1–2: "When Jesus had finished all these sayings, he said to his disciples, 'You know that after two days the Passover is coming, and the Son of man will be delivered up to be crucified.' " Before his Passion begins, the earthly Jesus speaks for the last time and in a solemn way of the future of the disciples and of the nations until his return and the end of the world. Mt 24–25 is thus both a vision of the future and a testament.

Overview of the Content of Mt 24–25

The Matthean eschatological discourse could be considered an expansion of that of Mark. Matthew uses and even copies Mk 13 with the exception of its last five verses. After Mk 13:32 (cf. Mt 24:37), however, he continues writing about the Parousia with the aid of Q and his *Sondergut*. Besides that of Mark, Matthew must have known another apocalyptic discourse, which Luke has also preserved in a more extensive way in his seventeenth chapter.

Matthew, however, uses only a few fragments of this second discourse: 24:26–28 (claims of the false prophets concerning the whereabouts of the Messiah, sayings about the Messiah's return like lightning, and his manifest coming) and 24:37–41 (comparison with Noah's time; the image of the two men in the field and the two women grinding at the mill). Furthermore, at the end of chap. 24 and within chap. 25 Matthew inserts three Parousia parables (the Burglar at Night, the Faithful or Wicked Servant, and the Talents), which also appear in Lk and which are thus likewise Q-material. Finally in chap. 25 there is the parable of the Ten Virgins and the pericope of the Last Judgment, both from Matthew's *Sondergut*.

We may accept that at the point where Matthew leaves his Marcan source (i.e., after Mk 13:32 = Mt 24:37), a new section of the discourse begins. But if only Matthew's sources are considered, the actual structure and line of thought of this discourse cannot be grasped. It is equally inadvisable in attempting to discern the structure of the discourse to divide it according to the literary forms employed, with sayings in the first half and parables in the second, or (more formally) information first and then exhortation. Rather, information and exhortation are interwoven, and in the first half there are also parables (see 24:27, 28), just as there are sayings and direct address in the second (see 24:42, 44; 25:13).

It seems that the whole of Mt 24–25 can best be divided into three large sections: (A) 24:4–35; (B) 24:36–25:30; and (C) 25:31–46. The *first part* supplies information concerning the end-time (and what can be considered a sign of it); it also foretells persecution, false prophecies, apostasy; it exhorts the disciples to fidelity and perseverance; it emphasizes the proximity and certainty of the Lord's coming. In the *second part* no actually new information is given. It is only said emphatically and, with or without illustrations, repeated again and again that this coming will be sudden, or better, unexpected, whence comes the summons to vigilance and responsible life, to an existence that faithfully fulfills the entrusted task. The exhortations use the motive of judgment, the prospect of reward or punishment according to conduct and achievements. The *third part* develops this judgment idea in a very graphic scene, a universal final happening that is dominated and led by the Lord. There is no longer any explicit exhortation; the disciples are not further appealed to or admonished. Here again, as in the first part, there is information. It is as if 25:31–32 ("When the Son of man comes in his glory, and all the angels with him, then he will sit on his glorious throne. Before him will be gathered all the nations . . . .") leads us back to 24:30–31 ("Then will appear the sign of the Son of man in heaven, and then all the tribes of the earth will mourn, and they will see the Son of man coming on the clouds of heaven with power and great glory; and he will send out his angels. . . ."). Here we find the same apocalyptic style, the same figurative language, and the same judgment theme.

Matthew thus begins by giving information about the course of history to the Parousia and the end of the world; for this part he follows his Marcan source very closely. He then depicts Jesus urging his disciples to be ready for his unexpected return; here he mainly uses parables from Q. Matthew concludes the discourse with a description of the universal judgment at the Parousia. He is the only evangelist to give such a description. The following plan shows how these three parts may be further subdivided:

Division and Overview
Introduction (24:1–4a)
A. 24:4b–35: *The Phases of the Future*
  1. *Not Yet the End* (vv. 4b–14)
     4b–5: false Christs, danger of being led astray
     6–8: wars, natural disasters, danger of disturbance
     9: persecution by all the nations
     10–13: internal divisions, false prophets, love growing cold, need of perseverance
     14: proclamation of the gospel before the end
  2. *The Great Persecution* (vv. 15–28)
     a) 15: the abomination of desolation
        16–22: the great persecution in Judea
     b) 23–26: false prophets try to mislead
        27–28: the manifest Parousia
  3. *The Parousia Itself* (vv. 29–31)
     29a: the exact time
     29b: concomitant natural phenomena
     30a: appearance of the Son of man
     30b: reaction of all the tribes of the earth

31a: sending out of the angels
31b: gathering of the elect
   4. *The Moment and Its Certainty* (vv. 32–35)
     a) 32–33: parable of the Fig Tree
     b) 34–35: all this is sure to take place
B. 24:36–25:30: *Exhortation to Vigilance*
   1. *Time of the Parousia Unknown* (24:36–44)
     36: neither the day nor the hour
     37–39: comparison with Noah
     40–41: two in the field, two grinding corn
     42: "Watch therefore, for . . ."
     43: the master of the house and the burglar
     44: "Be ready, for . . ."
   2. *Parable of the Faithful or Wicked Servent* (24:45–51)
     51b: weeping and gnashing of teeth
   3. *Parable of the Wise and Foolish Virgins* (25:1–13)
     13: "Watch therefore, for . . ."
   4. *Parable of the Talents* (25.14–30)
     30b: weeping and gnashing of teeth
C. 25:31–46: *The Last Judgment*

Exhortation to Vigilance

At the beginning of the second part, or as a transition from the first to the second, is found the controversial v. 24:36: "But of that day and hour no one knows, not even the angels of heaven, nor the Son. . . ." The Son does not know the moment of his own return! That the time of the, nonetheless, imminent return is not known could hardly be more strongly emphasized. Note that for Matthew this statement becomes the starting point for an extended exhortation. Because the time of the Parousia is at once unknown and imminent, i.e., it will take place within a short time, the only appropriate attitude is one of vigilance. This second part, which extends to 25:30 is one long exhortation, a parenesis. Expressions like "Watch therefore, for you do not know on what day your Lord is coming" (24:42; cf. also 24:44) and "Watch therefore, for you know neither the day nor the hour" (25:13) recur like a refrain. The comparisons and the parables all serve this pastoral plea for vigilance.

It seems best to divide this second unit into four paragraphs. All agree that the three parables, the Talents (par. 4), the Wise and Foolish Virgins (par. 3), and the Faithful or Wicked Servant (par. 2), are well-delimited and, as such, each forms a rather independent unit. The first paragraph on the other hand is composite, compiled from elements and fragments of diverse origin. A real parable is not found here. Rather, there are motivating comparisons (e.g., the days of Noah, the master of the house, the burglar). It is a figurative announcement of the unexpected coming which will strike the unprepared in a catastrophic way.

Watching and Working

On closer inspection, it is possible to pair off the four paragraphs mentioned above: 1 corresponds with 3, and 2 with 4. The first paragraph and the parable of the Wise and Foolish Virgins both deal with the unknown, unexpected time of the return. Both end with an appeal in the second person: "Watch therefore, for you do not know on what day your Lord is coming" (24:42) and "Watch therefore, for you know neither the day nor the hour" (25:13) (compare 24:44: "Therefore you must also be ready; for the Son of man is coming at an hour you do not expect"). In both we also meet the themes of vigilance (cf. 24:42, 43 and 25:13) and readiness (cf. 24:44 and 25:10). The second and fourth paragraphs also have much in common. Both are parables in which servants are given a task to fulfill during the absence of their master. On his return the master rewards or punishes the servants according to their conduct. In each case the reward consists in promotion to a more responsible position and a greater share in the master's authority. The punishment involves banishment to a dark place where there is weeping and gnashing of teeth.

It is clear that the second and fourth paragraphs respectively further define the first and third. They indicate what vigilance consists of. "Watching" is active, diligent, and responsible service. Thus, all four paragraphs ultimately teach the same lesson.

Conclusion

At the conclusion of these brief remarks concerning the structure of the Matthean eschatological discourse, and more particularly its second part, three observations regarding Matthew's intention can be added:

(a) Matthew obviously intends, through the figures of the disciples whom Jesus addresses, to exhort the Christians of his own time to vigilance and readiness which, as the explanation of the two parables about "servants" leads us to understand, implies an active and faithful service, a conscientious stewardship of the goods or talents with which one has been entrusted. This concern is typical for Matthew.

(b) One of the striking features of the second part of the discourse is that the theme of judgment comes to the fore in all four of its pericopes. The returning master will ask for an accounting; he will pass judgment. He will reward beyond all expectation, but will also punish in a frightening way. This motive of judgment gives an extremely serious and urgent character to Matthew's appeal for vigilance. Eschatological motivation and the idea of judgment are also favorite Matthean themes.

(c) The third observation concerns a difficulty of interpretation. Several exegetes give special attention to 24:48, "My master is delayed," and also to the remark in 25:19 that the master returns "after a long time." In their view, these temporal references, as well as other details of these parables, reflect the situation of the early Christians who had become conscious of the long delay of the Parousia. With the slackening of their initially intense expectation of Jesus' imminent coming the danger of a loss of zeal and fervor arose. Certain of these authors therefore conclude that it was no longer the proximity of the second coming but rather its unexpected, unforeseeable character which had become the real motive of Christian parenesis. In response to the above position, it may be said that all the time references in these parables may originally have functioned as unstressed, nonallegorical elements in the figurative part. It is further possible that Matthew subsequently (and perhaps also his source) understood them as pointing to the delay of the Parousia and thus saw them as more or less independent individual elements dealing in an allegorical way with the problem of the imminence of the second coming. Nevertheless, it does seem to us that in Matthew's conception the notions "imminent" and "unexpected" still belong together, and it would be unnatural to separate them.

In the light of the foregoing, we can now proceed to a detailed analysis of the parable of the Wise and Foolish Virgins.

II. Uncertainties and Disturbing Elements in Mt 25:1–13

1 "Then the Kingdom of heaven shall be compared to ten maidens who took their lamps and went to meet the bridegroom.

2 Five of them were foolish, and five were wise.

3 For when the foolish took their lamps, they took no oil with them;

4 but the wise took flasks of oil with their lamps.

5 As the bridegroom was delayed, they all slumbered and slept.

6 But at midnight there was a cry, 'Behold, the bridegroom! Come out to meet him.'

7 Then all those maidens rose and trimmed their lamps.

8 And the foolish said to the wise, 'Give us some of your oil, for our lamps are going out.'

9 But the wise replied, 'Perhaps there will not be enough for us and for you; go rather to the dealers and buy for yourselves.'

10 And while they went to buy, the bridegroom came, and those who were ready went in with him to the marriage feast; and the door was shut.

11 Afterward the other maidens came also, saying, 'Lord, lord, open to us.'

12 But he replied, 'Truly, I say to you, I do not know you.'

13 Watch therefore, for you know neither the day nor the hour."

The various problems concerning this parable can be placed under four headings. There is uncertainty with regard to Matthew's source. The translation of certain terms or expressions is debatable. On a first reading of the text one is confronted with some disturbing elements. And, the investigation is rendered more difficult by the lack of agreement which prevails in scholarly circles as to the parable's authenticity and, for those authors who admit a pre–Matthean form of the parable, as to the meaning of that form.

Matthew's Sondergut

In our survey of the parables (pp. 18–20), the Wise and Foolish Virgins (Mt 25:1–13) were listed under Matthew's *Sondergut*. Verses 11 and 12 of the parable, however, do have a parallel in Lk 13:25: "When once the householder has risen up and shut the door, you will begin to stand outside and knock at the door, saying, 'Lord, open to us.' He will answer you, 'I do not know where you come from.' " With respect to this Lucan parallel it must be asked: Is Lk 13:25 the displaced conclusion of the Matthean parable? Or is the parable presented by Matthew later than the short dialogue of Lk 13:25 (= Mt 25:11–12) and thus a secondary preface to it?

On the first supposition, Luke (or his source) would have known the parable of the Ten Virgins which would then have to be considered as Q-material. On the other hand, if the second alternative is correct, the pericope would still contain some Q-elements. Thus, in either case, if the designation "Matthean *Sondergut*" is to be retained for this parable, it must be nuanced.

The Translation

The RSV translation of v. 1, "Then the kingdom of heaven shall be compared to ten maidens . . ." is definitely too literal and misses the real point of the following parable. J. Dupont, among others, in a short study on the introductory formulas in the parables has shown that it is not completely correct to say in the parable of the Guests Invited to the Feast and also in the Wise and Foolish Virgins that the kingdom is like a king who gives a marriage feast for his son (Mt 22:2) or like the ten virgins who go to meet the bridegroom (Mt 25:1). It is rather the feast itself which represents the kingdom. Moreover, because both parables describe the behavior of those excluded from the banquet room, they are ultimately intended as a warning against an attitude which would lead to being banished from the kingdom.

A further remark can be made concerning Mt 25:1. The particle "then" can be related to the "then" in 25:31: "When the Son of man comes in his glory, and all the angels with him, *then* he will sit on his glorious throne." *Then* it will be with Christians, with us, as it was with the virgins at the coming of the bridegroom. The "then" in 25:1 thus refers to the time of the Parousia and the manifestation of the kingdom on the last day.

Some modern translations prefer to speak of "girls" or "bridesmaids," five of whom are "stupid" and five "clever" or "prudent" or "sensible." The traditional rendering was "foolish" and "wise" virgins. One can indeed hesitate as to the translation of *parthenoi* (literally: virgins, but not necessarily always in the strictly biological sense). On the other hand, the Greek adjectives *mōros* and *phronimos* in this context have little or nothing to do with intellectual ability, with stupidity or cleverness. They refer rather to being open or closed with respect to the right, existential, moral-religious attitude. The traditional "foolish" and "wise" seem therefore to render this meaning more adequately.

Disturbing Elements

Commentators call attention to a number of disturbing features in Mt 25:1–13:

(1) What can the girls do in the open air with their small oil lamps made of baked clay? Why, too, does the question of lighting receive such emphasis in the parable?

(2) Verse 1 says that the ten girls set out to meet the bridegroom. But where do they go? Do they stop on the way? Do they stop, rest, and fall asleep somewhere on the street, or at the city gate? And how can we imagine such a scene in the middle of the night when we take into account the strict morality of the East in the matter of feminine conduct?

(3) Normally one would think that the burning lamps would be turned down during the wait. But the neck gets dirty; the lamp has to be cleaned and trimmed (v. 7). The girls have to add more oil which they have brought with them in flasks. Why these flasks and why so much oil?

(4) The heartless refusal of the wise virgins is not in accordance with Christ's command of love of neighbor. It betrays a lack of human sympathy and social solidarity. Weren't all these girls friends?

(5) Can we really suppose that the dealers' shops would have remained open all night? After all, the incident does not take place in a big modern city.

(6) Specialists in Palestinian customs believe that at the time of Jesus men and women participated at wedding banquets in separate rooms. What then are the girls doing who accompany the bridegroom inside to celebrate the wedding?

(7) The angry bridegroom is solemnly addressed as "Lord, Lord." But was he not the girls' familiar friend and neighbor? Furthermore, his extremely severe and harsh reply, "Truly, I say to you, I do not want to know you any longer" (a possible translation

of the Greek expression *ouk oida humas*) seems out of all proportion to the negligence of the foolish virgins. His reply even becomes offensive in a certain sense if we take into account that the bridegroom himself, through his long delay, was in part responsible for their predicament.

(8) Is it not somewhat strange that the parable does not say a single word about the bride?

The accumulation of obscure details of this sort and the less than sympathetic, not to say heartless, behavior of the honored central figure have given rise to the question of whether it would not be better to drop this pericope from the church's lectionary. Is it still possible to save this Scripture passage for a modern critical audience? What can be done with it in catechetics and preaching?

Two Recent Positions

The two main positions held today regarding the literary form and authenticity of this parable are yet to be mentioned.

(a) Many exegetes, e.g., G. Bornkamm, contend that from the beginning Mt 25:1–13 was an allegory with which the early church answered questions arising from the experience of the delay of the Parousia. The parable would have contradicted the Jewish customs of the time because it was not the bridegroom but the bride who was escorted to the feast. Neither the delay of the bridegroom nor the late beginning of the feast are readily imaginable. But such "unnatural" features, it is said, would function very well within an allegory. The bridegroom is Jesus, the returning judge of the world, whose Parousia did not come as quickly as had initially been expected and whose delay had caused a kind of crisis in the early church. The allegory states that it is necessary for Christians to adapt to a longer period before the end. It is not sufficient to have lamps; one also has to keep a supply of oil on hand.

In this conception, Mt. 25:1–13 does not go back to Jesus himself. Rather, the text came into existence after Easter and was seen as an allegory from the start. This allegory of the Ten Virgins would represent the expansion of a figure of speech about the closed door (cf. Lk 13:25) which already existed in the tradition. The dominant intention of this new composition was to exhort Christians not to grow cold and dejected because time went on and the Lord's return was delayed. From the very beginning Mt

25:1–13 was thus a Parousia allegory. As such it originated in the Christian community which was conscious of the delay of the Parousia. Is Matthew the author of this allegory (as e.g., was recently proposed by K. Donfried) or was it a Christian writer before him?

(b) J. Jeremias is of the opinion that in Mt 25:1–13 an authentic parable of Jesus lies concealed, overlaid with a secondary allegorizing stratum. Jeremias tries to disengage this old parable from the present Matthean text and to recover the original meaning of that reconstructed parable.

It is above all the disturbing elements in the story and the lack of agreement in the conclusions of contemporary exegetes which urge us to an investigation of this text. At the outset we cannot avoid the impression that Matthew has integrated an already existing parable into his eschatological discourse. Will this initial impression prove itself correct in the following analysis?

III. Tradition and Redaction

The tension between the framework verses and the parable narrative itself seems to indicate that tradition and redaction must be distinguished here. Moreover, it can be demonstrated that many of the so-called disturbing features do, on the contrary, fit rather well with what is known about Palestinian customs of the time. These details, therefore, need not be allegorically intended and could very well belong to an old traditional parable.

Two Discrepancies

(a) The introductory Matthean particle "then" in 25:1 situates the parable in the context of the Parousia discourse. Verses 11–12 likewise clearly allude to Jesus' coming again: cf. "Lord, Lord" and the bridegroom's answer with its severe judgment, "Truly, I say to you, I do not know you." On the other hand, the parable itself has to do with the kingdom of heaven, as is explicitly stated in v. 1, and this is not exactly the same as the return of the Son of man.

(b) "Watch therefore, for you know neither the day nor the hour" (25:13) is Matthew's redactional refrain (cf. 24:42). But in the parable itself the emphasis is not on vigilance since all the girls, including the five wise ones, sleep. The stress is rather on "being ready" (cf. v. 10).

In consideration of these tensions between framework and narrative, it must be concluded that the redactor Matthew used an older traditional text here. This source-text was apparently a kingdom of God parable which was intended as an illustration of the motif of being ready.

A Palestinian Wedding Feast

In Jeremias's view there would be no unreal or unnatural features in the original parable. On the contrary, typical Palestinian wedding customs can be pointed out in it. His most important findings in this respect, listed according to the order of the verses of the parable, are the following:

Verse 1: Who . . . went out to meet. In the parable of the Guests Invited to the Feast (Mt 22:2–14), the narrative proper starts only with v. 3, "He sent his servants . . ." whereas v. 2 stands at the head of the narrative as a title or announcement of the theme: The kingdom of heaven may be compared to a marriage feast which a king gave for his son. We find a similar presentation in our parable. Verse 1 is a sort of title; the girls have not set out; they do so only after hearing that the bridegroom is coming (cf. v. 6). The *lamps* are not small clay oil lamps for use inside the house, nor lanterns for lighting, but torches. One has to think here of long sticks or rods at the end of which a big rag is wrapped which is soaked in olive oil prior to being lit. The bridesmaids carry these flaming torches in solemn procession to the house where the marriage feast is to take place. On arrival they perform various round dances until their torches burn out.

Verse 4: Flasks of oil. The large quantity of oil carried by the girls is thus not needed to fill the small lamps, but because a torch of this sort must be soaked repeatedly—otherwise it would burn only about a quarter of an hour. Jeremias notes that, with this background in mind, the negligence of the foolish virgins can no longer be regarded as a casual lack of foresight which could hardly be held against them in view of the unexpectedly long delay of the bridegroom. No, it is an incomprehensible, inexcusable fickleness and carelessness.

Verse 5: As the bridegroom was delayed. "After hours of waiting for the bridegroom, whose coming was repeatedly announced by messengers, at last he came, half an hour before midnight, to fetch the bride; he was accompanied by his friends, floodlit by burning candles, and received by the guests who had come out to meet him. The wedding assembly then moved off, again in a flood of light, in festal procession to the house of the bridegroom's father, where the marriage ceremony and fresh entertainment took place. Both the reception of the bridegroom with lights and the hour-long waiting for the bridegroom's arrival are frequently mentioned in modern reports of Arab weddings in Palestine. Even today the usual reason for delay is that agreement cannot be reached about the presents due to the relatives of the bride. To neglect this often lively bargaining might be taken to imply an insufficient regard for the relatives of the bride; on the other hand, it must be interpreted as a compliment to the bridegroom if his future relations show in this way that they give away the bride only with the greatest reluctance" (Jeremias, *The Parables of Jesus,* pp. 173–74).

They all slumbered and slept. The girls have not yet set out but are waiting together. Where? Most probably at the bride's house where they assist and adorn the bride. An atmosphere of anticipated festive joy prevails. The bridegroom (and his friends) will come to the house to fetch the bride and lead her, accompanied by the bridesmaids, to his father's house. Thus there is no need to think of the girls stopping along the way.

Verse 7: They trimmed their lamps. There is, then, no question of lamps which had been turned down, whose blackened necks had to be cleaned, but rather of torches that had not yet been lit. These torches would not be used for illumination, at least not primarily; they are processional torches. Upon arrival at the house the bridesmaids and the young men would start a dance with the flaming torches.

Verse 8: Our lamps are going out. That is: our torches will go out at once. Unless they are soaked in oil, they will not last long, certainly not long enough to finish the dance.

Verse 10: They went in with him to the marriage feast. It would be wrong to understand this statement as affirming that the girls would sit at the table with the men. Rather, the girls and the young men, along with the bridegroom and the bride, enter the inner courtyard of the house where the dance is performed until their torches burn out. Then the women leave the men to themselves and retire to another room.

Verse 12: I do not know you. This seems to be a formula employed by the rabbis with which, among other things, a teacher would exclude a pupil from his company for a certain time. It should thus be understood; "(Tonight, or, for a certain time) I will have nothing to do with you."

In connection with Jeremias's attempted explanation, it is of interest to refer to the recent note of A. W. Argyle (1975) in which he retracts what he had written in his earlier commentary on Matthew (1963) concerning the improbability of certain features in this parable. In this note he now stresses the normal character of the feast after sunset and of the torchlight procession (with singing) from the house of the bride to that of her in-laws and from there to the house of the bridegroom. Argyle refers to such Old Testament texts as Cant 3:6–11; Jer 7:34; 16:9 and 25:10: "I will banish from them the voice of mirth and the voice of gladness, the voice of the bridegroom and the voice of the bride, the grinding of the millstones and the light of the lamp" (cf. also Jer 33:11). On such occasions it is not improbable that some shops would remain open. Therefore, the advice of the wise virgins to the foolish ones would not have sounded strange or offensive to those hearing the story.

The Pre–Matthean Kingdom of God Parable

Even if all the details of the above reconstruction are not equally certain, it is no longer legitimate on the basis of the so-called puzzling or disturbing elements to consider Mt 25:1–13 as an artificial, late allegory created by a Christian writer. On the other hand, we need not suppose the original narrative to have been as devoid of allegorical elements as Jeremias is inclined to think. In fact, it is quite possible that the part concerning the "reality" already makes itself felt in the "figurative" part of the parable. So, e.g., the figure of the bridegroom, whether or not he was already addressed as "Lord" in the original version as is now the case in v. 11, was probably always intended as a metaphor.

In any event, the reconstruction confirms what the two above-mentioned discrepancies had led us to suppose, i.e., that a pre–Matthean parable can be discerned in Mt 25:1–13. If we remove the particle "then" in v. 1 and the entire v. 13, "Watch therefore, for you know neither the day nor the hour," what remains is a kingdom of God parable. What was the original meaning of this parable? Does it go back to Jesus?

IV. Jesus' Original Parable

Besides the addition of the particle "then," Matthew probably also rewrote the opening words of the parable in v. 1a. There is, however, no reason to suppose that the content of the expression "the kingdom of heaven shall be compared to . . ." in v. 1a is secondary. Moreover, the fact that Matthew is thinking concretely in chaps. 24–25 about the return of the Son of man which results in a certain tension between the manifestation of the kingdom of God (v. 1a) and the Parousia (= return of the Bridegroom, vv. 1b–13) strengthens the supposition that the pre–Matthean parable also began with a comparative introductory clause. Mt 25:1–12 was therefore originally a parable of the kingdom of God. We are dealing here with an imaginary story which, notwithstanding the introductory comparison which gives a direction to the whole, and the possible presence of a few metaphors, must be called a parable in the strict sense.

Jesus' Own Narrative?

If, in light of the foregoing, it is now assumed that a pre–Matthean parable of the Ten Virgins did exist, this does not *ipso facto* prove the authenticity of that parable. The parable could have been created after Easter at one or another stage in the development of the primitive church. The fact that Luke has preserved the final dialogue in 13:25 seems to indicate that he too (or the tradition prior to him) knew this parable—hence our hesitation in classifying Mt 25:1–13 as *Sondergut*. The parable is thus, in any case, not a late creation. Moreover, the possibility of understanding the narrative against the background of Judaeo–Palestinian customs strongly suggests its Palestinian origin. If it can be further demonstrated that the meaning and the message of the parable are in accord with what we know of Jesus' preaching, then it seems no longer legitimate to doubt the authenticity of the narrative.

Gift and Task

In trying to determine the original meaning of the parable of the Wise and Foolish Virgins the Parousia context of Mt 24–25 cannot be used because, as we have seen, the Ten Virgins was initially a kingdom of God parable. The bridegroom in the original story was not Jesus but God. In the Old Testament, this bridegroom metaphor is used several times with reference to God: "As a young man marries a virgin, so shall your sons marry you (or more probably: so He who builds you up will marry you; cf. Ps 147:2), and as the bridegroom rejoices over the bride, so shall your God rejoice over you" (Is 62:5). In our parable, however, the metaphor is not used in connection with the notion of the covenant which in the Old Testament is several times compared to a betrothal or marriage.

According to Jeremias, Jesus would have told the Ten Virgins as a *Krisisgleichnis*, a crisis parable: "The sudden coming of the bridegroom (v. 6) has its parallels in the sudden downpour of the Flood, in the unexpected entry of the thief, or the unlooked for return of the master of the house from the feast or the journey. The common element of suddenness is a figure of the unexpected incidence of catastrophe. The crisis is at the door. It will come as unexpectedly as the midnight cry in the parable, 'Behold the bridegroom cometh!' And it brings the inexorable severance, even where mortal eyes see no distinction (cf. Mt 24:40–41; Lk 17:34–35) Woe to those whom that hour finds unprepared! Hence it was as a cry of warning in view of the imminent eschatological crisis that Jesus uttered the parable, and as such the crowd understood it" (*Parables of Jesus*, p. 53). Elsewhere Jeremias writes in the same vein. For him the Ten Virgins is one of the crisis parables. It is intended as a warning against the fate of the foolish virgins. The emphasis lies on this warning. Why were the foolish virgins excluded? The answer is the same as in the sayings about Noah's contemporaries (Mt 24:37–39 = Lk 17:26–27) or those of Lot (Lk 17:28–30), the same also that is given to the man without a wedding garment (Mt 22:11–13). All these people have, with an incomprehensible carelessness and superficiality, neglected to prepare themselves for what was at hand, even in spite of the urgency of the hour.

Against this interpretation I. Maisch has rightly remarked that a marriage feast is not the most appropriate image for an approaching catastrophe and that in v. 6 there is, strictly speaking, no mention of a "sudden" coming. In the Ten Virgins the kingdom of God, God's kingly rule, is compared to a marriage feast, i.e., the time of salvation. God gives his dominion. People must be ready, prepared to receive it. Those who are found unprepared are excluded. God's coming means salvation for the righteous and disaster for the wicked. The parable speaks of that which Jesus also proclaimed on other occasions: God will soon establish his dominion over all people. We must be prepared to receive it.

With this intention, Jesus addressed the parable of the Ten Virgins to his audience. The narrative fits their familiar life and customs. Nevertheless, it does contain a few puzzling features which arouse attention. What is he saying? What is he getting at? The hearers are somewhat irritated, but also stimulated to further reflection. They enter into the story and know that they themselves are involved. They take part in it, they live it even before they fully realize what it is all about. When the meaning of the parable becomes clear to them, they not only grasp the point but are faced with a decision of existential significance. Through such parables Jesus confronted his hearers with a fundamental choice. What he called them to was nothing less than a conversion, an orientation of their lives towards God's new future for man, a future which is overwhelmingly full of happiness but also extremely serious. Man can, through his own fault, miss out on this future; it is possible to run away from the kingdom and ultimately to lose it.

V. Matthew's Allegorizing

After Easter the primitive church not only preserved and handed on this parable, but also actualized it. We possess the parable in Matthew's version. This leads us to ask what the evangelist has done with Jesus' original parable.

The Matthean Redaction

Matthew had the kingdom of God parable of the Wise and Foolish Virgins in his traditional material. He probably rewrote this narrative to an extent and presented it in his own words and style. A comparison with Lk 13:25 suggests that Matthew duplicated the appeal "Lord" in v. 11 (perhaps on the basis of Q; cf. Mt 7:21 = Lk 6:46: "Not every one who says to me 'Lord, Lord,' shall enter the kingdom of heaven"), and possibly also inserted the expression "Truly, I say to you" in v. 12.

More important is the new context which Matthew gives to the parable. The particle "then" with which the parable now begins undoubtedly stems from him. With this temporal adverb Matthew refers to the Parousia: "Then will appear the sign of the Son of man in heaven" (Mt 24:30); "When the Son of man comes in his glory, and all the angels with him, *then* he will sit on his glorious throne" (Mt 25:31; cf. the Parousia motif in 24:36–44, 45–51; 25:14–30). The concluding v. 13, "Watch therefore, for you know neither the day nor the hour," was also added by Matthew.

By means of these literary interventions, Matthew integrated the original parable of the Ten Virgins into the larger whole of his Parousia discourse. In this process the narrative lost something of its independent character. It now functions within Jesus' last major discourse as that was conceived, structured, and edited by Matthew.

From Parable to Allegory and Parenesis

Four shifts of content resulting from the Matthean reworking can be indicated: (1) For Matthew and his church the bridegroom is no longer God, but Jesus (cf. also 9:15), represented here as the Judge of the last days. In postpaschal preaching, to the expectation of God's kingdom was added that of the Son of man who is to come back. (2) The expression of v. 5, "as the bridegroom was delayed" was, in this new interpretation, most probably seen as an allusion to the delay of the Parousia of the Son of man. (3) This delay entailed certain dangers and therefore the implicit warning of the original parable to be prepared was changed into an explicit summons to vigilance; cf. v. 13. Even if the Lord tarries, we must remain prepared and be watchful. (4) The original parable was most probably addressed by Jesus to the crowd, to all those who happened to be present, without distinction. In the context of the Matthean gospel the hearers become the disciples who, in Matthew's view, represent the Christians of his time. The allegorized parable was thus used as an exhortation within the church.

To Do the Will of the Father in Heaven

With the mention of these various shifts of meaning, all is still not said. Within the second part of the Parousia discourse (Mt 24:36–25:30), the motif of vigilance is emphasized in the first (24:36–44) and third (the Ten Virgins) pericopes: cf. 24:42–44 and 25:13. The second (the Faithful or Wicked Servant) and the fourth (the Talents) pericopes more precisely define the first and third respectively by showing, through their images, that vigilance has to be understood as active, diligent service.

For Matthew the oil mentioned in the Ten Virgins undoubtedly refers to good works. The principle according to which the separation will take place at the Parousia is whether or not one has "oil," i.e., good works. Matthew wants his fellow Christians to become "wise virgins" by fulfilling the will of the Father in heaven.

At the end of the Sermon on the Mount, Matthew's first major discourse, there are two passages concerning the judgment at the Parousia which are very reminiscent of the parable of the Ten Virgins:

> Not every one who says to me, "Lord, Lord," shall enter the kingdom of heaven, but he who does the will of my Father who is in heaven. On that day many will say to me, "Lord, Lord, did we not prophesy in your name, and cast out demons in your name, and do many mighty works in your name?" And then will I declare to them, "I never knew you; depart from me, you evildoers." (7:21–23)

> Every one then who hears these words of mine and does them will be like a wise man who built his house upon the rock; and the rain fell, and the floods came, and the winds blew and beat upon that house, but it did not fall, because it had been founded on the rock. And every one who hears these words of mine and does not do them will be like a foolish man who built his house upon the sands; and the rain fell, and the floods came, and the winds blew and beat against that house, and it fell; and great was the fall of it. (7:24–27)

At the end of the liturgy of baptism the celebrant gives a lighted candle to the newly baptized (or to the parents or godparents who act on his behalf). He clearly reminds him of the parable of the Wise and Foolish Virgins when he exhorts him with the following prayer: "*Accipe lampadem ardentem, et irreprehensibilis custodi Baptismum tuum. . . .*" In a modern version:

> Parents and godparents, this light (i.e. of the child's candle, the torch of the parable) is entrusted to you to be kept burning brightly. This child of yours has been enlightened by Christ. He is to walk always as a child of the light. May he keep the flame of faith alive in his heart. When the Lord comes, may he go out to meet him with all the saints in the heavenly kingdom.

BIBLIOGRAPHY

Argyle, A. W., "Wedding Customs at the Time of Jesus," *ExpT* 86 (1974–1975) 214–15.

Bornkamm, G., "Die Verzögerung der Parusie. Exegetische Bemerkungen zu zwei synoptischen Texten," in Bornkamm, *Geschichte und Glaube* I. *Gesammelte Aufsätze*, Band III, BEvT 48, Munich, 1968, pp. 46–55.

Deiss, L., "La parabole des dix vierges. Mt 25,1–13," *AssSeign II* (1971) no. 63, pp. 20–32.

Donfried, K. P., "The Allegory of the Ten Virgins (Matt 25:1–13) as a Summary of Matthean Theology," *JBL* 93 (1974) 415–28.

Dupont, J., "Le royaume des cieux est semblable à. . . ," *Bibbia e Oriente* 6 (1964) 247–53.

Feuillet, A., "La parabole des vierges, Mt 25,1–13," *La Vie spirituelle* (1946) no. 75, pp. 667–77.

Gnilka, J., *Jesus Christus nach frühen Zeugnissen des Glaubens*, Biblische Handbibliothek 8, Munich, 1970, pp. 131–36.

Grässer, E., *Das Problem der Parusieverzögerung in den synoptischen Evangelien und in der Apostelgeschichte*, Beihefte zur ZNW 22, 2nd ed., Berlin, 1960 (especially pp. 91–92, 119–25).

Hoffmann, P., "*Pantes ergatai adikias.* Redaktion und Tradition in Lc 13,22–30," *ZNW* 58 (1967) 118–214.

Jeremias, J., "Lampades," *ZNW* 56 (1965) 196–201.

Lambrecht, J., "The Parousia Discourse. Composition and Content in Mt., XXIV–XXV," in *L'Évangile selon Matthieu. Rédaction et théologie*, BETL 29, ed. M. Didier, Gembloux, 1972, pp. 309–42.

Maisch, I., "Das Gleichnis von den klugen und törichten Jungfrauen. Auslegung von Mt 25,1–13," *BibLeb* 11 (1970) 247–59.

Massingberd Ford, J., "The Parable of the Foolish Scholars (Mt 25,1–13)," *NovT* 9 (1967) 107–23.

Meinertz, M., "Die Tragweite des Gleichnisses von den zehn Jungfrauen," in *Synoptische Studien. A. Wikenhauser dargebracht*, Munich, 1954, pp. 94–106.

Schenk, W., "Auferweckung der Toten oder Gericht nach den Werken. Tradition und Redaktion in Matthäus xxv 1–13," *NovT* 20 (1978) 278–99.

Strobel, A., "Zum Verständnis von Mt 25,1–13," *NovT* 2 (1958) 199–227.

———, *Untersuchungen zum eschatologischen Verzögerungsproblem auf Grund der spätjüdischen Geschichte von Habakuk 2,2ff.*, NovTSup 2, Leiden–Cologne, 1961, pp. 233–54.

Zorell, F., "De lampadibus decem virginum," *Verbum Domini* 10 (1930) 176–82.

Zumstein, J., *La condition du croyant dans l'évangile selon Matthieu*, Orbis biblicus et orientalis 16, Fribourg–Göttingen, 1977, pp. 271–81.

Seven

The Talents and the Pounds
(Mt 25:14–30 and Lk 19:11–27)

In the preceding chapter we dealt with the position and function of the parable of the Talents in the second part of the Matthean Parousia discourse (see pp. 150–51). The present chapter is devoted entirely to this parable which is often used in preaching and catechesis. It speaks of eternal reward and punishment and urges Christians to make the most of the talents which have been given them. At the last judgment they will be asked to give an account of their lives and actions. Two possible alternatives, heaven or hell, reward or punishment, must constantly be kept in mind. The parable of the Talents is thus very suitable as an exhortation, containing as it does both encouragement and warning.

Such an understanding is fully justified. Nevertheless, two features urge us to study this parable more closely. First, there is the fact that Luke in his parable of the Pounds (19:11–27) presents a parallel text, this being the reason why the Talents–Pounds were listed under the Q-material in our survey on p. 19. On the other hand, not only does Luke situate his parable in another context than does Matthew, but his version is also very different, in fact so different that many exegetes prefer not to speak of a Q-parable here. According to these scholars, the two evangelists would have found the parable in their respective *Sondergut*. In their view a long process of tradition separates the old common original text which is to be postulated and the two actual gospel versions. Moreover, the various differences between these versions cannot all be attributed to Matthew or Luke. Rather, their immediate sources were already divergent to a high degree.

In place of the simple schema:

$$\text{Jesus} \longrightarrow Q \underset{\longrightarrow\text{ Lk}}{\overset{\longrightarrow\text{ Mt}}{<}}$$

they propose a more complicated one:

$$\text{Jesus} \longrightarrow X \underset{\longrightarrow\text{ S(Lk)} \longrightarrow \text{Lk}}{\overset{\longrightarrow\text{ S(Mt)} \longrightarrow \text{Mt}}{<}}$$

in which X represents the common original version, and S(Mt) and S(Lk) the *Sondergut* or intermediary stage which these authors think it necessary to postulate. In a sense, the presence of a Lucan parallel to the Matthean Talents is to be welcomed because this makes comparison possible. On the other hand, the complicated presentation of the tradition process as schematized above can be intimidating. What is to be made of all this?

Also to be taken into account is the fact that those contemporary exegetes who regard this parable as authentic do not agree as to the meaning given to it by the earthly Jesus. Some think that Jesus used it to give a moralizing instruction concerning reward in accordance with one's works. Others are of the opinion that Jesus recounted the narrative to reproach his Jewish opponents, i.e., the religious authorities, Pharisees and scribes, for not having made their God-given talents (e.g., the Torah) bear fruit. Still others relate the parable directly to Jesus' preaching about the kingdom of God and to the challenge which it involved for all hearers. Keeping these two initial observations in mind, in this chapter we hope to gain a better insight into Jesus' intention in this parable and the adaptations of it made first by the early church and later by the evangelists Matthew and Luke.

Our analysis proceeds in five stages. First the Talents and the Pounds are compared with a view to reconstructing a sort of basic text which would have provided the starting point for the later divergent developments (I). It is then asked whether this basic text offers us the parable as it was spoken by the earthly Jesus or whether a pre- and a postpaschal version must be further distinguished. In the following two stages the earliest attainable interpretation of the primitive church (II) and Jesus' intention (III) are investigated. Thereafter attention is given to the specific characteristics of the Lucan (IV) and the Matthean (V) versions.

I. Comparison of the Talents and the Pounds
Mt 25   Lk 19

	11 As they heard these things, he proceeded to tell a parable, because he was near to Jerusalem, and because they supposed that the kingdom of God was to appear immediately. 12 He said therefore,
14 "For it will be as when a man going on a journey	"A nobleman went into a far country to receive kingly power and then return.
called his servants and entrusted to them his property; 15 to one he gave five talents, to another two, to another one, to each according to his ability.	13 Calling ten of his servents, he gave them ten pounds
	and said to them, 'Trade with these till I come.'
Then he went away. 16 He who had received the five talents went at once and traded with them; and he made five talents more. 17 So also, he who had the two talents made two talents more. 18 But he who had received the one talent went and dug in the ground and hid his master's money. and his his master's money.	
	14 But his citizens hated him and sent an embassy after him, saying, 'We do not want this man to reign over us.'

I. Comparison of the Talents and the Pounds (*Continued*)
Mt 25   Lk 19

Mt 25	Lk 19
19 Now after a long time the master of those servants came	15 When he returned,
	having received the kingly power, he commanded these servants, to whom he had given the money, to be called to him
and settled accounts with them.	that he might know what they had gained by trading.
20 And he who had received the five talents came forward, bringing five talents more, saying,	16 The first came before him, saying,
'Master, you delivered to me five talents; here I have made five talents more.'	'Lord, your pound has made ten pounds more.'
21 His master said to him, 'Well done, good and faithful servant; you have been faithful over a little, I will set you over much;	17 And he said to him, 'Well done, good servant! Because you have been faithful in a very little, you shall have authority over ten cities.'
enter into the joy of your master.'	
22 And he also who had the two talents came forward saying,	18 And the second came, saying,
'Master, you delivered to me two talents; here I have made two talents more.'	'Lord, your pound has made five pounds.'

Mt 25	Lk 19
23 His master said to him, 'Well done, good and faithful servant; you have been faithful over a little, I will set you over much;	19 And he said to him,
	'And you are to be over five cities.'
enter into the joy of your master.' 24 He also who had received the one talent came forward, saying, 'Master,	20 Then another came, saying, 'Lord, here is your pound, which I kept laid away in a napkin; 21 for I was afraid of you,
I knew you to be a hard man, reaping where you did not sow, and gathering where you did not winnow; 25 so I was afraid, and I went and hid your talent in the ground. Here you have what is yours.' 26 But his master answered him,	because you are a severe man; you take up what you did not lay down, and reap what you did not sow. 22 He said to him, 'I will condemn you out of your own mouth,
'You wicked and slothful servant! You knew that	you wicked servant! You knew that I was a severe man, taking up what I did not lay down
I reap where I have not sowed, and gather	and reaping what I did not sow?

I. Comparison of the Talents and the Pounds (*Continued*)
Mk 25   Lk 19

where I have not winnowed?
27 Then you ought to have invested
my money with the bankers,
and at my coming
I should have received
what was my own with interest.

23 Why then did you not
put
my money into the bank,
and at my coming
I should have collected
it with interest?
24 And he said to those who
stood by,

28 So take the talent from him,
and give it to him
who has the ten talents.

Take the pound from him,
and give it to him
who has the ten pounds.'
25 And they said to him,
'Lord, he has ten pounds!'
26 'I tell you,

29 For to every one who has
will more be given
and he will have abundance;
but from him who has not,
even what he has will be taken
away.
30 And cast the worthless servant into the outer darkness;
there men will weep
and gnash their teeth.' "

that to every one who has
will more be given;

but from him who has not,
even what he has will be taken
away.

27 But as for these enemies of
mine
who did not want me to reign
over them,
bring them here
and slay them before me.' "

Every word and expression in this comparison will not be discussed. Nevertheless, we shall try to reach a defensible view as to
the character of the parable prior to the emergence of its two divergent versions. This common original text must naturally be free

from all Matthean or Lucan additions and rewriting. And, even if it should appear that a particular secondary element preserved by only one of the evangelists could have belonged to the preredactional version, that element will not figure in our reconstructed text. The analysis proceeds in four stages: (1) In his version Luke speaks of a claimant to the throne. Is everything related to this theme to be considered as secondary? (2) The two versions designate the money given to the servants differently and also diverge as to the number of servants and talents or pounds involved. Which version is the more original on these points? (3) What is to be thought of those elements which Matthew has in addition to those preserved by Luke? (4) And, conversely, how are we to evaluate the material—beyond the claimant to the throne—offered by Luke alone?

The Claimant to the Throne

The first point which strikes us in comparing the two versions is that in 19:12–27 Luke presents a much more complicated parable than does Matthew in 25:14–30. The Matthean Talents is about a master who goes on a long journey for the duration of which he entrusts money to three servants. After his return he asks them to render an account. In the Lucan Pounds the central figure is a man of noble birth, a claimant to the throne, the purpose of whose journey to a far country is to receive the kingship there. He too entrusts money to his servants. But in addition to servants, there are also other people, the nobleman's fellow countrymen, who send a delegation after him in order to prevent him from being appointed king. Nevertheless, the man is appointed king and therefore on his return has to settle a double account: he calls his servants in order to find out how much each one has earned with the money entrusted to him and gives orders that his countrymen who had opposed him be put to death in front of him.

All the data concerning the claimant to the throne can readily be removed from the text. Thus in v. 12 the phrases "of noble birth" (the RSV has "a noble man"; in Greek, "a man of noble birth") and "to receive kingly power," and in v. 15a the clause "having received the kingly power" can be omitted. Also to be eliminated are all of v. 14, "But his citizens hated him and sent an embassy after him saying, 'We do not want this man to reign over us' " and the entire v. 27, "But as for these enemies of mine, who did not want me to reign over them, bring them here and slay them before me!" Furthermore, the reward "you shall have authority over ten cities" (end of v. 17) and "you are to be over five cities" (end of v. 19) also probably came from the story of the claimant to the throne since only such a figure would freely dispose of territory and cities. It may also have been because of the main figure's "noble birth" that the three servants of the original parable were secondarily multiplied: cf. "ten of his servants" (v. 13; see also v. 24: "those who stood by").

What convinces us that the simpler structure of Matthew's parable must also be the more original is not only the double activity narrated in the Lucan version and not only the fact that the elements relating to the claimant to the throne can be removed from the latter without difficulty, but also the observation that the discrepancies discoverable in the Lucan text are caused by the presence of just those elements. In fact, the claimant to the throne leaves clues within the present expanded story which betray its secondary character. Four such clues can be noted: (1) It is improbable that a future king who was going to give the government of cities as a reward would entrust the relatively small sum of ten pounds to his servants. (2) From the point of view of narrative technique, a certain tension exists between vv. 12 and 13. After hearing about a man who aspires to become king, one does not quite see the point of his giving the pounds to his servants and commanding them to trade with them. (3) It is also remarkable that only three of the ten servants do in fact give an account of their actions. (4) In v. 25 the bystanders remark that the first attendant already "has ten pounds." This remark indicates that the reward of the cities is, as it were, forgotten, and is thus perhaps not original. In any case, we read in Matthew's version "I will set you over much," i.e., money (25:21, 23).

A much-disputed question among scholars is whether the story of the claimant to the throne ever constituted an independent narrative prior to its combination with the parable of the Pounds. Many scholars think this is the case. However, such a supposition may be superfluous. It seems sufficient to admit that in the narrative elements dealing with the claimant to the throne allusion is made to well-known contemporary facts concerning the accession of Archelaus who, after the death of his father Herod the Great, travelled to Rome in 4 B.C. to have his kingship over Judea confirmed. The Jews sent a delegation after him petitioning the emperor to refuse him the appointment. And in fact Archelaus only became a tetrarch. On his return he punished the Jews in a terrible massacre. It is not impossible, although not very probable, that Jesus—or a Christian of the postpaschal period—would have composed a separate parable on the basis of this data. The Pounds is thus probably not the result of a fusion of two preexisting narratives. Rather, we should think of a simpler, more straightforward parable (cf. the Talents) which was later enlarged and enriched with details alluding to the story of Archelaus. The Pounds, before the addition of the claimant to the throne, would have lent itself to such an expansion since it had to do with a man who goes on a journey, as does the claimant, and on his return asks his servants for an account.

Who was responsible for this expansion of the Pounds? Was it Luke himself or someone before him? A. Weiser has made a very detailed study of the style and vocabulary of Lk 19:12–27, and he comes to the conclusion that at the pre–Lucan level the text existed more or less in its present form. Thus, in his view, the data concerning the claimant to the throne was added prior to Luke. In this connection it should be noted that Weiser is one of those recent authors who do not regard the Talents–Pounds as Q-material (see above p. 167). Rather, according to him both the Lucan and Matthean versions are *Sondergut*. It is true that one must question whether Luke could have written in this allusive sort of way ca. A.D. 80 for readers outside Palestine. On the other hand, the allegorizing—the claimant to the throne is Jesus, who after his death becomes king in far away heaven and who will return for judgment—is in complete agreement with Luke's presentation of Jesus' ascension and Parousia. Moreover, in an introductory verse of his own creation (19:11), Luke indicates his precise intention in making Jesus narrate this parable at this particular juncture in his gospel, an intention which is very well furthered by the details concerning the claimant to the throne. Finally, both the style and certain of the motifs are perhaps more Lucan than, e.g., Weiser is inclined to admit. In this connection we note the Lucan character of v. 15 and of the motifs of kingship (vv. 11, 12, 15), "to become

king" (vv. 14, 27; cf. also 19:38: "king"—a Lucan addition; otherwise Mk 11:10) and "to trade" (vv. 13, 15). All these considerations
incline us rather to the view that it was Luke himself who enriched
the parable with the data concerning the king. But be this as it
may, even on the alternative supposition the claimant to the
throne certainly did not belong to the basic text which we are
seeking to reconstruct.

Talents or Pounds? Which Numbers Are Original?

The "talents" of Matthew's version are probably secondary. It
has been shown that Luke appears inconsistent when he represents a future king as distributing a relatively small sum to his
servants. This would imply that, on this point, Luke did not alter
his source text. One pound was worth ten denarii (a denarius was
the average daily wage of a workman; cf. Mt 20:2 "one denarius a
day"). One talent was worth sixty (or, in another system of compu-
tation, a hundred) pounds. From this it appears that Matthew too
is inconsistent in his own way in that five talents is not really a
small sum and yet, in his version, the master says on his return,
"You have been faithful over a little" (vv. 21 and 23). Originally,
then, the parable must have concerned pounds. In any event, we
know that the tendency in the tradition process was to increase
numbers and quantities. But then it must be further asked
whether the original relatively small sums involved are in agreement with what Matthew says in 25:14: "he entrusted to them his
property." Was this word perhaps secondarily inserted (from the
parable of the Faithful or Wicked Servant, cf. Mt 24:47 = Lk
12:44) in function of the multiplication of the sums?

It has been indicated that the larger number of servants in Lk
(cf. 19:13: "ten of his servants") probably goes together with the
fact that in the Lucan version the master has become a claimant to
the throne and therefore must oversee more than three servants.
The original parable, on the contrary, only concerned three servants and even in Luke only three are actually asked to give an
account of their trading.

According to Matthew the distribution of the talents proceeds in
a decreasing fashion: five, two, and then one. The first servant
gains five more talents, the second only two. In Luke's version
each servant receives one pound. The first gains ten more, the

second five. It has been claimed that the gradation in the talents received, "each according to his ability" (Mt 25:15), is already a Christian allegory which refers to the different gifts and abilities of the faithful. Luke would have remained closer to the original on this point: each gets one pound (cf. 19:13). It seems more likely however that Luke omitted this gradation for the sake of his number "ten." This is supported by the fact that Luke does retain the gradation for the trading and the reward (ten and five). Moreover, his v. 25 with its "he [i.e., the first servant] already has ten pounds" is in fact incorrect (the servant has ten plus one, i.e., eleven pounds; perhaps the "ten" here is reminiscent of "five plus five," cf. Mt 25:20). Thus the numbers given by Matthew seem more original. Initially no allegory was intended by the gradation of the sums. It was rather a question of the storyteller's need for variation.

In the original parable the reward was that the servants were set over "much" (= over much *money*), because they had been faithful over a "little": see the Talents (cf. Lk 19:17: "a very little"). As already mentioned, the expansion of the parable with the data concerning the claimant to the throne resulted in the changes in Lk 19:17 and 19: "You shall have authority over ten cities" and "you are to be over five cities." In vv. 24–25, however, Luke makes no further mention of these cities. It could thus be asked what significance the addition of one pound would have for the servant who had been set over ten cities (see v. 17)!

Data Found Only in Matthew's Version

Some authors think that in Matthew's version vv. 16–18 (the description of what the different servants did with the money entrusted to them) are secondary because they anticipate what is said in vv. 20–25 and because the verses in question have no parallel in Luke's version. Neither of these reasons is convincing, however. The description in vv. 16–18 seems to be neither premature nor too explicit an explanation. It is more likely that the insertion of Lk 19:14 with its mention of the embassy of the nobleman's fellow citizens caused Luke to omit from his version the description found in Mt 25:16–18.

In vv. 21 and 23 the servants are not only rewarded by being set over "much," they also hear the command, "Enter into the joy of your master." Should we think of a cheerful banquet, or is the author referring to the joy of heaven here? Since the Lucan version does not contain this invitation and since above all vv. 21 and 23, in the light of the punishment described in v. 30, acquire an unmistakable eschatological significance (= heaven) which disrupts the figurative character of the narrative, these verses should most probably be considered as secondary.

The punishment mentioned in v. 30, i.e., being cast "into the outer darkness," also appears to be secondary. This verse vis à vis v. 28 contains an additional punishment. And just as is the case with the additional reward in vv. 21 and 23, this second punishment with its allegorical significance disrupts the figurative character of the image. Moreover, the punishment specified is typical for Matthew. He also uses the phrase "darkness outside" in 8:12 (cf. Lk 13:28) and in 22:13 (here he alone among the Synoptics does so). The statement "There men will weep and gnash their teeth" was already in Q (cf. Mt 8:12 = Lk 13:28). Matthew especially shows a distinct preference for the expression, reutilizing it in 13:42, 50; 22:13; 24:51, as well as here in 25:30.

In vv. 21 and 23 Matthew writes "good and *faithful* servant" while Luke in 19:17 has only "good servant" and drops the characterization of the servant altogether in 19:19. In Mt 25:26 we read "wicked and *slothful* servant" whereas Luke in 19:22 has only "wicked servant." Matthew elsewhere has the habit of adding adjectives. Also, the phrase "faithful servant" is found earlier in Mt 24:45 (= Lk 12:42). Finally, "slothful" is not an altogether accurate description of the behavior of the third servant. For all these reasons it seems that these two adjectives were added by Matthew.

There can moreover be no question but that it was Matthew who added the word "for" at the beginning of v. 14. In his conception the parable is an interpretation and an explication of the summons to vigilance in v. 13. And finally, with respect to the statement of v. 29, it was not Luke who in 19:26 omitted the phrase "and he will have abundance," but rather Matthew who added it here (the same phrase appears in Mt 13:12; it is absent from Mk 4:25).

Data Found Only in Luke's Version

The following details have already been noted as not belonging to the common original text: all those elements in Lk 19:12–27 connected with the theme of the claimant to the throne, i.e., vv. 14 and 27 in their entirety, as well as fragments of vv. 12, 13, 15, 17, and 19.

There is also general agreement as to the Lucan origin of v. 11. Luke, prior to resuming his travel narrative in 19:28 (which he had interrupted at Jericho: cf. 19:1), situated the parable by means of this verse. The parable of the Pounds is meant to tell the hearers that the entry into Jerusalem will not be the time of the public manifestation of the kingdom of God. This verse therefore stems from Luke who conceived the structure of the travel narrative. Furthermore, the style and vocabulary are thoroughly Lucan.

The secondary character of four explicit amplifications can also be admitted: (1) At the end of v. 13 we read, "He said to them, 'Trade with these till I come.' " This command is absent in Mt. In Lk it apparently takes the place of the description of what the servants did with the money entrusted to them (cf. Mt 25:16–18). (2) Similarly, the last remark in v. 15, "that he might know what they had gained by trading," sounds equally explanatory and secondary. The wording is in any case reminiscent of the end of v. 13. (3) In v. 22a we find, "I will condemn you out of your own mouth." This phrase is also explanatory since in v. 22b the king uses the words spoken by the servant in order to excuse himself in v. 21. One must admit that such an elucidatory remark appears quite secondary. If it was in the common source, we do not see why Matthew would have omitted it. (4) Finally there is v. 25. In Matthew's version the statement "for to every one who has . . ." (25:29) follows directly upon v. 28: "So take the talent from him and give it to him who has the ten talents". Luke interrupts this sequence by the remark, "And they [i.e., the bystanders] said, 'Lord, he has ten pounds!' " (19:25). Only then follows, "I tell you, that to every one who has . . ." (v. 26). In Luke's version v. 25 is clearly a preparation for the saying of v. 26. This addition is also connected to the beginning of v. 24: "And he said to those who stood by. . . ." Such interruptions enhance the liveliness of the scene and increase the element of dialogue. The beginning of v. 24 and the whole of v. 25 are thus clearly secondary. There is one further detail: the manner in which the third servant preserves the money entrusted to him. Is the "hiding in the ground" of the Talents (Mt) original or is it rather the "laying away in a napkin" (Lk)? A talent weighed approximately 25 kg. (= ca. 55 lbs.) and thus could not be easily wrapped in a napkin and hidden. Was the hiding in the ground then introduced in conjunction with the secondary use of the term "talents" by Matthew? Perhaps. But, J. Jeremias notes that while both ways of keeping money were used in Palestine, only burial in the ground was regarded as safe by the law. Would it not then be Luke's version which is secondary, his intention being to emphasize the carelessness of the third servant by means of this reference to the way in which he hides his money? It is probably best to leave this last question unresolved.

II. The Parable in Early Christian Preaching

Time and again the comparison of the Talents with the Pounds has led us to conclude: probably original, probably secondary. The whole discussion had as its goal the recovery of the source text, i.e., the single common text which must have existed before the divergent versions arose. Does the text which we are now in a position to reconstruct go back to Jesus himself? The concluding statement which (on the evidence of Mt 25:29 = Lk 19:26) the original text must have contained suggests a negative answer to this question. Our reconstructed parable is thus already an early Christian version.

The So–Called Original Text

We first attempt to reconstruct this so-called original text following the versification of Matthew. In doubtful cases the Matthean version is preferred. However, it should be repeated here that not every word and expression has been discussed and that, even after investigation, there still remains at times a certain margin of uncertainty.

14 "There was a man going on a journey, who called his servants and entrusted to them his money.
15 To one he gave five pounds, to another two, to another one, to each according to his ability. Then he went away.
16 He who had received the five pounds went at once and traded with them; and he made five more.
17 So also, he who had received the two made two pounds more.
18 But he who had received the one pound went and dug in the ground and hid his master's money.

19 Now after a long time, the master of those servants came and settled accounts with them.

20 He who had received the five pounds came forward bringing five pounds more, saying, 'Master, you delivered to me five pounds, here I have made five pounds more.'

21 His master said to him, 'Well done, good servant; you have been faithful over a little, I will set you over much.'

22 And he also who had the two pounds came forward, saying, 'Master, you delivered to me two pounds; here I have made two pounds more.'

23 His master said to him, 'Well done, good servant; you have been faithful over a little, I will set you over much.'

24 He also who had received the one pound came forward, saying, 'Master, I knew you to be a hard man, reaping where you did not sow, and gathering where you did not winnow;

25 so I was afraid, and I went and hid your pound in the ground. Here you have what is yours.'

26 But his master answered him, 'You wicked servant, you knew that I reap where I have not sowed and gather where I have not winnowed?

27 Then you ought to have invested my money with the bankers, and at my coming I should have received what was my own with interest.

28 So take the pound from him and give it to him who has the ten pounds.

29 For to every one who has will more be given; but from him who has not, even what he has will be taken away.' "

"For to Every One Who Has . . ."

It is possible that the phrase in v. 19, "after a long time," was very early interpreted in an allegorical way and related to the delay of the Parousia. But in the parable as Jesus told it during his earthly life this phrase could have functioned very well simply as such within the figurative part; a certain amount of time is required for trading and making money. Strictly speaking, only v. 29 militates against the authenticity of our reconstructed parable. Let us see why this is so.

The fact that this saying is also found in Mk 4:25 does not necessarily imply that it was originally an isolated logion which circulated independently, for Mark could have removed it from its parable context. On the other hand, we know that in the process of handing on the early Christian tradition, expanding, concluding, and applicatory remarks were often appended at the end of parables, cf. e.g., Lk 14:11; Mt 22:14; 20:16. Is the logion of v. 29 not a saying of this sort?

In light of v. 29, which in fact does function as a conclusion, the parable of the Pounds now represents an explication of that peculiar "giving and taking." But was this the original function of the parable? Probably not. One gets the impression that v. 29 was added to explain why the first servant is given the share of the third as well: he who has will get more. Would this feature have received so much attention in Jesus' own narration of the parable? It might also be noted that the second half of the statement in v. 29 is not altogether in accordance with what the parable itself gives us to understand: the pound is not taken away from the third servant precisely because he had only one pound, i.e., only "a little." His guilt lies rather in his lack of initiative or active engagement.

All these reasons taken cumulatively lead to the conclusion that the statement in v. 29 must have been added to the parable at an early stage by the primitive church. Originally it was a wisdom saying of a profane type, based on the observation made so often in life that those who already have many possessions get more, while the poor get still poorer! In its present position at the end of the parable, however, the saying takes on an eschatological significance. The giving or taking away occurs at the last judgment. But once again the question arises: is this eschatological motivation original? Should the servants make the most of their money (only) in order to get a greater reward, or out of fear that everything will be taken away from them? Or, in the original parable was it not the reception of a task which itself was the gift? In this latter interpretation, to have been given a task was to have already been gifted. And, the gift in itself leads to active work.

Conclusion

We have come to the conclusion that, by the addition of the statement in v. 29, the early church eschatologically motivated the exhortation to active service and the warning against a lack of engagement which were in Jesus' original parable. The parable as told by Jesus had already emphasized the fact of judgment: we shall have to give an account. In the appended statement of v. 29 attention is, however, now focused more on the—in a certain sense paradoxical—way in which this judgment will take place: he who has will get more; from him who has not, even that will be taken away!

Before proceeding to investigate what Jesus himself intended with this parable, let us first briefly consider another version of the same parable. The church historian Eusebius (ca. 260–ca. 340) tells us that in the apocryphal *Evangelium secundum Hebraeos* (dating perhaps from the first half of the second century A.D.), the parable goes like this: The three servants each behave in a different way. One wastes his master's money in loose living with "prostitutes and fluteplayers" (cf. the Prodigal Son). The second increases what was given to him, while the third hides his talent. The good servant is received by his master with joy. The first, wasteful servant is thrown into prison. The third who hid his talent is merely rebuked. From this account we can see how in the process of tradition in the early church offense was taken at the judgment passed on the third, according to Jesus, "wicked" servant. Some did not shrink from "correcting" this point in the prosaic and moralizing way just indicated.

III. The Parable in Jesus' Preaching

In order to grasp what Jesus during his earthly life intended by this parable, the concluding saying in v. 29 must be left out of consideration since, as we have seen in the preceding discussion, this saying was added after Easter by the early church. But apart from this there is no reason to doubt the authenticity of our reconstructed parable or of its parts. This narrative is a parable in the strict sense, i.e., an imaginary story about a purported historical event, formulated in the past tense, a story which corresponds to the life and customs of people in Palestine, but which nevertheless manifests a few odd features. The dialogue between the master and the third servant especially appears strange: "Master, I knew you to be a hard man, reaping where you did not sow. . . ." Since the master seems to agree with this negative view of himself, Jesus' hearers were thus compelled to reflect further. The parable ends abruptly. No explanation is given, no application made. The hearers must discover these for themselves. What does the story mean? We pose the same question. Our answer combines three different approaches.

Instruction

One cannot avoid the impression that Jesus, with his parable of the Pounds, seems to be teaching. His story contains a lesson and he wants to evoke an insight. But it would be wrong to restrict the teaching involved to moralizing preaching about general human truths. In this parable Jesus says more than that everyone "will get his due." His preaching cannot be separated from his mission. The story speaks of a master who demands of his servants that the capital entrusted to them be increased. Certainly the details of the narrative should not be understood in an allegorical way; the figurative part is only a figure. The reality with which Jesus was really concerned here was definitely not an abstract theodicy or a teaching about the divine attributes or ordinary human ethics. Rather, Jesus is concretely concerned with what God his Father is offering the world in him: God's "dominion" is revealed by Jesus.

In this parable instruction Jesus emphasizes that God indeed bestows his dominion as an undeserved gift but that, nevertheless, it also involves a task for man. He has to make the most of the gift given, make it bear fruit. Jesus indicates that an account will ultimately have to be rendered and thus emphasizes the seriousness of the matter. Two types of servants, two good, the third one bad, are successively brought on the scene. Jesus the teacher thus uses the Pounds to point to the challenge which his message involves for humankind, a challenge which must be taken up wholeheartedly. Jesus' teaching is a warning: in it reward, but also punishment, are announced as future possibilities.

Accusation

Our first approach to the parable as told by Jesus is thus definitely Christological. It speaks of what God in Jesus was achieving for the world then and there, at that particular point in time, and among the people of that country. In this approach it is also assumed that those addressed by Jesus were not specifically his disciples or still less his adversaries, but all his hearers without distinction.

Nevertheless, attention has rightly been drawn to certain features of the narrative which call for another approach. According to the parable "laws" (cf. p. 62), the end of the narrative has the greatest importance; it is there that the real point must be sought (the law of "end-stress"). It may therefore be assumed that the departure on a journey, the distribution of the pounds, and the trading are all mentioned in function of the necessity of giving an account, this being the element on which the stress is placed. Therefore, the first and second servants should not distract attention away from the account demanded at the conclusion of the parable. Their behavior is described in a brief stereotyped manner. They only serve as foils for the third servant. They merely form the bright background against which the dark figure of the third servant stands out all the more sharply. The space devoted to the latter is greater than that given to the first two servants together. And, it is precisely the excuse of the third servant and Jesus' answer to him which capture attention by their strange, even disturbing content. Can we then remain satisfied with our first explanation in which Jesus functions as a teacher who serenely and objectively describes two possible responses to the entrusted task?

The third servant defends his behavior. He takes his stand on the level of strict justice: "Here you have what is yours" (v. 25). He acted out of fear: "So I was afraid, and went and hid your talent in the ground" (v. 25). His fear is rooted in the idea which he has of his master. He knows him to be a hard man who reaps where he did not sow and gathers where he did not winnow (cf. v. 24). The master condemns the servant's behavior because it does not correspond to what the servant ought to have done considering his conception of his master. If the master does in fact demand more than he gave, then the servant should at least have put the money in the bank at interest (cf. vv. 26–27). Consequently, the pound is taken away from the wicked servant in punishment.

Nevertheless, it is difficult to imagine this servant, so emphatically characterized as "wicked," as representing all people who do not recognize God's gift as a task and thus fall short in living out that task. Rather, Jesus has a definite class of people in view with this figure of the "wicked" servant. Jesus is more than a mere teacher here. He is carrying on a concealed, indirect controversy with certain of his contemporaries who do not agree with him.

Who is, in fact, intended by the figure of the third servant? We think here of the scribes and Pharisees who opposed Jesus' view of God and thus the way in which God through Jesus brings his salvation to the world. They adhered strictly to the Law and took their stand on generally accepted norms. According to them God cannot be as Jesus depicts him in his preaching. They rise up in protest: such a God is unjust! They revolt against a God who asks more than the normal, who unexpectedly enters into their lives and throws everything into confusion, and who manifests, in such an astonishing and revolutionary way, his own being in this Jesus. They are deeply offended, just like the elder brother in Lk 15:11–32 and the workers of the vineyard in Mt 20:1–15. But Jesus, the persecuted prophet who is attacked and accused, does not give in. The parable functions then also as his apology, his self-defence. When God addresses man, Jesus says, man may not take refuge behind a prefabricated concept of justice or a legalistic, sterile image of God. He must abandon his complacent security, must be careful not to seek some theological alibi or take cover behind a mercantile contract mentality. With the parable of the Pounds, Jesus launches a counterattack. He defends himself and his message with this strange story about a master who represents God.

Our first approach therefore needs to be complemented. Within the wider group of his hearers, Jesus was especially speaking to the religious experts, the scribes and the Pharisees. The parable is more than teaching in the form of an illustrative story; it is also accusation and apology. Among his hearers Jesus above all has his opponents in view. Jesus is both the teacher and the persecuted prophet.

Challenge

The explication hitherto has led us to identify the master with God, the entrusted pounds with the breaking in of his dominion and the servants with humankind. With the figures of the servants Jesus is referring in the first place to his hearers, and with that of the third, more particularly to his opponents. It would be wrong for us to give in to the inclination to allegorize and, e.g., to ask whether the pounds concretely signify God's word which is entrusted to man and what is meant by the bank or what is intended by the sowing or the harvesting of which the third servant speaks.

It would be equally inappropriate to argue about whether the harsh master can really represent God. Such questions disrupt the dynamism of the narrative and distract attention from its main point.

Is everything thus said when, in line with the second approach, we call the Pounds a judgment parable? Was it in fact Jesus' ultimate intention to vindicate himself against his opponents? Once again we are led to view the parable as a word-event. Jesus' audience, including his opponents, is compelled to reflect upon the story. What is the sense of the parable? When its meaning is suddenly recognized Jesus' parable effects a "disclosure." The hearer understands in a new way. His present situation is unexpectedly illuminated: he "finds." But at the same time the hearer realizes that his previous conceptions, his thinking, and his attitudes must be radically changed. This involves a revolution: he "loses" his past, turns his back on it. The final aim of the parable is that he will start a new life in accordance with his new insight. He finds himself confronted with an existential decision: he "chooses" a new future.

The parable of the Pounds is, therefore, more than teaching, more even than self-defence. It is a word which radically changes people, challenges them, and places them at a crossroad. Jesus is more than a teacher, more than a prophet who defends himself. With this sort of parable, he wants to win people over and convert them. This includes his opponents. He is first and foremost God's envoy, sent to save what is on the point of being lost.

The three foregoing approaches are not identical as far as their results are concerned. Each has its own accent and also a certain onesidedness. None of these approaches should be denigrated or excluded. They should be recognized as interrelated and complementary. Speaking in parables is a very rich happening indeed!

IV. The Parable in Luke's Gospel

In the preceding analysis, the question as to whether everything peculiar to the Lucan version is to be ascribed to the evangelist himself did not receive a clear answer. Our preference in this matter was indicated, i.e., to attribute as much as possible to Luke himself. Nevertheless, we do not wish to hold at all costs to the position that Luke worked with the "bare" parable of the source-text which we think we have been able to reconstruct. Further investigation of this problem cannot be included here. Whenever, then, in what follows reference is made for the sake of brevity to "Luke's redaction," the possibility remains in some cases that the pre–Lucan tradition already contained certain elements of this "Lucan" redaction. Luke's version of the Pounds can be described with three terms: it reflects allegorizing, deeschatologizing, and moralizing. Each of these three characteristics must now be discussed in more detail.

Allegorizing

The original text of the Pounds was enriched in the Lucan version by the data concerning the claimant to the throne. The reader of the gospel thus had to interpret the parable in a radically allegorical way. The master is no longer God; the man of noble birth is Christ who leaves and disappears on a long journey. The far away country is heaven and the journey his ascension. There Christ will be enthroned as king, and it is as king that he will return for judgment. His Jewish compatriots who had rejected and crucified him will be punished. His servants—probably all Christians in Luke's conception—will have to give an account of what they have done with what has been entrusted to them.

This allegorizing is Christological. It offers a survey of Christ's past and future history. It has to do with what has already happened to Jesus, but above all with what will take place at the last judgment. This judgment motif parenetically underscores the necessity of zealously bearing fruit in the present interval. The less attractive features of the king's behavior were apparently not felt to be disturbing, however peculiar the modern reader may find them.

Deeschatologizing

For Luke the allegory of the Pounds has an even more concrete function. From 19:11 we learn that Jesus narrated this parable "because they supposed that the kingdom of God was to appear immediately." In Luke's gospel the whole section 9:51–19:46 concerns Jesus' long ascent to Jerusalem, the Lucan travel narrative. Towards the end of this section Jesus states in the Passion predic-

tion in 18:31 for the last time, "We are going up to Jerusalem.
. . ." In 19:41–44 he weeps over the holy city and in 19:45 enters
the temple. Earlier, in 18:35 Jesus is approaching Jericho and in
19:1 he arrives. There he goes into the house of Zacchaeus and,
before continuing his journey to Jerusalem (cf. 19:28), narrates the
allegory of the Pounds.

In light of the gospel context, and more particularly of the statement in 19:11, this allegory is then intended to show that the kingdom will not be manifested at the time of Jesus' entry into Jerusalem. A certain misconception on this point must be dispelled.
Jesus must first die and ascend to heaven. Only thereafter will he
return as king. In the meantime active service is called for.

From the context of chap. 19 the identity of Jesus' hearers is not
clear: the crowd (also his opponents? cf. 19:7) or only the disciples?
In Acts 1:6, just prior to the ascension, it is the apostles who ask
the risen Christ, "Lord, will you at this time restore the kingdom
to Israel?" This may be an indication that in Luke's conception the
allegory of the Pounds was especially intended for the disciples.
But through the disciples the evangelist also has his contemporaries, his fellow Christians, in mind. Luke thus deeschatologizes,
i.e., he explains why the kingdom of God has not yet been manifested. He uses the allegory to combat the enthusiastic expectation
of the end, the *Naherwartung*, among his Christian community (or
to alleviate their disappointment at the long delay of the Parousia).
At "this time" during Jesus' absence the believers must engage
themselves in the task of trading with the money entrusted to
them. In view of the coming judgment this is now their urgent
duty! Just as with his allegorizing, Luke's deeschatologizing of the
Pounds has a parenetic and moralizing intention.

Moralizing

In comparing the two versions, reference was made to Luke's
explanatory additions (cf. pp. 178–80). In the Lucan version Jesus
orders the disciples, "Trade with these till I come" (v. 13), and on
his return he wants to know "what they had gained by trading" (v.
15). The wicked servant had done no business and thus in Luke's
view is disobedient. His guilt is pointed out and emphasized.

In consideration of these insertions, the question might be
raised whether Luke in his explanations has fully respected Jesus'

original intention. Jesus' parable did not contain an explicit command. On the other hand, the gift of which Jesus spoke in itself implies a task. Nevertheless, the guilt of the wicked servant does not consist—as Luke would have it—in his formal disobedience, but rather in clinging to his own image of God, in revolting against the demand made by God with which Jesus suddenly breaks into his life. Luke no longer understood this first purpose of the parable. In his Q-material the Pounds may have followed the parable of the Faithful or Wicked Servant: cf. Mt 24:45–51 and 25:14–30 (thus separated in Mt only by the *Sondergut* of the Ten Virgins, 25:1–13). Luke presents the Faithful or Wicked Servant in 12:42–46. In 12:47–48 he adds, "And that servant who knew his master's will, but did not make ready or act according to his will, shall receive a severe beating. But he who did not know, and did what deserves a beating, shall receive a light beating. Every one to whom much is given, of him will much be required; and of him to whom men commit much they will demand the more." It is not impossible that Luke wrote these verses after reading the Pounds which followed next in his Q-source (on this hypothesis, he did not wish to use the Pounds immediately in chap. 12 but reserved it for his chap. 19). To know God's will and yet not to act according to it deserves severe chastisement. From those to whom much is entrusted, more will be demanded. In 12:47–48 Luke is thinking about levels of responsibility and he does so probably under the influence of the Pounds. Then in chap. 19, when he came to edit the Pounds itself, he probably still had this reflection in 12:47–48 in mind.

Conclusion

Is the Lucan interpretation of Jesus' original parable legitimate? This question is unavoidable after what has been discussed concerning Luke's allegorizing, deeschatologizing, and moralizing. A correct answer to this question must take into account the change brought about by the paschal event. The altered postpaschal situation was the primary driving force behind this reinterpretation and actualization. The fact that God had raised Jesus from the dead signified his lasting enthronement. After Easter one could no longer conceive of God apart from Jesus his Son. People were convinced henceforth that in the future God would also act through this Jesus. Jesus thus became the master of the parable. With their well-known freedom the early Christians resolutely began to allegorize.

Luke's deeschatologizing was also unavoidable in the long run and moreover salutary. The delay of the Parousia led to this reflection. The initially tense *Naherwartung* of the early church was rightly given up; at the same time stress was laid on the duties of this life. The judgment motif was nonetheless retained.

What are we to think of the way in which Luke moralizes, i.e., his speculation concerning a gradation in rewards? Such reflection is no longer specifically Christian, but it is not therefore necessarily wrong. In this connection we recall that the wisdom saying, "to every one who has will more be given" (Lk 19:26), added by the early church, in the context of the parable received a Christian eschatological meaning (see pp. 181–82). Luke, however, by his separation of the saying from the parable through the interruption of v. 25, once again deprived it to some extent of this Christian character.

At the end of these observations concerning Luke's reinterpretation it can still be asked whether we in our actualizing use of the parable of the Pounds must not also think back to what Jesus originally intended, i.e., he wanted to confront his hearers with a God who bestows his gifts generously but who also makes radical demands. In Jesus' view one should not so much (and certainly not primarily) pay heed to those demands because God gives an explicit and extrinsic command to do so (cf. Lk 19:13: "Trade with these till I come"). Rather, the dynamic gift of God's "dominion," well-understood and well-received, leads in itself to a generous response and actually results in the fulfillment of those radical demands.

V. The Parable in Matthew's Gospel

In structure, content, and vocabulary, Matthew's version has remained closer to the original text than Luke's did. But even Matthew has made alterations here and there, inserted a few additions and given the parable a very definite context. His redactional work is also a reinterpretation.

A Parousia Parable

Matthew situates the Talents within the last discourse of his gospel, the extended Parousia discourse (chaps. 24–25). In this discourse the parable stands at the end of the second section (24:36–25:30), which represents a long exhortation to vigilance. By means of the particle "for" in 25:14 the parable is linked with the final appeal in the Wise and Foolish Virgins: "Watch therefore, for you know neither the day nor the hour" (25:13). The parable thus explains what vigilance consists of. As such, it resembles another parable within the same section, the Faithful or Wicked Servant (24:45–51). Both are servant parables. The servant or servants receive a task which they must perform during the master's absence. Good and bad service is sharply contrasted. On his return the master rewards or punishes. The good servant receives a greater responsibility (cf. 24:47: "he will set him over all his possessions"; and 25:21, 23: "I will set you over much"), while the bad or wicked servant is cast outside where there is "weeping and gnashing of teeth" (cf. 24:51 and 25:30). Just like the Talents, the Faithful or Wicked Servant further explains the saying which immediately precedes: "Therefore you also must be ready; for the Son of man is coming at an hour you do not expect" (24:44; cf. 24:42: "Watch therefore, for you do not know on what day your Lord is coming"). Both parables explain that readiness and watching consist in active service, the fulfillment of the given task.

Sitting on the Mount of Olives, Jesus addresses his Parousia discourse to the disciples (cf. 24:3). He repeatedly summons them to hear. They should feel both comforted and admonished. While in the Lucan version of the Pounds the nobleman's hostile compatriots, representing the Jews, also make their appearance, in the Talents Matthew speaks only of servants. The disciples realize that these figures illustrate the positive and negative stances which they themselves can assume. But for Matthew, these servants to an extent represent his fellow Christians for whom he is writing. The Matthean church was a mixed congregation, a *corpus mixtum*, in which good and bad Christians (cf. Mt 22:10) were living together until the day of judgment. Matthew exhorts, admonishes, and warns them.

In a certain sense Matthew has also allegorized the parable. He does so by placing it in the Parousia context. The master is no longer God but Jesus, who now absent since his death and "on a journey" (cf. vv. 14–15), "after a long time" (v. 19) will return for judgment. Indeed, the whole Parousia discourse concerns Jesus' return. One gets the impression that at the time when Matthew wrote his gospel the delay of the Parousia was already consciously experienced: "after a long time" (v. 19). Nevertheless, the emphasis falls on the certainty and unexpectedness of the return, and on the consequent necessity for watchfulness, readiness, and service. Unlike Luke, Matthew does not use the narrative for the explicit purpose of solving the problem of the delay of the Parousia. Furthermore, the change of "pounds" into "talents" also seems to be a result of Matthew's allegorization. The gifts which Christians receive, each according to his ability, are valuable talents, certainly small in comparison to "eternal joy" (cf. vv. 21 and 23), but nevertheless as precious as a large sum of money!

Judgment

In vv. 21, 23, and 30 Matthew has expanded the parable with the addition of the phrases, "Enter into the joy of your master," and "cast the worthless servant into the outer darkness; there men will weep and gnash their teeth." Both these additions are connected with judgment. The idea of judgment was already present in the original parable, cf. "giving an account," but Matthew stresses this idea. He would hardly have noticed that in his version the images of the reward presented do not completely agree. Originally the reward consisted in being "set over much (money)." In his additions Matthew seems to think rather of the joy of the eschatological banquet and he thus goes beyond the figurative part, the imaginary story. For him reward and punishment already belong to the application, the part concerning reality. They are heaven and hell! The reality in question has emerged from the figurative part of the story. One should not lose sight of the fact that in Matthew's allegorized version of the Talents the dialogue takes place between Jesus, the Son of man who has returned as judge, and the disciples, i.e., the Christians. The parable concerns the last judgment of all Christians.

Making the Most of One's Talents

In Matthew's conception, the parable of the Talents illustrates the idea of watchfulness (cf. 25:13). It shows what vigilance consists of. To watch is to remain faithful, to be diligent, and not slothful.

Matthew probably added the adjective "wise" in 24:45 (compare "who then is the faithful and *wise* servant" with Lk 12:42 which has only "faithful" servant) and the adjective "wicked" in 24:48 (compare "but if that *wicked* servant says to himself" with Lk 12:45 which has only "that" servant). In 25:21 and 23, Matthew writes, "Well done, good and *faithful* servant" (Lk 19:17 reads simply, "Well done, good servant") and in 25:26, "You wicked and *slothful* servant" (Lk 19:22, "You wicked servant"). Matthew probably took over the word "faithful" from the parable of the Faithful or Wicked Servant (see 24:45). The concluding 25:30 is likewise Matthean; this verse also contains a remarkable adjective: "*worthless* servant." The inserted adjectives "faithful" and "slothful" reveal the Matthean emphasis. They have a function within the Matthean parenesis. For Matthew, watching is active service, making the most of one's gifts, bringing forth fruit and doing the will of the Father in heaven. The fact that Matthew motivates this emphatic exhortation by reference to the future judgment is equally characteristic for his gospel.

BIBLIOGRAPHY

Derrett, J. D. M., "Law in the New Testament: The Parable of the Talents and Two Logia," ZNW 56 (1965) 184–95; also in Derrett, *Law in the New Testament*, London, 1970, pp. 17–31.

Didier, M., "La parabole des talents et des mines," in *De Jésus aux Evangiles. Tradition et rédaction dans les Évangiles synoptiques*, BETL 25, ed. I. de la Potterie, Gembloux–Paris, 1967, pp. 248–71.

Dupont, J., "La parabole des Talents. Mt 25,14–30," *AssSeign* II (1969) no. 64, pp. 18–28.

———, "La parabole des talents (Mat. 25:14–30) ou des mines (Luc 19:12–27)," *RThPh* 49 (1969) 376–91.

Fiedler, P., "Die übergegebenen Talente. Auslegung von Mt 25,14–30," *BibLeb* 11 (1970) 259–73.

Foerster, W., "Das Gleichnis von den anvertrauten Pfunden," in *Verbum Dei manet in aeternum. Festschrift für O. Schmitz*, Witten, 1953, pp. 37–56.

Ganne, P., "La parabole des talents," *Bible et vie chrétienne* (1962) no. 45, pp. 44–53.

Joüon, P., "La parabole des mines et la parabole des talents," *RScR* 29 (1939) 489–94.

Kamlah, E., "Kritik und Interpretation der Parabel von den anvertrauten Geldern," *KD* 14 (1968) 28–38.

McGaughy, L. C. "The Fear of Yahweh and the Mission of Judaism: A Postexilic Maxim and Its Early Christian Expansion in the Parable of the Talents," *JBL* 94 (1975) 235–45.

Neuhäusler, E., "Mit welcher Massstab misst Gott die Menschen? Deutung zweier Jesussprüche," *BibLeb* 11 (1970) 104–13.

Weinert, F. D., "The Parable of The Throne Claimant (Luke 19:12, 14–15a, 27) Reconsidered," *CBQ* 39 (1977) 505–14.

Weiser, A., *Die Knechtsgleichnisse der synoptischen Evangelien*, StANT 29, Munich, 1971, pp. 226–72.

Zerwick, M., "Die Parabel vom Thronanwärter," *Bib* 40 (1959) 654–74.

Eight

The Last Judgment
(Mt 25:31–46)

It is well-known that the final pericope of the Matthean Parousia discourse (25:31–46) presents more than one difficulty for interpretation. Does the term "all the nations" (v. 32) refer only to the Gentiles or also to Christians and Jews? Who are "the least of my brethren" (v. 40; cf. v. 45): Are they all of the "little people" or a specific group of Christians? The exegesis of Mt 25:31–46, and to a significant degree also the interpretation of the "works of mercy" which are enumerated in this pericope, depend on the answer given to these two questions. Even the very traditional title of this parable suddenly becomes unclear in the light of such questions: does "last" also mean "general, universal" here?

The purpose of this chapter is to assist the reader in reaching a responsible position regarding these problems. This necessitates a certain insight into the intentions of the evangelist Matthew as these come to the fore in his gospel. Attention will therefore first be given to the context of the narrative (I). Then two series of remarks concerning the text itself will clarify the presence of tradition and redaction within the pericope (II). In a third section we will attempt to reconstruct the pre–Matthean version and also investigate whether this reconstructed text goes back to Jesus himself and what might be its original meaning (III). The investigation then returns to the Matthean version in order to determine to what extent Matthew's rewriting of the source and his incorporation of it within the whole of the Parousia discourse has changed its original meaning (IV). The fifth section deals with a difficulty related to our explanation of Matthew's interpretation (V). The final section is the conclusion to both this eighth chapter and also to the two previous ones; here the main characteristics of Matthew's Last Judgment and of the Parousia discourse as a whole are briefly discussed (VI).

I. The Context

Our sixth chapter (pp. 147–52) included a survey of the contents of the Parousia discourse, Mt 24–25. The pericope of the Last Judgment (25:31–46) constitutes the conclusion of that discourse. This conclusion, vis à vis 24:4b–35 and 24:36–25:30, was moreover identified as a more or less independent third section.

The Parousia Discourse

After the second section (24:36–25:30) with its exhortation to vigilance and responsible Christian living, the Last Judgment is couched in terms of information concerning the future. The first section (24:4b–35) already offers a certain amount of information about the future. Its various phases are distinguished: i.e., not yet the end (vv. 4b–14), the great persecution (vv. 15–28), and the Parousia itself (vv. 29–31). But at the same time, Jesus addresses himself repeatedly to his hearers, the disciples, with warnings and exhortations: "take heed that no one leads you astray" (v. 4b); "see that you are not alarmed" (v. 6b); "let the reader understand" (end of v. 15); various counsels are given (vv. 16–18); "pray that your flight may not be in winter or on a sabbath" (v. 20); ". . . do not believe it" (vv. 23 and 26); cf. also the similitude of the Fig Tree in vv. 32–33. Thereafter, in the second section Jesus makes his final appeal to the disciples: "watch therefore, for you know neither the day nor the hour" (25:13). Then follows the parable of the Talents (25:14–30) comprising simply a narrative, without application or explicit exhortation. In the third section (25:31–46) no further appeals for response are made to the disciples. Jesus speaks to them *about* the Last Judgment. He explains what will happen when the Son of man returns and takes his seat on his glorious throne. He imparts information, but no longer exhorts, at least not directly.

The second section of Matthew's Parousia discourse has been

sufficiently dealt with in our sixth and seventh chapters. For a better understanding of the Last Judgment, the first section of the discourse and the relation in content between chap. 23 and 24:1–3 are of great importance. We start therefore with a discussion of Jesus' prediction of the destruction of the temple in 24:1–4a.

Destruction of the Temple Predicted (24:1–4a)

1 Jesus left the temple and was going away, when his disciples came to point out to him the buildings of the temple.
2 But he answered them, "You see all these, do you not? Truly, I say to you, there will not be left here one stone upon another, that will not be thrown down."
3 As he sat on the Mount of Olives, the disciples came to him privately saying, "Tell us, when will this be, and what will be the sign of your coming, and of the close of the age?"
4 And Jesus answered them. . . .

The discourse proper starts in 24:4b. What precedes in 24:1–4a forms the introduction indicating the occasion for that which follows. These verses indicate a change of place (on the way after leaving the temple; seated on the Mount of Olives). Twice the disciples approach Jesus, first gesturing towards the temple buildings (v. 1), and then asking him a question (v. 3). Jesus responds to the disciples' gesture by announcing the destruction of the temple. Then he answers their urgent question (when, what sign) with a long discourse.

When the text and context here are compared with those in Mk a number of differences are evident. For our purposes, it is not so important to note that in Mt 24:1–3 the disciples approach Jesus twice in a group: the first time *after* leaving the temple, still in the presence of the people, the second on the Mount of Olives, when they are alone. Matthew's source, i.e., Mk 13:1–5a, gives another presentation of this:

1 And as he [Jesus] came out of the temple, one of his disciples said to him, "Look, Teacher, what wonderful stones and what wonderful buildings!"
2 And Jesus said to him, "Do you see these great buildings? There

will not be left here one stone upon another, that will not be thrown down."

3 And as he sat on the Mount of Olives opposite the temple, Peter and James and John and Andrew asked him privately,

4 "Tell us, when will this be, and what will be the sign when these things are all to be accomplished?"

5 And Jesus began to say to them. . . .

In Mk 13:1–4 it is initially one of the disciples who draws Jesus' attention to the buildings as they are leaving the temple. Afterwards on the Mount of Olives only four of the disciples, Peter, James, John, and Andrew, question Jesus about the time and the sign. Thus in Mark in the discourse in 13:5b–37 there is a separation between these four disciples and the others (cf. also 13:37: "And what I say to you I say to all: Watch"), whereas in Matthew the separation is between the disciples as a whole and the people who probably include the Pharisees and the scribes as well as the city of Jerusalem (cf. chap. 23).

The fact that Matthew has omitted the section about the widow's mite (Mk 12:41–44) is more significant. Due to this omission, Matthew's introduction to the eschatological discourse follows immediately on the woes in chap. 23:

Compare:

Mt	Mk	
22:41–46	12:35–37a	son and lord of David
23:1–39	12:37b–40	against the (Pharisees and) scribes
————	12:41–44	the Widow's Mite
24:1–3	13:1–4	destruction of the temple predicted

The omission in question was probably intentional. Matthew obviously wanted to connect the announcement of 24:2 with that of 23:38. Much has been written about the arrangement and the editing of the woes in Mt 23. We limit ourselves to the following remarks. After the seventh woe, in 23:29–31, Matthew switches in vv. 32–36 to a very direct accusation and announcement of punishment which is repeated in an emphatic and pathos-filled way in the conclusion where Jerusalem is addressed.

29 "Woe to you, scribes and Pharisees, hypocrites! for you build the tombs of the prophets and adorn the monuments of the righteous,

30 saying, 'If we had lived in the days of our fathers, we would not have taken part with them in shedding the blood of the prophets.'

31 Thus you witness against yourselves, that you are sons of those who murdered the prophets.

32 Fill up, then, the measure of your fathers.

33 You serpents, you brood of vipers, how are you to escape being sentenced to hell?

34 Therefore I send you prophets and wise men and scribes, some of whom you will kill and crucify, and some you will scourge in your synagogues and persecute from town to town,

35 that upon you may come all the righteous blood shed on earth, from the blood of innocent Abel to the blood of Zechariah the son of Barachiah, whom you murdered between the sanctuary and the altar.

36 Truly, I say to you, all this will come upon this generation.

37 O Jerusalem, Jerusalem, killing the prophets and stoning those who are sent to you! How often would I have gathered your children together as a hen gathers her brood under her wings, and you would not!

38 Behold, your house is forsaken and desolate.

39 For I tell you, you will not see me again, until you say, 'Blessed is he who comes in the name of the Lord.' "

In the seventh woe reference is made to the hypocritical behavior of the scribes and Pharisees. They build tombs and decorate the monuments of the prophets whom they themselves have put to death (v. 29); they consider themselves righteous (v. 30), but are in fact, as sons of the prophets' murderers, no better than their forefathers (v. 31). With an ironic imperative they are now summoned to fill up the measure of their fathers (v. 32) by persecuting to death the prophets, wise men, and scribes, whom Jesus ("I"!) sends to them (v. 34). All the righteous blood which was shed, from that of Abel to that of Zechariah son of Barachiah, their contemporary, will come upon them, this generation (vv. 35–36), i.e., they will be judged and punished for all those crimes (vv. 33, 35–36).

It is striking that Jesus addresses the scribes and Pharisees in very hostile fashion here. In accusing them not only of their ancestors' murder of the prophets but also of the persecution which will occur after Jesus' death and resurrection, Matthew uses words of Jesus to refer to persons both in Jesus' time and in the time of the primitive church. R. Walker has, rightly in our view, stated that for Matthew the scribes and Pharisees are "an undifferentiated unity," who as such represent the guilty Israel of Jesus' days and of the years before A.D. 70. In its own way the term "Jerusalem" (v. 37) functions analogously in Matthew. Thus, it is possible for Matthew, without the least difficulty, to pass from the "scribes and Pharisees" (v. 29) to "Jerusalem" (v. 37, cf. also v. 36: "this generation").

What kind of punishment does Matthew concretely envision? Verses 37–39 elucidate this point. Initially it should be noted that in vv. 37–39 the reason for the punishment is somewhat different from that given in vv. 32–36 where punishment is announced because the scribes and Pharisees had rejected the prophets sent by God and Jesus. In vv. 37–39 the reason for the punishment is, beyond the persecution of the prophets, above all the rejection of Jesus himself: "How often would I have gathered your children together . . . , and you would not" (v. 37). The punishment itself is mentioned in v. 38: "Behold, your house is forsaken and desolate." It is not immediately evident what is meant by "house" here—spontaneously one would think of the temple which will be abandoned by God and delivered up to destruction.

Matthew makes a causal connection between this "leaving the house desolate" and the disappearance of Jesus himself: "*For* I tell you, you will not see me again until . . ." (23:39). Some exegetes think that this disappearance is already suggested in 24:1 when Jesus leaves the temple. Although one could consider Jesus' departure here as a first step leading to the complete abandonment and destruction of the temple (and thus Jerusalem with its rejection of Jesus would already realize and not merely motivate her own rejection), the clause "you will not see me again until . . ." (= the disappearance of Jesus) in 23:39 refers to Jesus' death, not to his departure from the temple in 24:1. On the other hand, 24:1–3 must in fact be read in the light of 23:29–39 and vice versa. Matthew omits Mk 12:41–44 because he wishes the disciples' pointing to the temple buildings (24:1) to become a reaction to

Jesus' announcement about the desolation of Jerusalem's "house" in 23:38. Jesus' answer in 24:2, "Truly, I say to you, there will not be left here one stone upon another, that will not be thrown down" is, in this context, undoubtedly a further specification of the announcement in 23:38: "your house" (23:38) is the temple of Jerusalem. The destruction will come as the punishment for the reasons enumerated in 23:32–37. This prediction of punishment is introduced by the solemn formula "Truly, I say to you" (23:36; 24:2) or "For I tell you" (23:39). The threat becomes clearer from one text to the next.

The redactional emphasis on the destruction of the temple as a punishment does not, however, prevent Matthew from distinguishing more clearly than Mark between the destruction of the temple and the Parousia/end of the world. In the question in Mk 13:4 ("Tell us, when will this be, and what will be the sign when these things are all to be accomplished?") by paralleling the terms "this" and "these things," these two events are very much intertwined. On the other hand, Mt 24:3 reads, "Tell us, when will this be, and what will be the sign of your coming (*parousia*) and of the close of the age?" It is well-known that of the three Synoptics only Matthew, and he only in this discourse (vv. 3, 27, 37, 39), uses the term "Parousia" (= advent, presence; but in this context meaning more specifically "return, coming again"). Matthew, under the influence of the verb "to be accomplished" (literally: to be fulfilled) in Mk 13:4, also uses the expression "the close of the age" (= the fulfillment of the world) in 24:3. This phrase is found only in Matthew and not in the other two Synoptics (see Mt 13:39, 40, 49; 28:20). We would expect Matthew's Parousia discourse then to answer the double question in 24:3—what is the connection between the destruction of the temple and the Parousia, between the end of the temple and the end of the world? Is it not true that the redactional rewriting of the second question in 24:3 already leads us to surmise that it is the Parousia and the end of the world which above all will be the focus of Matthew's attention in chaps. 24–25? With the expression "your Parousia" (24:3) Matthew has further rewritten Mk 13:4b in a christological way and in so doing prepares for what he will emphasize in 24:27, 30, 37–39, and 25:31: the coming of the Son of man. His whole discourse will be dominated by this idea.

Not Yet the End (vv. 4b–14)

4b "Take heed that no one leads you astray.
5 For many will come in my name, saying, 'I am the Christ,' and they will lead many astray.
6 And you will hear of wars and rumors of wars; see that you are not alarmed; for this must take place, but the end is not yet.
7 For nation will rise against nation, and kingdom against kingdom, and there will be famines and earthquakes in various places:
8 all this is but the beginning of the sufferings.
9 Then they will deliver you up to tribulation, and put you to death; and you will be hated by all nations for my name's sake.
10 And then many will fall away, and betray one another, and hate one another.
11 And many false prophets will arise and lead many astray.
12 And because wickedness is multiplied, most men's love will grow cold.
13 But he who endures to the end will be saved.
14 And this gospel of the kingdom will be preached throughout the whole world, as a testimony to all nations; and then the end will come."

People will come claiming to be the Christ, whence the danger of being misled; war and disasters will occur, whence the danger of disturbance. All this is, however, just the beginning of the woes, not yet the end (vv. 4v–8). In those days ("then") there will also be oppression and persecution unto death, hatred on the part of all nations (v. 9). "And then" too there will be scandal and betrayal in the Christian community. False prophets will arise, sin will increase, love will grow cold, whence the danger of infidelity (vv. 10–12). But he who endures to the end will be saved (v. 13). First, however, the gospel of the kingdom must be preached to the whole world as a testimony to all nations; then, and only then, the end will come (v. 14).

Like Mark in his parallel text 13:5b–13, Matthew also gives a warning in 24:4b–14. The information imparted should keep the disciples from panicking and inspire them to remain faithful in persecution. Unlike Mark, however, Matthew clearly lets it be felt that in his church, among his fellow Christians, not everything is still zeal and sinlessness; the love of many is growing cold. In this part of the discourse there is a certain sadness of tone. Finally, more so than Mark, Matthew emphasizes the universal proclamation of the gospel. This is shown by his placing the affirmation about world-wide preaching at the end of this section.

In vv. 4b–8 Matthew follows his source (Mk 13:5b–8) very closely, whereas in vv. 9–14 he diverges from its continuation, i.e., Mk 13:9–13. Matthew had, however, already used Mk 13:9–13 in 10:17–22, i.e., in his missionary discourse:

Mk 13	Mt 10
9 But take heed to yourselves;	17 Beware of men;
for they will deliver you up	for they will deliver you up
to councils;	to councils,
and you will be beaten	and flog you
in synagogues;	in their synagogues,
and you will stand	18 and you will be dragged
before governors and kings	before governors and kings
for my sake,	for my sake,
to bear testimony	to bear testimony
before them.	before them and the Gentiles.
10 And the gospel must first	
be preached to all nations.	
11 And when they	19 When they
bring you to trial	
and deliver you up,	deliver you up,
do not be anxious beforehand	do not be anxious
	how you are to speak or
what you are to say;	what you are to say;
but say whatever	for what you are to say
is given you in that	will be given to you in that
hour,	hour;
for it is not you who speak,	20 for it is not you who speak,
but the Holy Spirit.	but the Spirit of your Father
	speaking through you.
12 And brother will deliver	21 Brother will deliver
up brother to death,	up brother to death,
and the father his child,	and the father his child,
and children will rise against	and children will rise against
parents	parents
and have them put to death;	and have them put to death;
13 and you will be hated by	22 and you will be hated by
all for my name's sake.	all for my name's sake.
But he who endures to the	But he who endures to the
end will be saved.	end will be saved.

It is striking that in 10:17–22 Matthew has omitted Mk 13:10, the verse concerning the proclamation of the gospel to all nations. Those nations are, however, mentioned later in an emphatic way in 24:9 and 14. Verses 9 and 14 with their mention of "all nations" frame the intervening passage, vv. 10–13. But while 24:14 deals expressly and in a very positive way with the proclamation of the gospel to the whole inhabited world, as a testimony to all nations (differing to a certain extent from Mk 13:10 in this regard), 24:9 refers to persecution at the hands of those very nations! The disciples will be oppressed and persecuted; they will be hated by all nations (Note: Mk 13:13 does not have "by all *nations*," but only "by all"). In 24:9 we do not read anything further about persecution by the Jews as this is described in the parallel texts Mk 13:9, 11, and Mt 10:17–18, 19–20, and also in Mt 23:34–38. In Mt 24 it is a question of being delivered up to "tribulation," not to Sanhedrins and synagogues! The standpoint has thus shifted: Mt 10 and 23 (and 24:1–2) concern rejection and persecution by the Jews and their punishment; 24:9, the hostile attitude of the nations. In Matthew's conception those nations are apparently the Gentiles.

It does not seem advisable to postulate a special source for 24:10–13. Matthew himself composed these verses, in large part with the help of words and ideas offered him by the context. The result is typically Matthean in its content and of importance for an insight into the evangelist's conceptions. Matthew announces division and hatred, error and slackness in the Christian ranks. All this is, however, not completely unrelated to the persecution by the Gentiles described in v. 9. In fact, the phrase "and then" of v. 10 even indicates a causal connection between the two. In this verse "and then" means "after this"; the phrase refers back to what has just been said, it points to the consequence of this.

Verse 6 reads, "For this is not yet the end;" v. 8 notes, "All this is but the beginning of the sufferings." In v. 13 and again in v. 14 the end is mentioned once more. One gets the impression that the persecution by the Gentiles and the intraecclesial crisis (the false prophets, mutual hatred, increase of sin, love growing cold) are for Matthew more connected with this end—also for what concerns the time—than vv. 5–6 initially would lead us to suppose: "he who endures to the end will be saved" (v. 13). Meanwhile the universal proclamation of the gospel proceeds. Only then will the end come (v. 14).

The Great Tribulation (vv. 15–28)

15 "So when you see the desolating sacrilege spoken of by the prophet Daniel, standing in the holy place (let the reader understand),

16 then let those who are in Judea flee to the mountains;

17 let him who is on the housetop not go down to take what is in his house;

18 and let him who is in the field not turn back to take his mantle.

19 And alas for those who are with child and for those who give suck in those days!

20 Pray that your flight may not be in winter or on a sabbath.

21 For then there will be great tribulation, such as has not been from the beginning of the world until now, no, and never will be.

22 And if those days had not been shortened, no human being would be saved; but for the elect those days will be shortened.

23 Then if any one says to you, 'Lo, here is the Christ!' or 'There he is!' do not believe it.

24 For false Christs and false prophets will arise and show great signs and wonders, so as to lead astray, if possible, even the elect.

25 Lo, I have told you beforehand.

26 So, if they say to you, 'Lo, he is in the wilderness,' do not go out; if they say, 'Lo, he is in the inner rooms,' do not believe it.

27 For as the lightning comes from the east and shines as far as the west, so will be the coming of the Son of man.

28 Wherever the body is, there the eagles [or vultures] will be gathered together."

In vv. 15–22 Matthew describes the great tribulation in Judea more or less à la Mark, although shortening or elucidating the description here and there. The abomination of desolation which will stand in a holy place—in the Greek text there is no definite article and thus the expression remains rather vague—alludes to the siege of Jerusalem and to the fate of the temple. All of these verses are a reminiscence of the tragic Jewish war of the years 66–70, an event which for Matthew already belongs to past history. The fall of Jerusalem, i.e., the great tribulation, is for Matthew, as for Mark, the answer to the disciples' first question at the beginning of the discourse: "Tell us, when will this be?" In vv. 23–26 Matthew twice emphatically warns against false prophets. Such will be present not only in the period before the end, but also during the great tribulation which will immediately precede the end. False Christs will arise. Do not believe them. Do not follow them. In vv. 27–28 the motive for this command is given: the Parousia of the Son of man will be as clearly visible as lightning in the sky; it will be as easily recognizable for everyone as a corpse is discovered by the vultures!

Like vv. 4b–14, vv. 15–28 form part of the Parousia discourse and as such are addressed to the same disciples. But how are we to understand vv. 15–22 which are so closely linked to Judea, after vv. 4b–14, where every reference to the Jews is deliberately avoided and where a divided but, at the same time, missionary Christian community living among the Gentiles stands in the foreground?

First, the fact that Matthew to a certain extent wants to respect the presentation of his Marcan source must be taken into account. Moreover, it should be kept in mind that he is here making the Lord speak prior to his Passion. He is seated on the Mount of Olives answering a question about his previous prediction concerning the destruction of the temple. But is there not, nevertheless, a certain tension here in relation to the more universalistic character of vv. 4b–14? We do not think so, because in vv. 15–22 not all the disciples but only "those who are in Judea" (v. 15) are warned in a special way. Those who are there at that time must flee to the mountains for the tribulation will be great, the greatest the world has ever known and ever will know. The tribulation will last for a certain time ("those days," vv. 19, 22, 29; "then," vv. 21, 23). The signal for the flight is the presence of the abomination of desolation standing in a holy place; then the really bad times will begin. In those days false Christs and false prophets will arise. For Matthew it is still less likely than it is for Mark, however, that these false prophets will be able to lead the elect astray.

Like v. 5, vv. 23–28 concern the identification of the true Christ. For the disciples the true Christ is Jesus who must return as Son of man (v. 28; cf. v. 3); vv. 29–31 will deal explicitly with his return, the Parousia. The coming will not take place during, but immediately after, the tribulation of those days (v. 29). The mention of the appearance of false Christs in both sections (cf. vv. 4b–5 and vv. 23–26) confirms our previous conclusion that it is not so obvious that Matthew sees a radical time difference between the events of vv. 4b–14 and those of vv. 15–28. On the other hand, it is true that the second section focuses attention on the Jewish war, the fall of Jerusalem, and the destruction of the temple with all the ensuing messianic unrest, while vv. 4b–14 have a more universalistic character. In any case, it should be noted that both the persecution by the Gentiles and the internal confusion described in vv. 4b–14 do announce the end.

The Parousia (vv. 29–31)

29 "Immediately after the tribulation of those days the sun will be darkened, and the moon will not give its light, and the stars will fall from heaven, and the powers of the heavens will be shaken;
30 then will appear the sign of the Son of man in heaven, and then all the tribes of the earth will mourn, and they will see the Son of man coming on the clouds of heaven with power and great glory;
31 and he will send out his angels with a loud trumpet call, and they will gather his elect from the four winds, from one end of heaven to the other."

From v. 23 on (also already in vv. 4b–5!) Matthew takes up the disciples' second question: "What will be the sign of your coming and of the close of the age?" (v. 3c). False Christs and false prophets can mislead with signs and miracles (vv. 4b–5, 24). What then is the sign of Jesus' Parousia? Verses 27–28 represent the Parousia as a manifest, undeniable fact. According to v. 29 the Parousia will be accompanied by miraculous, universal, cosmic phenomena. Nonetheless, those phenomena are not that sign, since subsequently v. 30a explicitly concerns the appearance of the sign of the Son of man. The expression "the sign of the Son of man" here probably means the sign which the Son of man himself is, the sign which Jesus as the returning Son of man becomes. It can hardly be doubted that it was Matthew who added v. 30a and that he did so with a double purpose: (1) to give a clearer answer to the question in v. 3c and (2) to make of v. 30, together with the whole of vv. 27–31 (the coming of the Son of man), a counterbalance to vv. 23–26 (the presence of false Christs and false prophets).

The presence of the abomination in the temple and the great tribulation are, for Matthew, temporally connected with the Parousia of the Son of man. His coming will happen not long after the tribulation, even "immediately" after it, as we read in v. 29. But what is the effect of the appearance of the sign and what does the coming of the Son of man involve? Just as for Mark, so also for Matthew, Jesus' purpose in his coming is to definitively assemble the elect who are scattered throughout the world. Matthew however adds something further. While Mark states, "And then *they* (indefinite plural) will see the Son of man coming . . ." (Mk 13:26), Matthew first mentions the appearance of the sign of the Son of man (v. 30a), and then affirms that at the sight of it all *the tribes of the earth* will mourn (v. 30b). It is these same "tribes of the earth" who will see the Son of man coming (v. 30c). This Matthean addition and change in v. 30 with respect to Mk will assist us in coming to a correct understanding of the Last Judgment pericope.

Certainty (vv. 32–35)

32 "From the fig tree learn its lesson: as soon as its branch becomes tender and puts forth its leaves, you know that summer is near.

33 So also, when you see all these things, you know that he is near, at the very gates.

34 Truly, I say to you, this generation will not pass away till all these things take place.

35 Heaven and earth will pass away, but my words will not pass away."

All has now been said. There has been talk, mostly by way of warning, of all kinds of events which announce the end but are not yet themselves the end. The fate of Jerusalem and the appearance of many false prophets and false Christs in the period of the great tribulation were dealt with. Finally the Parousia itself was treated and the return of the Son of man was briefly described. Now in this last section, in which Matthew follows Mark very closely, the temporal connection between the events announced and the Parousia is once more confirmed by means of the parable of the Fig

Tree—a sign of the imminence of summer (cf. "as soon as" in v. 32 and "when" in v. 33). All these things will surely, still during this generation, come to pass.

Conclusion

The first part of the Parousia discourse comprises prophetic announcements, often couched in apocalyptic language, which present a seemingly careful prospectus of the future, a schema of the end-time with the following phases: (1) "not yet the end"; (2) the destruction of the temple and the great tribulation of the Jewish war; and (3) the Parousia. This periodization is, however, not perfect in that not everything mentioned in the first section necessarily precedes the great tribulation in Judea portrayed in the second. Persecution by the Gentiles, false prophets, the appearance of false Christs, mutual hatred, division, love growing cold among Christians, the proclamation of the gospel to the Gentiles—all these events too lead to the verge of the end.

This investigation of Mt 24:4b–35 has confirmed what our analysis of the connection between chap. 23 and Mt 24:1–3 had already indicated. In chap. 23 Jesus addresses himself for the last time to the scribes and Pharisees (and the Jews). The discourse about punishment in chap. 23 ends with an announcement of judgment—a judgment which was to become a historical fact in the fall of Jerusalem and the destruction of the temple. In Matthew's view God has apparently carried out his judgment on Israel in history. In this connection other passages in his gospel can be recalled: e.g., 21:43, "Therefore, I tell you, the kingdom of God will be taken away from you and given to a nation producing the fruits of it" (the parable of the Wicked Tenants), and 22:7, "The king was angry, and he sent his troops and destroyed those murderers and burned their city" (the parable of the Guests Invited to the Feast). From these passages it appears that the evangelist can already look back upon the actual course of historical events which Jesus in his discourse is as yet only predicting. At any rate, Matthew clearly distinguishes the judgment of Israel and the end of the world (compare 24:3b and 3c). Consequently, it is hardly thinkable that in this context the last judgment in 25:31–46 would (still) concern the Jews who, according to Matthew, have already been condemned.

In the first part of the Parousia discourse the expression "all nations" occurs twice (24:9 and 14; cf. also "all the tribes of the earth" in v. 30). Each time it refers to the Gentiles. Does the expression thus have the same meaning in 25:32?

II. The Text of the Last Judgment

25:31 "When the Son of man comes in his glory, and all the angels with him, then he will sit on his glorious throne.

32 Before him will be gathered all the nations, and he will separate them one from another as a shepherd separates the sheep from the goats,

33 and he will place the sheep at his right hand, but the goats at the left.

34 Then the King will say to those at his right hand, 'Come, O blessed of my Father, inherit the kingdom prepared for you from the foundation of the world;

35 for I was hungry and you gave me food, I was thirsty and you gave me drink, I was a stranger and you welcomed me,

36 I was naked and you clothed me, I was sick and you visited me, I was in prison and you came to me.'

37 Then the righteous will answer him, 'Lord, when did we see thee hungry and feed thee, or thirsty and give thee drink?

38 And when did we see thee a stranger and welcome thee, or naked and clothe thee?

39 And when did we see thee sick or in prison and visit thee?'

40 And the King will answer them, 'Truly, I say to you, as you did it to one of the least of these my brethren, you did it to me.'

41 Then he will say to those at his left hand, 'Depart from me, you cursed, into the eternal fire prepared for the devil and his angels;

42 for I was hungry and you gave me no food, I was thirsty and you gave me no drink,

43 I was a stranger and you did not welcome me, naked and you did not clothe me, sick and in prison and you did not visit me.'

44 Then they also will answer, 'Lord, when did we see thee hungry or thirsty or a stranger or naked or sick or in prison, and did not minister to thee?'

45 Then he will answer them, 'Truly, I say to you, as you did it not to one of the least of these, you did it not to me.'
46 And they will go away into eternal punishment, but the righteous into eternal life.'"

The current interpretation of Mt 25:31–46 runs more or less as follows: When the Lord returns at the end of the world he will judge all nations, Gentiles, Jews, and Christians, i.e., the whole of humankind without distinction. The one and only criterion in this judgment will be the attitude the person judged has adopted towards the "least." These are the people, it is said, with no prestige or standing, the rejected, the prisoners, the sick, the hungry, the poor of this world. All people are brothers of Jesus; the poor are the least of his brothers! The surprising thing at the universal judgment will be that we neither knew nor realized how we were in fact touching Christ himself in our love or hate for our fellow men: "as you did it to one of the least of these my brethren, you did it to me" (v. 40, cf. v. 45). This pericope would thus be about the meaning and fruitfulness of all human love, especially love for the least, whoever they may be.

Can we subscribe to this explanation without further investigation? For a responsible exegesis it is methodologically necessary that we try to ascertain whether, and if so where, Matthew rewrote and altered his source text, if he used one. On the basis of the discrepancies present in the text and of the typically Matthean features it contains we shall now, accordingly, attempt to identify the Matthean redaction in the Last Judgment pericope.

Discrepancies in the Present Text

Some exegetes are of the opinion that Mt 25:31–46 should not be called a parable or a similitude. For, although the passage does contain a comparison in vv. 32c–33 ("as a shepherd separates the sheep from the goats, and he will place the sheep at his right hand, but the goats at the left"), nevertheless, the course of the judgment itself which follows is described in the style of a direct dialogue. In other words, from the figurative part statements emerge which concern reality. On the other hand, it is precisely in this second section of the Last Judgment (vv. 34–46) that we find another metaphor, that of the "King." Thus, while there is not an independent, fully-developed similitude here, in our view the shepherd-comparison and the King-metaphor do allow us to use the term "parable" for this text, even if not in the strict sense.

In this context we might note that in the Bible translations of several languages the two opposed groups of animals in our text are rendered as "(female) sheep and *rams*" rather than "sheep and *goats*" (so the RSV; cf. above). The Greek word *eripha* or *eriphia* permits either translation. The latter opposition is probably that intended by the narrator: "In Palestine mixed flocks are customary; in the evening the shepherd separates the sheep from the goats, since the goats need to be kept warm at night, for cold harms them, while the sheep prefer open air at night" (Jeremias, *The Parables of Jesus*, p. 206). There is an additional reason for the choice of this rendering: it reflects the contrast between white sheep and black goats—colors with an obvious symbolic value. On the other hand, the alternate translation "(female) sheep and rams" could be the correct one if it could be shown that Ezek 34:17–22 formed the background for the opposition developed in Mt 25:32–33: "Therefore, thus says the Lord God to them: Behold, I, I myself will judge between the fat sheep and the lean sheep. Because you push with side and shoulder, and thrust at all the weak with your horns, till you have scattered them abroad, I will save my flock, they shall no longer be a prey; and I will judge between sheep and sheep" (vv. 20–22). This prophecy concerns strong and weak animals. Perhaps a distinction between "male and female" is also involved here (cf. v. 17: "Behold I judge between sheep and sheep, rams and he-goats"). However, we need not resolve this detailed question of translation here.

For our purposes the discrepancies in the text are of greater importance. We note three such:

(a) Allusion has already been made to the possibility of some tension which, however, should not be exaggerated. What is the relation between the comparison in vv. 32c–33 and the appearance of the King in vv. 34–46? The transition from shepherd to King and from beasts to people is unexpected. Further, the juxtaposition of the comparison and the pronouncement of judgment by the King is disturbing to a certain extent because of the different literary forms involved. But even if the transition is somewhat abrupt, one can hardly speak of real tension here.

(b) The second feature is of greater significance. In v. 31 we read, "When the Son of man comes in his glory, and all the angels with him, then he will sit on his glorious throne." For Matthew this coming Son of man is certainly Christ. He is the judge, the King who in vv. 37 and 44 is addressed as "Lord." That in Matthew's conception the Son of man–King is Christ is also confirmed by v. 34 where the King says to those at his right hand, "Come, O blessed of my Father." The Father is God, the Son is Jesus Christ. We should not, however, overlook the shift in the titles used: the "Son of man" appears only at the beginning, while the dialogue in vv. 34–46 is conducted by the "King." It is hardly conceivable that an author who was writing spontaneously and not using a source would introduce such a change of title. The question arises, therefore, whether we are not dealing here with a combination of tradition and redaction, each having its own proper title.

(c) There is still more tension. Who are those who are gathered together and separated? Verse 32 states that all the nations will be gathered before the Son of man. Here the emphasis lies on the universal aspect: all the nations! But from v. 34 on attention is directed much more to individuals. It is not nations or groups of people who are separated but particular persons. Within the pericope there is thus a shift from "nations" to "individuals." Here again one may ask whether this tension might not be the consequence of Matthew's rewriting and redactional reinterpretation. The source text could, for example, have concerned the separation of individuals; the criterion would have been one's personal attitude. But the redactor, wishing to stress the universal character of the judgment, would therefore speak of "all the nations."

This first series of remarks has been concerned with three discrepancies in the text. We are very well aware that this type of analysis is rather intricate and easily becomes hypercritical. One detects tensions where there are none; minor, accidental, and unavoidable unevenness is exaggerated. Yet, it is just these small discrepancies, the involuntary, scarcely noticeable incongruities, which betray the hand of the redactor. It seems to us that at least the tension between the two titles and that between nations and individuals are indications of the presence of tradition and redaction in the Last Judgment.

Matthean Style and Thematic

Is it possible to further specify the contribution of the redactor Matthew to the text of the Last Judgment? In content this pericope does fit in well at the end of the whole discourse. Its themes of the return of the Lord and judgment were repeatedly mentioned in both the first and the second parts of the discourse. Its words and ideas are rooted in what precedes. The term "Son of man" (v. 31) is used in 24:27, 30, 37, 39, 44; the expression "all the nations" (v. 32) in 24:9, 14 (cf. 24:30: "all the tribes of the earth"). "When the Son of man comes in his glory, and all the angels with him" (v. 31) is clearly reminiscent of 24:30–31: ". . . and they will see the Son of man coming on the clouds of heaven with power and great glory; and he will send out his angels . . . ," just as "inherit the kingdom prepared for you" (v. 34) recalls 25:21, 23: "I will set you over much." The same is the case for the punishment in "eternal fire" (v. 41): cf. 24:51; 25:30 (a place of "weeping and gnashing of teeth"). This series of agreements suggests that this pericope is very Matthean, although this does not necessarily mean that Matthew created it *ex nihilo*.

This supposition finds further confirmation when not only the immediate context of the Parousia discourse but also the whole gospel is considered. Thus the introductory verse (25:31) evidences a great similarity with 16:27, "For the Son of man is to come with his angels in the glory of his Father, and then he will repay every man for what he has done," and with 19:28, ". . . when the Son of man shall sit on his glorious throne. . . ." It can further be shown that the conclusions of most of the other discourses in Matthew's gospel contain allusions to the judgment. Noteworthy in this respect is, for example, the parable discourse of Mt 13 whose Marcan source has been expanded by Matthew. While Mark in chap. 4 presents only three parables, Matthew in chap. 13 has seven. In the Matthean parable discourse the parable of the Tares and its interpretation (13:24–30, 36–43, *Sondergut*) as well as the concluding parable of the Net (13:47–50, *Sondergut*) concern the separation of the good and evil who are brought together by the angels, the kingdom of the Father as a reward, and a (fiery) place of weeping and gnashing of teeth. All these motifs are also present in Mt 25:31–46.

Several exegetes have made a detailed investigation of the Matthean character of the thematic and the choice of words in this pericope. We note their main findings:

(1) Verses 31–32a seem to be completely Matthean (cf. the use of the term "Son of man," the emphasis on the glorious Parousia, the close connection between Parousia and judgment, the fact that it is Jesus who will pass judgment and that the glory and the angels have become, as it were, his property; cf. also the use of expressions like "his glorious throne" [literally: "the throne of his glory"] and "all the nations"). All these elements taken cumulatively lead to the conclusion that vv. 31–32a are thoroughly Matthean and thus were not, it would seem, part of the pre–Matthean tradition.

(2) The same cannot be said of v. 34, although the terms "then," "to come," "to inherit," and the expression "my Father" do betray the presence of Matthew's editing in this verse. While these characteristic words and phrases do not prove that this verse is a purely Matthean creation, they do in any case indicate that Matthew has rewritten it in a thorough way.

(3) In other verses of the pericope Matthean redactional intervention can also be noted. For example, the word "righteous" in vv. 37 and 46 was perhaps inserted by Matthew, as was certainly the term "brethren" in v. 40 and probably the phrase "Truly, I say to you" in vv. 40 and 45. It is also possible that the expression "eternal fire" in v. 41 came from Matthew.

Conclusion

When looking back over the preceding analysis, it is evident that the cumulative force of all this data is impressive. Small discrepancies in the text and the evidence of Matthew's reworking destroy the naive conception that Mt 25:31-46 is a smooth text without difficulties which has simply unchangingly reproduced Jesus' original parable. When the two foregoing series of remarks are considered together, they strengthen the hypothesis that Matthew used a tradition or a "source" for this text. Is it still possible for us to remove the Matthean redaction and thus to uncover that pre–Matthean tradition?

III. The Pre–Matthean Tradition or Text

An Extreme Position

Following J.A.T. Robinson, S. Légasse did a long analysis of the pericope of the Last Judgment. In his opinion not only are vv. 31–32a a Matthean creation, but v. 34 is also. Matthew would have used the latter to link two traditional fragments, i.e., the remnant of a parable (vv. 32c–33) and the "antitheses" in vv. 35–36. Both Robinson and Légasse refer to the many Matthean features of vocabulary and thematic within this pericope. According to them, the convergence of all these elements leads to the conclusion that the Last Judgment parable as such did not exist prior to Matthew. Rather, to such possibly traditional elements as the comparison with the shepherd and the "antitheses" concerning the judgment Matthew added introductory and transitional verses designed to fit them into the discourse context. The perhaps originally disparate elements were thus related and shaped into an impressive scene. In this conception Matthew would be the true author of the Last Judgment.

Reconstruction of the Text

In his recent study, I. Broer proceeds more cautiously. He too recognizes the Matthean redactional character of vv. 31–32a, as well as of expressions such as "my Father" (v. 34), "my brethren" (v. 40), "eternal fire" (v. 41), "truly, I say to you" (vv. 40 and 45), "the righteous" (vv. 37 and 46), and the frequent use of "then." On the other hand, he notes the many *hapaxlegomena* in this pericope and also calls attention to the probably non–Matthean traditional character of some of them. Thus, he focuses attention on "punishment" (v. 46) and "curse" (v. 41) which are not typical for Matthew. In Mt 24:31, and also in 13:41 and 49, it is the angels who are sent out to gather and then to separate those who are judged; and so it appears strange that in 25:32b it is the Son of man himself who makes the separation, while the angels mentioned in v. 31 apparently remain inactive. Equally remarkable is the fact that the Son of man–Judge is only called "King" in Matthew's gospel in 25:34 and 40. Broer further remarks that elsewhere in his gospel Matthew does not show much interest in "corporal works" of mercy; in 10:42 it is not so much the act of giving

a cup of cold water as the intention of the giver in doing this deed
that is stressed (cf. 5:3 where "poor" is understood figuratively:
"the poor in spirit;" otherwise in the Lucan parallel text 6:20 and
most probably also in Q). Finally, there is also v. 34a: "Then the
King will say to those at his right hand" (cf. v. 41a: "those at his
left hand"). "Then" is definitely Matthean, but there is nothing
further in this verse which would suggest that this half of v. 34
constitutes a Matthean editorial transition connecting two disparate traditional fragments (comparison and antitheses). Rather, v.
34a clearly resumes the theme of separation present in vv. 32bc–
33 and, after the comparison developed in these verses, carries
the story further. But if v. 34a is thus essentially traditional, then
it is no longer necessary to regard the two pre–Matthean fragments, which respectively precede and follow it, as having been
independent from one another prior to their combination by Matthew. These two elements probably always belonged together and
from the beginning formed part of the one narrative of the Last
Judgment. The only peculiar detail is that suddenly a "King"
speaks. It is, however, probable that the pre–Matthean source did
not contain the title "Son of man"; we may suppose that in the
introduction of this source text a "King" was mentioned.

All this shows how cautiously one must proceed in distinguishing tradition and redaction. What was the content of the pre–
Matthean Last Judgment pericope? Whoever wishes to reconstruct
Matthew's source must remove all Matthean elements. This implies that the entire introduction up to and including v. 32a cannot
be referred to the source; it was created by Matthew. The mention
of the Parousia within it is designed to fit the Last Judgment into
the context of the Parousia discourse. This result, however, should
not lead to the conclusion that the Last Judgment contained no
introduction in its pre–Matthean form. We can perhaps (with
Broer) reconstruct this original introduction as follows: "At the end
of time (or: at his coming) the King will act like a shepherd who
. . . ." The content of v. 32b is incorporated in this reconstructed
introduction. Matthew rewrote it as v. 32b now stands. Verses
32c–33 then followed: "(who) separates the sheep from the goats;
and he will place the sheep at his right hand, but the goats at his
left." Thereafter, with the exception of its initial adverb "then," v.
34a is retained for the source, whereas at least the expression "of

my Father" must be excised from v. 34b. In v. 40 we eliminate "of my brethren" (cf. v. 45: "as you did it not to one of the least of these;" here Matthew forgets to add "my brethren").

Other words and expressions would probably have to be removed or replaced, but those mentioned in the foregoing reconstruction are, from the point of view of content, the most important. This suffices in order that we may now proceed to a discussion of the meaning of this pre–Matthean pericope.

The Original Meaning

In Broer's opinion there is no reason to deny this passage, which is to be regarded as a unity, to Jesus and to ascribe its origin rather to a Jewish–Christian milieu. The passage fits very well in Jesus' preaching about an inescapable judgment. It can also be attributed to Jesus in so far as attention is not focused on a reward-righteousness (one does not even realize that one is serving God in the neighbor) and since the radical and universal love of neighbor is obviously given precedence over fidelity to the Law, a fidelity which is not even mentioned in the passage.

In this parable of the Last Judgment, Jesus did not speak about himself. It can hardly be supposed that the earthly Jesus would have announced his own Parousia. Moreover, it has been noted that the entire introduction (vv. 31–32a) which does mention the return of the Son of man is Matthean. Similarly, the expression "of my Father" in v. 34 was added by Matthew. That Jesus would have referred to himself using the metaphor of the "King" is highly improbable and moreover would have been incomprehensible to his Palestinian hearers.

In the original version the King was therefore God who, according to Jesus, identifies himself with every wretched, needy, or suffering person. God is the Judge who will judge people according to their attitude towards the "least." Jesus compares God to a shepherd who separates the sheep from the goats. God will act in this way at the Last Judgment, the day on which his dominion will be realized and his kingdom definitively and visibly established.

Jesus used this parable to exhort his hearers—the people, his opponents, and his disciples—to a radical practice of love of neighbor. It is a matter of life and death, because in one's fellow man God himself is encountered. The Law is not mentioned. The only criterion of judgment is love for the neighbor in need. This "new" commandment of Jesus can, at times, oblige us to go beyond the stipulations of the Law.

IV. Matthew's Interpretation

The findings set forth in our previous paragraphs can be briefly summarized as follows: (1) Although Matthew's redaction of 25:31–46 has admittedly been very radical, we nevertheless retain the opinion that Matthew possessed an authentic narrative of Jesus about the Last Judgment in his traditional material (in this case in his *Sondergut*). This original narrative already had essentially the same structure as the present Last Judgment pericope. The Last Judgment, therefore, is not Matthew's own composition (e.g., put together on the basis of so-called traditional fragments, cf. Robinson and Légasse). (2) There seems to be no conclusive argument against attributing this pre–Matthean text unit to Jesus himself. To doubt the parable's authenticity would betray a hypercritical mentality. (3) What is most surprising is the original meaning of the narrative. In the Last Judgment scene Jesus does not speak of himself and the angels, nor of his "brethren" and all the nations. Jesus simply teaches his hearers that God the King will judge all without distinction. The only norm for his judgment will be the attitude one has adopted towards the "least" ones. These are people without prestige or status, the rejected, prisoners, the sick and the hungry, the naked and homeless. At the judgment those condemned will be amazed at the verdict, because they never realized that God is vulnerable in their neighbor: All that you did or did not do for one of these, the least ones, you did or did not do for God (cf. vv. 40 and 45). The original parable speaks indeed of the meaning of love of neighbor.

What we have above (p. 212) called the current interpretation thus seems, in fact, to have been the original meaning of the pericope, that intended by Jesus himself. It should however be emphasized once again that with the metaphor of the King, Jesus—just as the Old Testament—refers not to himself but to God. What has Matthew done with his source? How has he actualized it? Is his actualization a betrayal of Jesus' original message?

Matthew's Reworking

According to the results of our analysis, Matthew would have found the unit which we have reconstructed in his *Sondergut*. He reworked this source in three ways:

(a) The original introduction was broken off and Matthew created a new, longer introduction in its place. The Son of man comes in his glory, accompanied by all the angels; he takes his place on the judgment seat; all the nations are assembled before him and he separates them. By virtue of the fact that the coming of the Son of man is the return, the Parousia of Jesus, Jesus now becomes the King who judges and identifies himself with the "least." It was in this way that the double title in the pericope arose; Jesus is first Son of Man and then King. Moreover, Matthew in this introduction forgets that elsewhere (even in 24:31 where he follows Mk 13:27; cf. also Mt 13:41–42 and 49–50) he has accorded an active role to the angels. Finally, the mention of "all the nations" stands in a certain tension with the further development of the narrative in which the King addresses himself instead to individuals. These discrepancies have shown how difficult it is to completely harmonize later additions with the details of an older text.

(b) Matthew adds "of my brethren" in v. 40 (but not in v. 45!). By means of this addition he more closely specifies the broad category of the least ones as a group of "brethren." Who are these "brethren"?

(c) Matthew's contextualization of this pericope also constitutes a reinterpretation of the text. How does the parable function as the conclusion of the Parousia discourse addressed by Jesus to his disciples? How does this pericope relate to the broader context of Mt 23? Does the expression "all the nations" in 25:32 have the same meaning as elsewhere in Matthew's gospel?

At this point in our investigation we are trying to discover the vision which guided Matthew in his reworking. In this connection three main questions have to be answered: (1) Who are "all the nations"? Three possible interpretations are: all humankind (Gentiles, Jews, and Christians); all non–Christian peoples; only the Gentiles, excluding Jews and Christians. (2) Who are "the least of these my brethren"? Are they all those in need, without distinction, or only needy Christians, or a particular group of Christians? (3) The third question concerns the criterion of judgment, i.e., the corporal works of mercy. Is the reference to these works to be taken literally or in a more figurative way? The answer to this last question depends on those given to the first two. Finally, it should be repeated once again here that our discussion of these three questions in what follows no longer concerns Jesus' original intention. It is directed to Matthew's interpretation.

All the Nations

"Before him will be gathered all the nations" (Mk 25:32). The nations were already mentioned several times in chaps. 24–25. They are the nations spread throughout the whole world, to whom according to 24:14 (cf. 26:13), the gospel of the kingdom must be preached before the end comes (Mt 28:19 states that these nations must be made disciples). It is these nations too who, according to 24:9, will hate the disciples because of Jesus' name, but who then in 24:30 (here: "all the tribes of the earth") will mourn when they see the returning Son of man–Judge. "All the nations" in this pericope are thus apparently all the Gentile nations who are confronted with God's message in Christ as it is proclaimed by the disciples. In response to this proclamation they will either become disciples themselves or will be brought to hate the disciples. Mt 25:31–46 thus does not intend to describe the judgment of the apostles or the disciples of Jesus' earthly life, but rather that of the people to whom they are sent. Matthew develops the short, negative, and somewhat one-sided note in 24:30 (". . . all the tribes of the earth will mourn, and they will see the Son of man coming on the clouds of heaven with power and great glory") in 25:41–46, after having first portrayed the positive counterpart to this in vv. 34–40.

The wider context which we discussed above makes it clear that the Jewish people do not belong to these nations. *Panta ta ethnē* (25:32) are the *gôyîm*, the Gentiles; Israel herself is already condemned. At the end of the parable of the Wicked Tenants, Jesus declares to the high priests, elders, and Pharisees, "Therefore I tell you, the kingdom of God will be taken away from you and given to a nation (singular!) producing the fruits of it" (21:43). The Jewish "nation" is rejected. In the following parable, the Guests Invited to the Feast, Matthew states that the angry king "destroyed those murderers and burnt their city" (22:7)—an unmistakable allusion to the punishment which will befall Jerusalem. The destruction of the temple is foretold in 23:38 and 24:2. Just before the crucifixion the people shout, "His blood be on us and on our children!" (27:25). The Parousia discourse itself and the statements just mentioned refer to the judgment of Israel which had been realized in history before Matthew wrote his gospel. Nowhere in his gospel does it appear that Matthew still thinks of a mission to the Jewish people. In his view this people is already condemned and will, therefore, not be a part of the peoples who on the last day will stand assembled before the throne of the Son of man.

Neither, however, do the Christians belong to the nations. This will become clearer after our analysis of the term "brethren." To be sure, according to Matthew Christians will certainly be judged on the last day. The criterion will be their vigilance, their having done the will of the Father in heaven, their good works. This was the theme of the second section of the Parousia discourse (24:36–25:30). But in the third and final section of the discourse the perspective widens. After having dealt with the condemnation of Israel at the end of chap. 23 and the beginning of chap. 24, and after having exhorted Christians by means of the judgment motif in the discourse itself, Matthew now speaks at the end of the discourse about the judgment of the Gentile nations. The judgment of Jews, Christians and Gentiles is referred to by Matthew in chaps. 23–25, but the judgment of all three groups is not described in 25:31–46. In 25:32 "all the nations" are the Gentile nations; Jews and Christians are not included in this expression.

The Least of These My Brethren

Are the "least" in 25:40 and 45 still the vague, undefined category of all wretched people?

(a) At the end of the missionary discourse in Mt 10 we read, "And whoever gives to one of these little ones (*mikroi*) even a cup of cold water because he is a disciple, truly, I say to you, he shall not lose his reward" (10:42). In chap. 18 it is said that he who wishes to be the greatest among the disciples must consider himself as small as the child whom Jesus demonstratively places in their midst. To do this is even a condition for entering the kingdom of heaven (cf. vv. 2–4). Thereafter Jesus adds, "Whoever receives one such child in my name receives me" (v. 5). It would be wrong to focus on the physical smallness of the child here, because Jesus continues, "but whoever causes one of these little ones (*mi-kroi*) who believe in me to sin . . ." (v. 6). The little ones are thus the disciples who believe in Jesus. They are, in the proper sense of the word, Jesus' brothers, for in 12:49–50 we find, "And stretching out his hand toward his disciples, he said, 'Here are my mother and my brothers! For whoever does the will of my Father in heaven is my brother, and sister, and mother' " (cf. "brothers" or "brethren" = Christians also in 18:15–35; 23:8; 28:10). Perhaps these "small ones" have a weak faith; they can be misled and scandalized and go astray, but they are not to be despised (cf. 18:10). The shepherd searches out the lost sheep. It is the will of the heavenly Father that not one of these little ones should perish (cf. 18:12–14).

After having now explained—correctly, we hope—the expression "all the nations" and "the least of my brethren," and having taken into account the context and the Matthean accents elsewhere in the gospel, we are brought to a new insight into the judgment described in Mt. 25:31–46. The nations will be judged according to their attitude towards Christians. Whoever touches a Christian, touches Christ. In the already quoted missionary discourse in Mt 10 this is stated very clearly, "He who receives you receives me" (v. 40), and, "A disciple is not above his teacher, nor a servant above his master; it is enough for the disciple to be like his teacher, and the servant like his master" (vv. 24–25), while in vv. 11–15 we read:

> "And whatever town or village you enter, find out who is worthy in it, and stay with him until you depart. As you enter the house, salute it. And if the house is worthy, let your peace come upon it; but if it is not worthy, let your peace return to you. And if any one will not receive you or listen to your words, shake off the dust from your feet as you leave that house or town. Truly, I say to you, it shall be more tolerable on the day of judgment for the land of Sodom and Gomorrah than for that town."

From these texts we cannot avoid the impression that Jesus will be as radical in judging the attitude people have taken toward his disciples as he is in judging their attitude toward himself (cf. 10:32–33). The norm for the judgment will be acceptance or rejec-

tion of the disciple and his message about Christ. This acceptance
by the nations manifests itself in "works of mercy": in welcoming
and feeding, clothing and visiting that marginal, excluded, despised, reviled, and vulnerable "third" race which Christians constitute alongside the Gentiles and the Jews. It is not to be doubted
that to receive and welcome a disciple into one's home is practically equivalent to becoming a disciple oneself. Be this as it may,
however, the parable does not deal with the judgment of Christians as Christians. Rather, Mt 25:31–46 has to do with the fate of
all the Gentile nations who, before the end of the world, in some
way or another must accept or reject, receive or persecute the
Christians. The saying "He who is not with me is against me" (Mt
12:30) is also applicable to this encounter.

(b) Perhaps it is possible to be even more specific. In Mt 25:40
we read, "as you did it to one of the least of these my brethren."
The term translated "least" here is a superlative in Greek: *elachistos.* Although it is quite possible in biblical Greek for a positive
or comparative form to have a superlative meaning, so that there
need not necessarily be a difference of meaning among the terms
mikros, mikroteros, and *elachistos* (little, lesser and least), it is
nevertheless clear that Matthew deliberately uses the superlative
form in 25:40 in order to distinguish a particular group of brethren.
It would seem that he employs the demonstrative pronoun "these"
for the same reason. If, on the other hand, he had written, e.g.,
the positive form "little" and the article "the" (the little brethren),
this could give the impression that he was characterizing all the
brethren (= Christians) as small. But since, in fact, he does write
"one of the least of these my brethren" (superlative and demonstrative pronoun), it would appear that he has a specific group of
Christians in mind. Note further that "the little ones who believe
in Jesus" in 18:6 are also not all the disciples, but a determined,
limited group or category.

Who are these least or little ones in the Last Judgment pericope? Mt 10:40–42 brings us nearer the answer. In the discourse
in chap. 10 Matthew is clearly thinking about mission. In 10:40 we
read, "He who receives you receives me, and he who receives me
receives him who *sent* me." That this special group in Matthew's
view consists of those who are sent, of missionaries, is confirmed
by v. 42: "And whoever gives to one of these little ones even a

cup of cold water because he is a disciple, truly, I say to you, he shall not lose his reward." This verse has four points in common with the judgment scene in 25:31–46: (1) the expression "one of these little ones" (cf. "one of the least of these my brethren" in 25:40, and "one of the least of these" in 25:45); (2) "disciple" (cf. "brethren" in 25:40); (3) "reward" (cf. the giving of the reward in 25:34); and (4) the material criterion of loving reception and welcome: a cup of cold water (cf. the corporal works of mercy in 25:34–45). Thus, just as there is a missionary context in Mt 10, there is also in 25:31–46. And is such a context not already present in 24:14: "And this gospel of the kingdom will be preached throughout the whole world, as a testimony to all nations" (cf. 24:9)? Mt 10 deals with the mission to the "lost sheep" of Israel; Mt 24:14 and 25:31–46 concern the mission to the Gentiles.

The Criterion

If Mt 25:31–46 therefore has to do with missionary disciples and their being accepted or rejected by the Gentile nations, how is it that the whole emphasis in the judgment lies on the corporal works of mercy? Why is the criterion merely material? Of course it is true that external help is an expression of an inner acceptance of the message, even of becoming a Christian. But why is this not said explicitly? And why in Mt 25:41–44 is there also no mention of persecution such as in 24:9 ("Then they will deliver you up to tribulation, and put you to death; and you will be hated by all nations for my name's sake"), or in 23:32–38?

The real answer to such questions must, it would seem, be sought in the distinction between tradition and redaction. For Jesus, the works of mercy were the proof of a radical and universal love towards men. In Matthew's Christological and ecclesiological rewriting this material assistance now functions, not quite as appropriately, as a sign of acceptance and welcome for those sent and their message.

Conclusion

Our three earlier questions have now been answered. We know that for Matthew "all the nations" are the Gentile peoples. And, the "least of these my brethren" in Matthew's view are Christians, more specifically the particular group sent out to preach Christ among the Gentiles. According to Matthew, the criterion of judgment is the attitude which the Gentiles adopt towards these Christian missionaries. In the Matthean version of the Last Judgment, "all the nations" are the Gentiles who, confronted with God's message in Christ as this is preached by the disciples, must either welcome or reject this proclamation. Mt 25:31–46 does not describe the judgment of the disciples but only that of the Gentiles to whom the disciples are sent (cf. Mt 28:18–20). Nor is anything said about Israel here. Israel is already condemned.

V. "Smallness" and Poverty

One further difficulty remains: How is it possible that the same author, Matthew, should have used almost the same terminology with two radically different meanings? In chap. 10 the "little ones" and in chap. 25 "the least of these my brethren" refer to a specific group of disciples, the missionaries. In chap. 18 the "little ones who believe in me" (cf. 18:10, 14: "these little ones") are also a particular group which does not include all the disciples without distinction. They are, rather, marginal Christians who run the risk of losing their way and getting lost. Their smallness lies in their vulnerability. Because of their weakness other disciples may easily scandalize them (cf. v. 6) and may despise them (cf. v. 10). Jesus warns, it is the will of my Father that not one of these little ones should perish (cf. v. 14). What then does seeking out the lost ones involve, or better, in what does the care which will keep them from going astray consist? "Whoever receives one such child (probably in addition to real children this also meant "one of the little ones who believe in me") receives me" (v. 5). Here too it is a matter of acceptance; but while 10:40–42 and 25:31–46 point to the duties of those who must receive the little ones and those sent out, i.e., non–Christians, all Gentile nations, in chap. 18 it is the disciples themselves who must receive and seek out the little ones.

Does the group of little ones differ then according to the context? From the point of view of the vocabulary, this is not likely. The "little ones" and the "least" appear in Matthew only in 10:42; 18:6, 10, 14; and 25:40, 45. It is difficult to suppose that Matthew was inconsistent in his use of these terms. Further, both in the missionary (cf. chaps. 10 and 25) and community (cf. chap. 18) contexts, it is a question of a limited group of Christians. Therefore, we may accept that there is a common element in Matthew's references to the "little ones." Specifically we think here, with Légasse, of a group or class which can include both those whose faith is weak and preachers of the faith. They are the poor, those without social status, those who even in a Christian community are easily despised, neglected, and disdained and so run the risk of being lost. At the same time it is quite possible that the material criteria mentioned (cf. 10:42 and 25:35–45) would indicate that the traveling missionaries were poor Christians. Perhaps most of them came from the above-mentioned group of, socially speaking, "little people"; in any case, during their missionary journeys they were completely dependent on the material help offered by the "nations" to whom they were sent.

In this way it is possible, though not without some difficulty, to regard the use of the terms "little" and "least" in Mt 10, 18, and 25 as consistent to a certain extent. Wherever these terms occur in Matthew's gospel they do not refer to all disciples, but only to a few, a special group of Christians characterized by a certain inferiority. Chapter 18 points out a consequence of this "inferiority": moral and religious vulnerability. Jesus warns the other disciples not to despise them; he appeals to them to care for this group. From 10:40–42 and 25:31–46 it can perhaps be concluded that the traveling missionaries came mostly from the ranks of the "little people"; in any case, whatever their social origins might have been, these missionaries became poor and in need of help from the day they departed for their work of preaching. Jesus exhorts all those to whom they are sent to receive them well. In both the missionary as well as the community context, Jesus identifies himself with these poor disciples: he who receives you receives me; he who receives one such child in my name receives me!

VI. The Last Judgment in the Parousia Discourse

The explanation in the foregoing paragraph will not completely satisfy all. For, the fact remains that these "little ones" (cf. chap. 25:40: "the least of these my brethren") refer to two different groups of Christians. In chap. 18 they are those weak in faith; in chaps. 10 and 25 those of strong faith, preachers of the gospel! Is it, then, absolutely necessary to postulate a common element uniting these two practically opposite groups? Would that common element be the fact that both are poor? Are the two groups called "little ones" because of their need of special assistance and because, on account of their poverty, they are so vulnerable? This is possible, but ultimately these points should not be overemphasized. It remains possible that in this case Matthew did not fully harmonize his terminology.

Of far greater importance is Matthew's radical reinterpretation of Jesus' vision of the Last Judgment. Our detailed analysis has shown that Matthew had a very personal opinion about what is to take place when the Son of man comes in glory with all his angels and sits on his glorious judgment seat.

The Matthean Emphasis and Contemporary Objections

Matthew's rewriting and interpretation are influenced by his Christology and his image of the church. That after the resurrection the original King of the parable, i.e., God, becomes for Christians and for Matthew Christ the Son of man can hardly surprise us. But what are we to think of Matthew's restriction of the "little ones" to a particular group, and the new criterion of judgment which he proposes? And what about those who are judged? In Matthew's version the Last Judgment is no longer strictly universal. All humankind is not involved but only all Gentiles. They are judged according to the attitude they have adopted towards Christian missionaries. What they have done for one of these disciples, they have done to Jesus. In this postconciliar period when great attention is given in discussion and preaching to "horizontal," a-confessional human fellowship (and rightly so—see the original meaning, pp. 219–20), Matthew's radical reworking of the Last Judgment will hardly receive an enthusiastic reception. On the other hand, when the unique and definitive character of Jesus' mission is sufficiently elucidated, it may be recognized that Matthew's reinterpretation is not illegitimate. Man's destiny is always and radically called into question by an encounter with Jesus, whether in person or as present in his messengers: "Who is not with me is against me" (Mt 12:30).

There is a second point. What was Matthew's view about the time of Jesus' return? In the years 75–85 Matthew and his fellow believers no longer lived in a tense state of *Naherwartung*. In the last verse of Matthew's gospel we find Jesus' promise: "And lo, I am with you always, to the close of the age" (28:20). It would, however, be wrong to read our modern conceptions of an ongoing, open future into this verse. As far as we can see, Matthew probably still expected Jesus' soon return, the close of the age. In his Parousia discourse he preserves the statement in 24:34: "Truly, I say to you, this generation will not pass away till all these things take place" (cf. Mk 13:30). In the second section of this discourse he stresses the need to remain alert, because we do not know the day or the hour when the Son of man will come (cf. 24:42 and 25:13). Indeed, he will come at a moment when we least expect him (cf. 24:44). On the other hand, we read in the same Parousia discourse, "And this gospel of the kingdom will be preached throughout the world, as a testimony to all nations; and then the end will come" (24:14). Thus in Matthew's conception the nations will only be judged after they have been confronted with the Christian message. According to Mt 25:31–46, the judgment criterion is precisely the attitude adopted by those nations towards the missionaries in this confrontation.

In the early church there was a general expectation of an imminent Parousia. We no longer share this view of the future. But a correct understanding of Matthew's conception helps us to recognize why he does not speak (and apparently could not speak) about the problem of "anonymous" Christians, i.e., all those people who do not have the opportunity to meet Christ or to hear of his message, but who nonetheless lead an honest and moral life, without realizing that they implicitly desire to become Christians. All this lay outside Matthew's range of vision. We cannot address Matthew with these questions which so vitally concern us. In his time questions of this sort simply did not exist.

But we are still left with the criterion of judgment. For Matthew himself the pericope of the Last Judgment only concerns what applies to one class of people. Elsewhere in his gospel he discusses other norms. For him, *the Jews* are already condemned because they have rejected their Messiah and have persecuted and killed his messengers. This is the criterion of their judgment. According to the same Matthew, *Christians* also will be judged. What is the norm for their judgment? Matthew indicates that Christians must do the will of their heavenly Father. "Not every one who says to me, 'Lord, Lord,' shall enter the kingdom of heaven, but he who does the will of my Father who is in heaven. On that day many will say to me, 'Lord, Lord, did we not prophesy in your name, and cast out demons in your name, and do many mighty works in your name?' And then will I declare to them, 'I never knew you; depart from me, you evildoers' " (Mt 7:21–23). The expression "I never knew you" recurs in the parable of the Ten Virgins: "Afterwards the other maidens came also, saying 'Lord, Lord, open to us.' But he replied, 'Truly, I say to you, I do not know you' " (Mt 25:11–12). This could be called the moral criterion of judgment. It has to do with a denial of Christ through a lack of love and committing sin after having become a Christian (cf. also the exhortations in Mt 13). For *the Gentiles* it was Matthew's deepest conviction that the acceptance or rejection of Christ or his messengers was a matter of life or death. Already in the discourse in chap. 10, on the occasion of the Galilean mission, it appears that people can reject both the messenger and his message. A severe sentence awaits such people:

"And if any one will not receive you or listen to your words, shake off the dust from your feet as you leave that house or town. Truly, I say to you, it shall be more tolerable on the day of judgment for the land of Sodom and Gomorrah than for that town." (10:14–15)

Compare also 11:20–24:

Then he began to upbraid the cities where most of his mighty works had been done, because they did not repent. "Woe to you, Chorazin! woe to you, Bethsaida! for if the mighty works done in you had been done in Tyre and Sidon, they would have repented long ago in sackcloth and ashes. But I tell you, it shall be more tolerable on the day of judgment for Tyre and Sidon than for you. And you, Capernaum, will you be exalted to heaven? You shall be brought down to Hades. For if the mighty works done in you had been done in Sodom, it would have remained until this day. But I tell you that it shall be more tolerable on the day of judgment for the land of Sodom than for you."

The Jews not only rejected the Old Testament prophets, John the Baptist, and Jesus himself, but also the Christian missionaries sent to them by Jesus. Matthew explicitly connects the fate of Jerusalem with this rejection: "O Jerusalem, Jerusalem, killing the prophets and stoning those who are sent to you! How often would I have gathered your children together as a hen gathers her brood under her wings, and you would not! Behold, your house is forsaken and desolate" (Mt 23:37–38). Can we, then, interpret the rejection of the missionaries by the Gentiles referred to in 25:31–46 otherwise than as a rejection of Jesus himself and his message and as a refusal to become Christians, disciples (cf. Mt 28:19)?

The Parousia Discourse

The eschatological discourse in Mt 24–25 clearly has a composite character. The sources are a Marcan discourse and a number of sayings, exhortations, images, comparisons, similitudes, and parables of diverse origin. The result of Matthew's redactional work is most striking. Within the discourse three major sections must be distinguished:

The *first* section gives a schematic survey of the different phases of the coming future which was interpreted by the first Christians as the end of the world—there is still a short time before the Lord's Parousia. This section, with its announcements often couched in apocalyptic style, is imbued with a great pastoral concern. The disciples should not be credulous or overanxious; they must persevere till the end of the age in spite of persecution and the cooling of the love of many. The information imparted here serves this exhortation.

The *second* part is devoted completely to exhortation. Because neither the day nor the hour of the imminent Parousia is known, the disciples must watch and be ready. A more emphatic and detailed exhortation is hardly imaginable. We saw that two parables, that of the Faithful or Wicked Servant and that of the Talents, indicate what such "watching" concretely involves: faithfully performing the task assigned, making one's talents bear fruit. The judgment theme strengthens this exhortation by supplying a motive for it.

This theme of judgment dominates all of the *third* part which deals with the way in which the Son of man will judge the Gentiles. The criterion in this judgment will be the attitude which the Gentiles have adopted towards those "poor" Christians who by proclaiming the gospel bear a missionary witness to the "nations." Jesus is present in these preachers.

This last criterion may not, however, be absolutized. The requirement of an upright Christian life is by no means absent in Mt. The Christ of Matthew is the teacher of a higher righteousness (cf. Mt 5:20–48). It could even be supposed that Matthew would have affirmatively answered this question: Will the many people (nations) who have never known Christ and have never encountered his missionaries also not be judged according to their deeds (cf. 16:27)? But this problematic, which is of such importance in connection with the question of the salvation of non–Christians, does not, as we have seen, appear to have concerned the evangelist. Just as Israel's destiny was determined by the attitude which she assumed towards her Messiah, so too, according to Matthew, will all the nations be confronted with Christ (and also with his moral demands) before the end. The judgment will bear upon the acceptance of Christ *and* the higher righteousness implied by that acceptance.

The Three Aspects of the Discourse

Matthew 24–25 is a *prophetic salvific-historical* sketch of the future. After Jesus' first coming, the disciples live in expectation of his second coming as Judge. In this discourse there is still mention of the fall of Jerusalem (24:15–22; cf. 24:2–3). In 23:38 (cf. 22:7) this event is characterized as the judgment and punishment of Israel (cf. "scribes and Pharisees" in chap, 23; the authorities and the Pharisees in chaps. 21–22; but also the whole people: see 27:24–25). On the other hand, the question of Israel's punishment is no longer in the foreground in Mt 24–25. All attention goes rather to the disciples and the Gentiles. For Matthew, the redactor, Israel's history ends with the fall of Jerusalem in A.D. 70!

Matthew 24–25 is also an *ecclesial parenetic* plea. The writer Matthew is pastorally engaged. He exhorts his fellow Christians to live a responsible life. The second part of the discourse is devoted to this exhortation. But in the first part this concern also makes itself felt. Christians must stand firm in the dangerous final phase which puts their faith and love in jeopardy. Even the third part which deals with the judgment of the Gentiles is not without its admonition for the disciples. The righteous Gentiles take their place at the right hand of the Judge. As such, they are really no longer Gentiles, but in Matthew's way of thinking they have become Christians by their acceptance of Christian missionaries. They have heard the Word and borne fruit (cf. 13:18–23). The mention of active service, of welcoming and providing for others is, however, not meant merely as a statement of what the criterion of judgment will be for the "Gentiles." Their example in accepting missionaries also contains an implicit exhortation to the disciples and, ultimately, to the readers of the gospel.

Matthew 24–25 is finally a *Christological* document. Just as the Jewish war with the destruction of the temple represents the Jews' punishment for their rejection of Christ and his messengers, and just as for the Christians Jesus is the Son of man–Judge whose coming is both longed for and feared, so for all Gentiles the same Son of man is the future King–Judge. The attitude people take toward him, his message and those he sends, is decisive with respect to their eternal, ultimate future.

BIBLIOGRAPHY

Bligh, P. H., "Eternal Fire, Eternal Punishment, Eternal Life (Mt. 25:41, 46)," *ExpT* 83 (1971–1972) 9–11.

Bonnard, P., "Matthieu 25,31–46. Questions de lecture et d'interprétation," *Foi et vie* 76:5 (1977) (=Cahiers bibliques 16), pp. 81–87.

Broer, I., "Das Gericht des Menschensohnes über die Völker. Auslegung von Mt 25,31–46," *BibLeb* 11 (1970) 273–95.

Brown, S., "The Matthean Apocalypse," *Journal for the Study of the New Testament* 4 (1979) 2–27.

Cadoux, A. T., "The Parable of the Sheep and the Goats (Mt. 25:31–46)," *ExpT* 41 (1929–1930) 559–62.

Catchpole, D. R., "The Poor on Earth and the Son of Man in Heaven. A Re-Appraisal of Matthew xxv.31–46," *BJRL* 61 (1979) 355–97.

Cerfaux, L., "La charité fraternelle et le retour du Christ (Jo, XIII,33–38)," *ETL* 24 (1948) 321–32 (see especially pp. 325–29).

Cope, L., "Matthew 25,31–46, 'The Sheep and the Goats' Reinterpreted," *NovT* 11 (1969) 32–44.

Dupont, J., "L'Eglise et la pauvreté," in *L'Eglise de Vatican II. Etudes autour de la Constitution conciliaire sur l'Eglise II*, Unam Sanctam 51b, ed. G. Baraúna, Paris, 1966, pp. 339–72 (especially pp. 365–70).

Duprez, A., "Le Jugement dernier. Mt 25,31–46," *AssSeign II* (1973) no. 65, pp. 17–28.

Friedrich, J., *Gott im Bruder?* *Eine methodenkritische Untersuchung von Redaktion, Überlieferung und Tradition in Mt 25,31–46*, Calwer Theologische Monographien. Reihe A: Bibelwissenschaft 7, Stuttgart, 1977.

Gewalt, D., "Matthäus 25,31–46 im Erwartungshorizont heutiger Exegese," *LB* (1973) no. 25–26, pp. 9–21.

Gross, G., "Die 'Geringsten Brüder' Jesu in Mt 25,40 in Auseinandersetzung mit der neueren Exegese," *BibLeb* 5 (1964) 172–80.

Haufe, G., " 'Soviel ihr getan habt einem dieser meiner geringsten Brüder . . . '," in *Ruf und Antwort. Festgabe Em. Fuchs,* Leipzig, 1964, pp. 484–93.

Ingelaere, J.-C., "La 'parabole' du Jugement Dernier (Matthieu 25,31–46)," *RHPR* 50 (1970) 23–60.

Lambrecht, J., "The Parousia Discourse. Composition and Content in Mt., XXIV–XXV," in *L'Évangile selon Matthieu. Rédaction et théologie,* BETL 29, ed. M. Didier, Gembloux, 1972, pp. 309–42.

Légasse, S., *Jésus et l'enfant. "Enfants", "petits" et "simples" dans la tradition synoptique,* EBib, Paris, 1969, pp. 85–100.

Maddox, R., "Who are the 'Sheep' and the 'Goats'? A Study of the Purpose and Meaning of Mt. 25,31–46," *AusBR* 13 (1965) 19–28.

Mánek, J., "Mit wem identifiziert sich Jesus? Eine exegetische Rekonstruktion ad Matt. 25:31–46," in *Christ and Spirit in the New Testament: In Honour of C.F.D. Moule,* ed. B. Lindars and S. S. Smalley, Cambridge, 1973, pp. 15–25.

Martin, F., "The Image of Shepherd in the Gospel of St. Matthew," *Science et Esprit* 27 (1975) 261–301.

Michaels, J. R., "Apostolic Hardships and Righteous Gentiles: A Study of Matthew 25, 31–46," *JBL* 84 (1965) 27–37.

Robinson, J. A. T., "The 'Parable' of the Sheep and the Goats," *NTS* 2 (1955–1956) 225–37; also in Robinson, *Twelve New Testament Studies,* SBT 34, London, 1962, pp. 76–93.

Turner, H. E. W., "The Parable of the Sheep and the Goats (Mt 25:31–46)," *ExpT* 77 (1965–1966) 243–46.

Walker, R., *Die Heilsgeschichte im ersten Evangelium,* FRLANT 91, Göttingen, 1967.

Wikenhauser, A., "Die Liebeswerke im Gerichtsgemälde," *BZ* 20 (1932) 366–77.

Wilckens, U., "Gottes geringste Brüder—zu Mt. 25,31–46," *Jesus und Paulus. Festschrift für W.G. Kümmel,* ed. E. E. Ellis and E. Grässer, Göttingen, 1975, pp. 363–83.

Winandy, J., "La scène du Jugement Dernier (Mt 25,31–46)," *ScEccl* 18 (1966) 169–86.

Zumstein, J., *La condition du croyant dans l'évangile selon Matthieu,* Orbis biblicus et orientalis 16, Fribourg–Göttingen, 1977, pp. 327–50.

Index of Biblical References

I. OLD TESTAMENT

Genesis
22   53
37:20   130

Leviticus
19:18   64
21:1-4   71
   11   71

Deuteronomy
6:4-5   64

2 Samuel
12:1-3   4
   4   4

2 Chronicles 69-70

Psalms
118:22-23   129-31
126:5-6   102
147:2   162

Canticle of Canticles
3:6-11   160

Sirach
27:11   9

Isaiah
5:1-2   130-1
6:9-10   93, 108, 141
29:13   123
62:5   162

Jeremiah
7:34   160
16:9   160
25:10   160
33:11   160

Ezekiel
17:22-24   108
34:17-22   213

Habakkuk
2:2-4   166

II. NEW TESTAMENT

The list of Synoptic parables is found on pages 18-20

Matthew
5:3   218
   15   95
   20-48   233
   46   81
6:33   95
7:2   95
   21-23   165, 231

21	163
24-27	165
8:12	178
9:15	164
10:11-15	224
14-15	231
17-22	204-5
24-25	224
26	95
32-33	224
40-42	225-6, 227, 228
42	217, 223
11:20-24	231
12:22-45	119
28	104
30	225, 229
31-32	120
49-50	224
13	215, 231
13:12	178
18-23	234
24-30	8, 215
01 00	06, 108
31-32	99
33	100
36-43	215
37-39	8
39	202
40	202
41-42	221
41	217
42	178
44-46	16, 26
47-50	215
49-50	221
49	202, 217
50	178
16:27	215, 233
17:25	38
18	228
18:2-5	36
2-4	223
6-20	36
6	224, 225, 227-8
8-14	55
10	37, 224, 227
12-14	25, 28, 35-43, 224
14	227-8
15-35	224
21	36
22-35	36
19:1	36

28	215
29	10
20:1-16	32
1-15	186
2	176
16	182
21	233
21:28-31	31
33-43	145
33-46	144
43	210, 222
22	233
22:1-14	9
2-14	32, 158
2	154
7	9, 210, 222, 233
10	192
11-13	162
13	178
14	182
17	38
34-40	59, 64-5
41-46	199
42	38
23:1-39	198, 199, 210, 221, 223, 233
8	224
29-39	199-202
32-38	226
34-38	205
37-38	232
38	223, 233
24:1-25:46	146, 147-52, 161, 192, 197, 232-4
1-4	198-202
1-3	210
1-2	204
2-3	233
2	223
3	192, 202, 207, 208
4-35	197, 210
4-14	203-5, 207, 208
4-5	208
9	211, 215, 222, 225
14	211, 215, 222, 225, 230
15-28	206-8
15-22	233
23-26	208
26-28	148
27-28	208
27	202, 215
29-31	207

30-31	149, 208-9, 215	2:19-20	104, 111
30	164, 202, 211, 222	3	112, 138, 140
31	217, 221	3:6	94
32-35	209-10	7-12	90
34	215, 230	11-12	105
26-25:30	150-2, 164, 192, 197, 223	13-19	111, 113
36-44	164	20-4:34	109, 144
36	150	20-35	114-8, 121, 144
37-41	148	20-30	118, 119
37-39	162, 202	20-21	113-4
37	147, 148, 202, 215	22-30	94, 112-21
39	202, 215	22	73, 123
40-41	162	23-27	17, 112, 126, 132, 139
42-44	164	23-26	2
42	148, 150, 151, 157, 192, 230	23-25	112
		23	127
43	151	27	104
44	148, 150, 151, 192, 215, 230	31-35	90, 113-4, 119, 141, 142
		4	21, 112, 121, 138, 139, 140, 142, 215
45-51	137, 164, 190, 192		
45	178, 194	4:1-34	85-109, 110
47	176	1-20	124-5
48	152, 192	1-2	90-2
51	178, 215	2	112, 127, 139
25:1-13	31, 146-66, 190	3-9	102-4, 110
11-12	231	3-8	139
13	192, 193, 197, 230	3-4	3
14-30	18, 137, 146, 167-95, 197	3	116, 142
		9	116, 142
19	152	10-34	126-7
29	95	10-13	92-4
30	150, 215	10	112, 126
31-46	146, 196-235	10-12	25, 110, 121, 126, 140, 142, 143
31-32	149		
31	154, 164	11	105 7, 128, 139
26.1-2	142	13	112, 125, 142
13	222	14-20	8, 97-8
27:24-25	233	21-25	87, 95-6
25	223	21-22	142
28:10	224	21	111
18-20	227	24	111
19	222, 232	25	178, 181
20	202, 230	26-32	87-8
		26-29	2, 99-102, 110
Mark		26	3
1:2-3	111	30-32	2, 99-102, 110
5	111	30-31	3
10	111	30	112
17	111	33-36	89
21-22	111	33-34	90-2
22	111	33	112, 142
24-25	105	34	112, 141, 142

35-41	105
35-36	92
36	90
6:11	110
34	111
45-52	105
51-52	125
7	112, 132, 138, 140
7:1-23	121-7, 144, 145
14-23	109, 121-2, 124-7
14-18	94
15	112, 139, 143
17-23	92, 139
17-22	107
17-18	142
17	112
18-23	140
27-28	111
8:11-12	119, 120
11	73
14-21	109
15	111, 125
17-21	107, 125, 142
22-26	106
24	111
27-30	105
29	105
32-33	142
9:26	111
28-29	107
32-34	142
10:10-12	107
15	111
17-31	76
17	64, 66
35-45	142
38-39	111
11:1-11	128
10	176
12-14	111
15-19	111
16-17	128
17	111
18	128, 133, 142
19	128
20-27	128
20-21	111
27-12:12	128-9
27	112
32	128
33	131
12	112, 138, 140
12:1-12	127-32, 143, 144
1-11	110, 112, 139
1	112
10	111
12-13	128
12	112, 133, 142
14-17	113
17	133
18-44	113
25	111
28-34	59, 62-5, 68, 75, 81
31	111
33	66
34	133
35-40	141
35-37	199
37-40	199
37	133
38-40	133
41-44	199, 210
13	112, 129, 132-5, 138, 140, 144
13:1-5	108-9, 145, 147
3-37	92, 107
3	138
4	222
5-37	199
5-13	203
5-8	204
9-13	204-5
26	209
27	221
28-37	135-9
28-29	2, 110, 112, 132-9, 144
29	2, 140
30	230
32	147, 148
33-37	7, 144
34-36	110, 132-9, 144
37	107, 138, 143, 199
14:1-2	129, 133
2	142
22-25	111
36	111
48	111
Luke	
3:10-14	79
5:11	80
28	80
6:20	80, 218

24	80	14:1	26
38	95	11	182
46	163	28-32	26
7:36-50	58-9	33	80
8:4-18	118	15:1-32	24-56
10	25	1-2	26, 72
19-21	119	3-7	25
21	79	4-10	26-8
31	79	4-7	37-43
9:51-19:46	77, 188	8-10	18
51	25, 26	11-32	26, 29-33, 45-51, 186
52-56	77-8	11-12	3
53	26	11	59
56	26	16:1	3, 26, 59
57	26	9	80
10:1	26	15	40, 66
25-37	57-84	19-31	32, 80
25-28	62-4	19	59
29	7, 40	17	135
36-37	67-8	17:11-19	78
36	7	11	26
38	26	28-30	162
11:1-13	119	34-35	162
14-26	118-20	18:9-14	31
21-22	121	10-14	7
23	73	10	59
27-28	119	18-30	62, 64, 76
29-32	119	18	66
33	95	22	80
12:2	95	31	26, 189
10	120	35	26, 189
15	7	19:1	26, 179
16-21	59	7	189
16-20	7	8	80
20-21	80	11-27	167-95
31	95	11	26, 189
33-34	80	12-27	18, 137
35-38	137	26-27	162
42-46	137, 190	26	95
42	178, 194	28	26, 179, 189
44	176	29	26
45	194	37	26
47-48	190	38	176
13:1-9	34-5	41-44	189
18-21	26, 108	45	26, 189
18-19	99	20:9-19	144
20-21	100	28	59
22-30	166	39-40	59
22	26		
25	153-4, 156, 161, 163	**John**	
28	178	13:33-38	234
33	26	20:11-13	75

Acts

1:6	189
8	78
2:37	79
44-45	80
4:32	80
34-37	80
8:1-25	78
14	78
30	1
9:31	78
15:3	78

Romans

9-11	94

Index of Authors

Aland, 42
Alexandre, 21
Almeida, 21
Antoine, 53
Arai, 53
Argyle, 160, 166
Armstrong, 20
Aurelio, 21

Balz, 144
Banks, 143
Baraúna, 234
Beirnaert, 53
Bent, 20
Berger, 20, 143
Best, 108
Binder, 83
Biser, 21
Black, 108
Blank, 143
Bligh, 234
Böcher, 84
Bonnard, 54, 234
Bornkamm, 84, 156, 166
Boucher, 21
Bovon, 53
Broer, 54, 217, 219, 234
Brown, R. E., x
Brown, S., 105, 107, 234
Bultmann, 20, 108
Buzy, 20

Cadoux, 20, 234
Cantinat, 54
Carlston, 20, 54, 143
Casalegno, 108

Casper, 55
Catchpole, 234
Cerfaux, 20, 234
Colwell, 22
Conzelmann, 108, 145
Cope, 234
Cothenet, 143
Crespy, 83, 84
Crossan, 16, 17, 21, 23, 54, 83, 84, 108, 144

Dahl, 22
Daniel, 83
de Halleux, 144
Deiss, 166
de la Potterie, 55, 194
Derrett, 54, 83, 194
Descamps, 144
Didier, 166, 194, 235
Dietzfelbinger, 108
Dodd, 5, 10, 20
Donfried, 157, 166
Dupont, 20, 44, 54, 108, 144, 154, 166, 194, 234
Duprez, 234

Eichholz, 20
Ellis, 108, 235
Eulenstein, 83

Feuillet, 166
Fiedler, 194
Foerster, 194
Frankemölle, 103, 108
Friedrich, 144, 235
Fuchs, Em., 235

Fuchs, Ernst, 21, 54, 83
Funk, 22, 83, 84, 108

Ganne, 194
Geischer, 108
George, 20
Gerhardsson, 83
Gewalt, 83, 235
Giblet, 54
Giblin, 54
Gide, 24
Gnilka, 93, 108, 109, 143, 166
Goguel, 83
Goulder, 20
Grässer, 108, 166, 235
Grelot, 54
Gross, 235
Güttgemanns, 22, 54, 84

Haacker, 84
Hahn, 108, 144
Harnisch, 22
Harrington, 21, 23
Hartman, 144
Haufe, 235
Hengel, 144
Hermaniuk, 21
Hermann, 83
Hickling, 54
Hoffmann, 108, 166
Hofius, 54
Hooke, 20
Hoskins, 23
Hubaut, 108, 144
Hübner, 144
Huffman, 22

Ingelaere, 235

Jane, 144
Jeremias, 6, 10, 20, 22, 33, 48, 55, 93, 97,
    98, 108, 157, 158, 159, 160, 162, 166,
    180, 213
Jervell, 22
Jörns, 22
Jones, 21
Joüon, 194
Jülicher, 5, 10, 11, 20, 108
Jüngel, 22, 84

Kahlefeld, 21
Kamlah, 194

Kiefer, 83
Kissinger, 23
Klauck, 22, 23, 144
Klemm, 22, 83
Kossen, 55
Kümmel, 108, 144, 235
Kuhn, 108
Kuss, 108

Lambrecht, 21, 83, 108, 109, 144, 166,
    235
Lampe, 109
Laufen, 109
Le Du, 55
Leenhardt, 83
Légasse, 55, 83, 217, 220, 235
Lemcio, 109
Léon-Dufour, 109, 144
Lindars, 235
Linnemann, 22
Linton, 22
Little, 23
Lövestam, 144
Lohfink, 55
Lohse, 22, 108

Maddox, 235
Magass, 22, 55
Maillot, 22
Maisch, 162, 166
Mánek, 235
Marsh, 20
Martin, 235
Massingberd Ford, 166
McArthur, 109
McEleney, 144
McGughy, 195
Mecks, 22
Mees, 22
Meinertz, 21, 166
Merkel, 144
Metzger, 42
Michaelis, 21, 235
Miller, 53
Minette de Tillesse, 109
Monselewski, 83
Moule, 235
Mussner, 84

Nellessen, 109
Neuhäusler, 195
Newell, 144

O'Rourke, 55

Paschen, 145
Patte, 22, 55, 84
Payne, 109
Pépin, 22
Perrin, 22, 23
Pesch, 55, 144, 145
Petersen, 84
Pöhlmann, 55

Räisänen, 109
Rahner, 84
Ramaroson, 55, 84
Ramsey, 17, 21
Rasco, 55
Reicke, 84
Rengstorf, 55
Richards, 55
Ricoeur, xii, 11, 16, 21, 22, 23
Rigaux, 144
Robinson, J. A. T., 145, 217, 220, 235
Robinson, J. M., 23
Rouiller, 83

Sabbe, 108
Sanders, 55
Satake, 53
Schelkle, 109
Schenk, 166
Schillebeeckx, 23
Schlier, 84
Schmid, 108
Schmitz, 194
Schnackenburg, 109, 144
Schnider, 55
Schottroff, 55
Schulz, 144
Schwidler, 21
Scott, 56
Sekine, 53
Sellin, 68, 69, 84
Seven, 84
Smalley, 235

Smith, 21
Stählin, 84
Strecker, 108, 145
Strobel, 166
Stuhlmann, 109
Sturdy, 22

Tannehill, 84
Ternant, 84
TeSelle, 21
Tissot, 53
Tolbert, 56
Trilling, 145
Trocmé, 109
Trotter, 23
Trudinger, 84
Turner, 235

Van den Hougen, 56
Via, 17, 23, 56, 84
Vögtle, 144
von der Osten-Sacken, 145

Waelkens, 56
Walker, 201, 235
Weder, 23
Weinert, 195
Weiser, 145, 175, 195
Wikenhauser, 166, 235
Wilckens, 235
Wilder, 23, 109
Wilson, R. McL., 108
Wilson, R. R., 109
Winandy, 235
Wrede, 109

Young, 84

Zerwick, 195
Zimmermann, 84, 109
Zmijewski, 109
Zorell, 166
Zumstein, 166, 235